THE EXPERIMENTAL NOVEL

THE

EXPERIMENTAL NOVEL

AND OTHER ESSAYS

BY

ÉMILE ZOLA

AUTHOR OF "THE DOWNFALL" (LA DÉBÂCLE)

TRANSLATED FROM THE FRENCH BY

BELLE M. SHERMAN

———

HASKELL HOUSE
Publishers of Scholarly Books
NEW YORK
1964

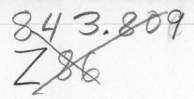

First published in 1893

HASKELL HOUSE

Library of Congress Catalog Card Number: 65-15864

Haskell House Catalogue Item # 697

PRINTED IN UNITED STATES OF AMERICA

INTRODUCTION.

FIVE of these articles first appeared, translated into Russian, in the *Messager de l'Europe*, a St. Petersburg review. The two others, entitled " The Novel " and " Criticism," are but the gathering together of articles selected from a large number published in *Le Bien Public* and *Le Voltaire*.

Allow me to publicly express my gratitude to the great nation which welcomed me so warmly, and adopted me, at a time when not a journal in Paris would accept what I wrote and everyone was my enemy in my literary battle. Russia, in one of my hours of pain and discouragement, revived my faith in myself, renewed my strength, and gave me a public, and that the most critical and impassioned of publics. Her criticism of my writings made me what I am to-day. I cannot speak of her without emotion, and I shall keep her in eternal remembrance.

They are therefore polemics, manifestoes, if you will, written in the first flush of the idea, without any rhetorical subtilities. As they were to be translated into another tongue, I paid little attention to their literary form. My first intention was to rewrite them before publishing them in France. But on reading them over I realized that it would be better to leave them as they were, with their faults and the outlines of their rather angular style, lest I should make the mistake of disfiguring them. I send them forth, then, as they have returned to me, encumbered with repetitions, loose in construction, with too much simplicity in their style, too much dryness in their reasoning. Doubts assail me, and I ask myself, Is it possible that these articles will be found to be my best work? For I am overcome with shame when I think of the enormous pile of romantic rhetoric which lies behind me.

ÉMILE ZOLA.

CONTENTS.

THE

EXPERIMENTAL NOVEL.

———

IN my literary essays I have often spoken of the
application of the experimental method to the novel
and to the drama. The return to nature, the naturalistic evolution which marks the century, drives little
by little all the manifestation of human intelligence
into the same scientific path. Only the idea of
a literature governed by science is doubtless a surprise, until explained with precision and understood.
It seems to me necessary, then, to say briefly and to
the point what I understand by the experimental
novel.

I really only need to adapt, for the experimental
method has been established with strength and marvelous clearness by Claude Bernard in his "Introduction à l'Étude de la Médecine Experimentale." This
work, by a savant whose authority is unquestioned,
will serve me as a solid foundation. I shall here find
the whole question treated, and I shall restrict myself
to irrefutable arguments and to giving the quotations
which may seem necessary to me. This will then be
but a compiling of texts, as I intend on all points to
intrench myself behind Claude Bernard. It will often
be but necessary for me to replace the word "doctor"

by the word "novelist," to make my meaning clear and to give it the rigidity of a scientific truth.

What determined my choice, and made me choose "L'Introduction" as my basis, was the fact that medicine, in the eyes of a great number of people, is still an art, as is the novel. Claude Bernard all his life was searching and battling to put medicine in a scientific path. In his struggle we see the first feeble attempts of a science to disengage itself little by little from empiricism,* and to gain a foothold in the realm of truth, by means of the experimental method. Claude Bernard demonstrates that this method, followed in the study of inanimate bodies in chemistry and in physics, should be also used in the study of living bodies, in physiology and medicine. I am going to try and prove for my part that if the experimental method leads to the knowledge of physical life, it should also lead to the knowledge of the passionate and intellectual life. It is but a question of degree in the same path which runs from chemistry to physiology, then from physiology to anthropology and to sociology. The experimental novel is the goal.

To be more clear, I think it would be better to give a brief *résumé* of "L'Introduction" before I commence. The applications which I shall make of the texts will be better understood if the plan of the work and the matters treated are explained.

Claude Bernard, after having declared that medicine enters the scientific path, with physiology as its foundation, and by means of the experimental method, first

* Zola uses empiricism in this essay in the sense of "haphazard observation" in contrast with a scientific experiment undertaken to prove a certain truth,—TRANSLATOR,

explains the differences which exist between the sciences of observation and the sciences of experiment. He concludes, finally, that experiment is but provoked observation. All experimental reasoning is based on doubt, for the experimentalist should have no preconceived idea, in the face of nature, and should always retain his liberty of thought. He simply accepts the phenomena which are produced, when they are proved.

In the second part he reaches his true subject and shows that the spontaneity of living bodies is not opposed to the employment of experiment. The difference is simply that an inanimate body possesses merely the ordinary, external environment, while the essence of the higher organism is set in an internal and perfected environment endowed with constant physico-chemical properties exactly like the external environment; hence there is an absolute determinism in the existing conditions of natural phenomena; for the living as for the inanimate bodies. He calls determinism the cause which determines the appearance of these phenomena. This nearest cause, as it is called, is nothing more than the physical and material condition of the existence or manifestation of the phenomena. The end of all experimental method, the boundary of all scientific research, is then identical for living and for inanimate bodies; it consists in finding the relations which unite a phenomenon of any kind to its nearest cause, or, in other words, in determining the conditions necessary for the manifestation of this phenomenon. Experimental science has no necessity to worry itself about the "why" of things; it simply explains the "how."

After having explained the experimental considerations common to living beings and to inanimate, Claude Bernard passes to the experimental considerations which belong specially to living beings. The great and only difference is this, that there is presented to our consideration, in the organism of livings beings, a harmonious group of phenomena. He then treats of practical experiments on living beings, of vivisection, of the preparatory anatomical conditions, of the choice of animals, of the use of calculation in the study of phenomena, and lastly of the physiologist's laboratory.

Finally, in the last part of " L'Introduction," he gives some examples of physiological experimental investigations in support of the ideas which he has formulated. He then furnishes some examples of experimental criticism in physiology. In the end he indicates the philosophical obstacles which the experimental doctor encounters. He puts in the first rank the false application of physiology to medicine, the scientific ignorance as well as certain illusions of the medical mind. Further, he concludes by saying that empirical medicine and experimental medicine, not being incompatible, ought, on the contrary, to be inseparable one from the other. His last sentence is that experimental medicine adheres to no medical doctrine nor any philosophical system.

This is, very broadly, the skeleton of " L'Introduction" stripped of its flesh. I hope that this rapid *exposé* will be sufficient to fill up the gaps which my manner of proceeding is bound to produce ; for, naturally, I shall cite from the work only such passages as are necessary to define and comment upon the experimental novel.   I repeat that I use this treatise merely as a solid foundation on which to build, but a foundation very rich in arguments and proofs of all kinds. Experimental medicine, which but lisps as yet, can alone give us an exact idea of experimental literature, which, being still unhatched, is not even lisping.

I.

THE first question which presents itself is this: Is experiment possible in literature, in which up to the present time observation alone has been employed?

Claude Bernard discusses observation and experiment at great length. There exists, in the first place, a very clear line of demarcation, as follows: "The name of 'observer' is given to him who applies the simple or complex process of investigation in the study of phenomena which he does not vary, and which he gathers, consequently, as nature offers them to him; the name of 'experimentalist' is given to him who employs the simple and complex process of investigation to vary or modify, for an end of some kind, the natural phenomena, and to make them appear under circumstances and conditions in which they are not presented by nature." For instance, astronomy is a science of observation, because you cannot conceive of an astronomer acting upon the stars; while chemistry is an experimental science, as the chemist acts upon nature and modifies it. This, according to Claude Bernard, is the only true and important distinction which separates the observer from the experimentalist.

I cannot follow him in his discussion of the different definitions given up to the present time. As I have said before, he finishes by coming to the conclusion that experiment is but provoked observation. I repeat his words: "In the experimental method the search after facts, that is to say, investigation, is always accompanied by a reason, so that ordinarily the experimentalist makes an experiment to confirm and verify the value of an experimental idea. In this case you can say that experiment is an observation instigated for the purpose of verification."

To determine how much observation and experimenting there can be in the naturalistic novel, I only need to quote the following passages:

"The observer relates purely and simply the phenomena which he has under his eyes. . . He should be the photographer of phenomena, his observation should be an exact representation of nature. . . He listens to nature and he writes under its dictation. But once the fact is ascertained and the phenomenon observed, an idea or hypothesis comes into his mind, reason intervenes, and the experimentalist comes forward to interpret the phenomenon. The experimentalist is a man who, in pursuance of a more or less probable, but anticipated, explanation of observed phenomena, institutes an experiment in such a way that, according to all probability, it will furnish a result which will serve to confirm the hypothesis or preconceived idea. The moment that the result of the experiment manifests itself, the experimentalist finds himself face to face with a true observation which he has called forth, and which he must ascertain, as all observation, without any preconceived idea. The experimentalist should then disappear, or rather transform himself instantly into the observer, and it is not until after he has ascertained the absolute results of the experiment, like that of an ordinary observation, that his mind comes back to reasoning, comparing, and judging whether the experimental hypothesis is verified or invalidated by these same results."

The mechanism is all there. It is a little complicated, it is true, and Claude Bernard is led on to say: "When all this passes into the brain of a savant who has given himself up to the study of a science as complicated as medicine still is, then there is such an entanglement between the result of observation and what belongs to experiment that it will be impossible and, besides, useless to try to analyze, in their inextricable *mélange*, each of these terms." In one word, it might be said that observation "indicates" and that experiment "teaches."

Now, to return to the novel, we can easily see that the novelist is equally an observer and an experimentalist. The observer in him gives the facts as he has observed them, suggests the point of departure, displays the solid earth on which his characters are to tread and the phenomena to develop. Then the experimentalist appears and introduces an experiment, that is to say, sets his characters going in a certain story so as to show that the succession of facts will be such as the requirements of the determinism of the phenomena under examination call for. Here it is nearly always an experiment "*pour voir*," as Claude Bernard calls it. The novelist starts out in search of a truth. I will take as an example the character of the *Baron Hulot*, in "Cousine Bette," by Balzac. The general fact observed by Balzac is the ravages that the amorous temperament of a man makes in his home, in his family, and in society. As soon as he has chosen his subject he starts from known facts; then he makes his experiment, and exposes *Hulot* to a series of trials, placing him amid certain surroundings in order to exhibit how the complicated machinery of his passions works. It is then evident that there is not only observation there, but that there is also experiment; as Balzac does not remain satisfied with photographing the facts collected by him, but interferes in a direct way to place his character in certain conditions, and of these he remains the master. The problem is to know what such a passion, acting in such a surrounding and under such circumstances, would produce from the point of view of an individual and of society; and an experimental novel, "Cousine Bette," for example, is simply the report of the experiment that the novelist conducts before the eyes of the public. In fact, the whole operation consists in taking facts in nature, then in studying the mechanism of these facts, acting upon them, by the modification of circumstances and surroundings, without deviating from the laws of nature. Finally, you possess knowledge of the man, scientific knowledge of him, in both his individual and social relations.

Doubtless we are still far from certainties in chemistry and even physiology. Nor do we know any more the reagents which decompose the passions, rendering them susceptible of analysis. Often, in this essay, I shall recall in similar fashion this fact, that the experimental novel is still younger than experimental medicine, and the latter is but just born. But I do not intend to exhibit the acquired results, I simply desire to clearly expose a method. If the experimental novelist is still groping in the most obscure and complex of all the sciences, this does not prevent this science from existing. It is undeniable that the naturalistic novel, such as we understand it to-day, is a real experiment that a novelist makes on man by the help of observation.

Besides, this opinion is not only mine, it is Claude Bernard's as well. He says in one place: " In practical life men but make experiments on one another." And again, in a more conclusive way, he expresses the whole theory of the experimental novel: " When we reason on our own acts we have a certain guide, for we are conscious of what we think and how we feel. But if we wish to judge of the acts of another man, and know the motives which make him act, that is altogether a different thing. Without doubt we have before our eyes the movements of this man and his different acts, which are, we are sure, the modes of expression of his sensibility and his will. Further, we even admit that there is a necessary connection between the acts and their cause; but what is this cause? We do not feel it, we are not conscious of it, as we are when it acts in ourselves; we are therefore obliged to interpret it, and to guess at it, from the movements which we see and the words which we hear. We are obliged to check off this man's actions one by the other; we consider how he acted in such a circumstance, and, in a word, we have recourse to the experimental method." All that I have spoken of further back is summed up in this last phrase, which is written by a savant.

I shall still call your attention to another illustration of Claude Bernard, which struck me as very forcible: " The experimentalist is the examining magistrate of nature." We novelists are the examining magistrates of men and their passions.

But see what splendid clearness breaks forth when this conception of the application of the experimental method to the novel is adequately grasped and is carried out with all the scientific rigor which the matter permits to-day. A contemptible reproach which they heap upon us naturalistic writers is the desire to be solely photographers. We have in vain declared that we admit the necessity of an artist's possessing an individual temperament and a personal expression; they continue to reply to us with these imbecile arguments, about the impossibility of being strictly true, about the necessity of arranging facts to produce a work of art of any kind. Well, with the application of the experimental method to the novel that quarrel dies out. The idea of experiment carries with it the idea of modification. We start, indeed, from the true facts, which are our indestructible basis; but to show the mechanism of these facts it is necessary for us to produce and direct the phenomena; this is our share of invention, here is the genius in the book. Thus without having recourse to the questions of form and of style, which I shall examine later, I maintain even at this point that we must modify nature, without departing from nature, when we employ the experimental method in our novels. If we bear in mind this definition, that " observation indicates and experiment teaches," we can even now claim for our books this great lesson of experiment.

The writer's office, far from being lessened, grows singularly from this point of view. An experiment, even the most simple, is always based on an idea, itself born of an observation. As Claude Bernard says: " The experimental idea is not arbitrary, nor purely

imaginary; it ought always to have a support in some
observed reality, that is to say, in nature." It is on
this idea and on doubt that he bases all the method.
"The appearance of the experimental idea," he says
further on, "is entirely spontaneous and its nature
absolutely individual, depending upon the mind in
which it originates; it is a particular sentiment, a *quid
proprium*, which constitutes the originality, the invention, and the genius of each one." Further, he makes
doubt the great scientific lever. "The doubter is the
true savant; he doubts only himself and his interpre-
tations; he believes in science; he even admits in the
experimental sciences a criterion or a positive principle,
the determinism of phenomena, which is absolute in
living beings as in inanimate bodies." Thus, instead of
confining the novelist within narrow bounds, the experimental method gives full sway to his intelligence as
a thinker, and to his genius as a creator. He must
see, understand, and invent. Some observed fact
makes the idea start up of trying an experiment; of
writing a novel, in order to attain to a complete knowledge of the truth. Then when, after careful consideration, he has decided upon the plan of his experiment,
he will judge the results at each step with the freedom
of mind of a man who accepts only facts conformable
to the determinism of phenomena. He set out from
doubt to reach positive knowledge; and he will not
cease to doubt until the mechanism of the passion,
taken to pieces and set up again by him, acts according
to the fixed laws of nature. There is no greater, no
more magnificent work for the human mind. We shall
see, further on, the miseries of the scholastics, of the
makers of systems, and those theorizing about the

ideal, compared with the triumph of the experimentalists.

I sum up this first part by repeating that the naturalistic novelists observe and experiment, and that all their work is the offspring of the doubt which seizes them in the presence of truths little known and phenomena unexplained, until an experimental idea rudely awakens their genius some day, and urges them to make an experiment, to analyze facts, and to master them.

II.

SUCH, then, is the experimental method. But for a long time it has been held that this method cannot be applied to living beings. This is the important point in the question that I am going to examine with Claude Bernard. The reasoning subsequently will be of the simplest; if the experimental method can be carried from chemistry and physics into physiology and medicine, it can be also carried from physiology into the naturalistic novel.

Cuvier—to cite the name of only one scientific man—pretended that experiment as applied to inanimate bodies could not be used with living beings; physiology, according to his way of thinking, should be purely a science of observation and of anatomical deduction. The vitalists even admit a vital force in unceasing battle with the physical and chemical forces neutralizing their action. Claude Bernard, on the contrary, denies all presence of a mysterious force, and affirms that experiment is applicable everywhere. " I propose," he says, " to establish the fact that the science of the phenomena of life can have no other basis than the science of the phenomena of inanimate bodies, and that there are, in this connection, no differences between the principles of biological science and those of physics and chemistry. In fact, the end the experimental method proposes is the same everywhere; it consists in connecting, by experiment, the natural phenomena

to their conditions of existence or to their nearest
causes."

It seems to me useless to enter into the complicated
explanations and reasonings of Claude Bernard. I
have already said that he insists upon the existence of
an interior condition in living beings. "In experimenting on inanimate bodies," he says, "there is only
one condition to be considered, that is, the exterior
earthly condition; while among the higher living
organisms there are at least two conditions to consider:
the exterior condition or extra-organic, and the interior
or inter-organic. The complexity due to the existence
of an interior organic condition is the only reason for
the great difficulties which we encounter in the experimental determination of living phenomena, and in the
application of the means capable of modifying them."
And he starts out from this fact to establish the principle that there are fixed laws governing the physiological elements plunged into an interior condition, as there
are fixed laws for governing the chemical elements
which are steeped in an exterior condition. Hence,
you can experiment on a living being as well as on an
inanimate one; it is only a question of putting yourself in the desired conditions.

I insist upon this, because, I repeat once more, the
important point of the question is there. Claude
Bernard, in speaking of the vitalists, writes thus:
"They consider life as a mysterious and supernatural
agent, which acts arbitrarily, free from all determinism,
and they condemn as materialists all those who
endeavor to trace vital phenomena to definite organic
and physico-chemical conditions. These are false ideas,
which it is not easy to root out once they have become

domiciled in the mind; only the progress of science can dissipate them." And he lays down this axiom: " With living beings as well as inanimate, the conditions of the existence of each phenomenon are determined in an absolute manner."

I restrain myself for fear of complicating the argument to too great an extent.

Thus you see the progress which science has made. In the last century a more exact application of the experimental method creates physics and chemistry, which then are freed from the irrational and supernatural. Men discover that there are fixed laws, thanks to analysis, and make themselves masters of phenomena. Then a new point is gained. Living beings, in which the vitalists still admitted a mysterious influence, are in their turn brought under and reduced to the general mechanism of matter. Science proves that the existing conditions of all phenomena are the same in living beings as in inanimate; and from that time on physiology assumes little by little the certainty of chemistry and medicine. But are we going to stop there? Evidently not. When it has been proved that the body of man is a machine, whose machinery can be taken apart and put together again at the will of the experimenter, then we can pass to the passionate and intellectual acts of man. Then we shall enter into the domain which up to the present has belonged to physiology and literature; it will be the decisive conquest by science of the hypotheses of philosophers and writers. We have experimental chemistry and medicine; we shall have an experimental physiology, and later on an experimental novel. It is an inevitable evolution, the goal of which it is easy to see to-day.

All things hang together ; it is necessary to start from the determinism of inanimate bodies in order to arrive at the determinism of living beings ; and since savants like Claude Bernard demonstrate now that fixed laws govern 'the human body, we can easily proclaim, without fear of being mistaken, the hour in which the laws of thought and passion will be formulated in their turn. A like determinism will govern the stones of the roadway and the brain of man.

This opinion is to be found in " L'Introduction." I cannot repeat too often that I take all my arguments from Claude Bernard's work. After having explained that any completely special phenomena may be the result of the more and more complex combination and co-operation of the organized elements, he writes the following : " I am persuaded that the obstacles which surround the experimental study of psychological phenomena are in great measure due to difficulties of this order ; for notwithstanding the marvelous nature and the delicacy of their manifestations, it is impossible, so it seems to me, not to bring cerebral phenomena, like all the phenomena of living bodies, under the laws of a scientific determinism." This is clear. Later, without doubt, science will find this determinism for all the cerebral and sensory manifestations of man.

Now, science enters into the domain of us novelists, who are to-day the analyzers of man, in his individual and social relations. We are continuing, by our observations and experiments, the work of the physiologist, who has continued that of the physicist and the chemist. We are making use, in a certain way, of scientific psychology to complete scientific physiology ;

and to finish the series we have only to bring into our studies of nature and man the decisive tool of the experimental method. In one word, we should operate on the characters, the passions, on the human and social data, in the same way that the chemist and the physicist operate on inanimate beings, and as the physiologist operates on living beings. Determinism dominates everything. It is scientific investigation, it is experimental reasoning, which combats one by one the hypotheses of the idealists, and which replaces purely imaginary novels by novels of observation and experiment.

I certainly do not intend at this point to formulate laws. In the actual condition of the science of man the obscurity and confusion are still too great to risk the slightest synthesis. All that can be said is that there is an absolute determinism for all human phenomena. From that on investigation is a duty. We have the method; we should go forward, even if a whole lifetime of effort ends but in the conquest of a small particle of the truth. Look at physiology: Claude Bernard made grand discoveries, and he died protesting that he knew nothing, or nearly nothing. In each page he confesses the difficulties of his task. " In the phenomenal relations," he says, " such as nature offers them to us, there always reigns a complexity more or less great. In this respect the complexity of mineral phenomena is much less great than that of living phenomena; this is why the sciences restricted to inanimate bodies have been able to formulate themselves more quickly. In living beings the phenomena are of enormous complexity, and the greater mobility of living organisms renders them more difficult to grasp and to define." What can be said, then, of the difficulties to be encountered by the experimental novel, which adds to physiology its studies upon the most delicate and complex organs, which deals with the highest manifestations of man as an individual and a social member? Evidently analysis becomes more complicated here. Therefore, if the physiologist is but drawing up his principles to-day, it is natural that the experimental novelist should be only taking his first steps: We foresee it as a sure consequence of the scientific evolution of the century; but it is impossible to base it on certain laws. Since Claude Bernard speaks of "the restricted and precarious truths of biological science," we can freely admit that the truths of the science of man, from the standpoint of his intellectual and passionate mechanism, are more restricted and precarious still. We are lisping yet, we are the last comers, but that should be only one incentive the more to push us forward to more exact studies; now that we possess the tool, the experimental method, our goal is very plain—to know the determinism of phenomena and to make ourselves master of these phenomena.

Without daring, as I say, to formulate laws, I consider that the question of heredity has a great influence in the intellectual and passionate manifestations of man. I also attach considerable importance to the surroundings. I ought to touch upon Darwin's theories; but this is only a general study of the experimental method as applied to the novel, and I should lose myself were I to enter into details. I will only say a word on the subject of surroundings. We have just seen the great importance given by Claude Bernard to the study of those inter-organic conditions which must be taken into account if we wish to find the determinism of phenomena in living beings. Well, then! in the study of a family, of a group of living beings, I think that the social condition is of equal importance. Some day the physiologist will explain to us the mechanism of the thoughts and the passions; we shall know how the individual machinery of each man works; how he thinks, how he loves, how he goes from reason to passion and folly; but these phenomena, resulting as they do from the mechanism of the organs, acting under the influence of an interior condition, are not produced in isolation or in the bare void. Man is not alone; he lives in society, in a social condition; and consequently, for us novelists, this social condition unceasingly modifies the phenomena. Indeed our great study is just there, in the reciprocal effect of society on the individual and the individual on society. For the physiologist, the exterior and interior conditions are purely chemical and physical, and this aids him in finding the laws which govern them easily. We are not yet able to prove that the social condition is also physical and chemical. It is that certainly, or rather it is the variable product of a group of living beings, who themselves are absolutely submissive to the physical and chemical laws which govern alike living beings and inanimate. From this we shall see that we can act upon the social conditions, in acting upon the phenomena of which we have made ourselves master in man. And this is what constitutes the experimental novel: to possess a knowledge of the mechanism of the phenomena inherent in man, to show the machinery of his intellectual and sensory manifestations, under the influences of heredity and environment, such as physiology shall give them to us, and then finally to exhibit man living in social conditions produced by himself, which he modifies daily, and in the heart of which he himself experiences a continual transformation. Thus, then, we lean on physiology; we take man from the hands of the physiologist solely, in order to continue the solution of the problem, and to solve scientifically the question of how men behave when they are in society.

These general ideas will be sufficient to guide us to-day. Later on, when science is farther advanced, when the experimental novel has brought forth decisive results, some critic will explain more precisely what I have but indicated to-day.

Elsewhere Claude Bernard confesses how difficult it is to apply the experimental method to living beings. "The living body," he says, "especially among the higher animals, never falls into chemical or physical indifference with the exterior conditions; it possesses an incessant movement, an organic evolution apparently spontaneous and constant; and notwithstanding the fact that this evolution has need of exterior circumstances to manifest itself, it is, however, independent in its course and movement." And he concludes as I have: "In short, it is only in the physical and chemical conditions of the interior that we shall find the principle that governs the exterior phenomena of life." But whatever complexities may present themselves, and even when extraordinary phenomena are produced, the application of the experimental method is imperative. If the phenomena of life have a complexity and an apparent difference from those of inanimate bodies, they do not offer this difference, except by reason of determined or determinable conditions which belong to them. Therefore, even should the sciences dealing with life differ from the others in their application and in their special laws, they are not to be distinguished by their scientific method."

I must say one word as to the limits which Claude Bernard assigns to science. According to him we shall always be ignorant of the "why" of things; we can only know the "how." It is this that he expresses in the following terms : "The nature of our minds urges us to seek the essence or the 'why' of things. In this we see further than the goal it has been given us to attain to ; for experiment soon teaches us that we must not go beyond the 'how'; that is to say, beyond the nearest cause or the condition of the existence of any phenomenon." Further on he gives this example : " If we can discover 'why' opium and its alkaloids produce sleep, we shall know the mechanism of such slumber, and know ' how ' opium or its essence produces sleep ; for slumber only takes place because the active substance is about to put itself in contact with certain organic elements which it modifies." The practical conclusion of all this is the following : "Science has precisely the privilege of teaching us what we are ignorant of, through its substitution of reason and experiment for sentiment, and by showing us clearly the limit of our actual knowledge. But, by a marvelous compensation, in proportion as science humbles our pride, it strengthens our power." All these considerations are strictly applicable to the experimental novel. In order not to lose itself in philosophical speculations, in order to replace idealistic hypothesis by a slow conquest of the unknown, it must continue the search after the " how " of things. This is its exact rôle, and it is from this that it must draw, as we are going to see, its reason for being and its moral.

I have reached this point: the experimental novel is a consequence of the scientific evolution of the century; it continues and completes physiology, which itself leans for support on chemistry and medicine; it substitutes for the study of the abstract and the metaphysical man the study of the natural man, governed by physical and chemical laws, and modified by the influences of his surroundings; it is in one word the literature of our scientific age, as the classical and romantic literature corresponded to a scholastic and theological age. Now I will pass to the great question of the application of all this, and of its justification.

III.

THE object of the experimental method in physiology and in medicine is to study phenomena in order to become their master. Claude Bernard in each page of " L'Introduction " comes back to this idea. He declares: " All natural philosophy is summed up in this: To know the laws which govern phenomena. The experimental problem reduces itself to this: To foresee and direct phenomena." Farther on he gives an example: " It will not satisfy the experimental doctor, though it may the merely empirical one, to know that quinine cures fever; the essential thing is to know what fever is, and to understand the mechanism by which quinine cures. All this is of the greatest importance to the experimental doctor; for as soon as he knows it positively, the fact that quinine cures fever will no longer be an isolated and empirical fact, but a scientific fact. This fact will be connected then with the conditions which bind it to other phenomena, and we shall be thus led to the knowledge of the laws of the organism, and to the possibility of regulating their manifestations." A striking example can be quoted in the case of scabies. " To-day the cause of this disease is known and determined experimentally; the whole subject has become scientific, and empiricism has disappeared. A cure is surely and without exception effected when you place yourself in the conditions known by experiment to produce this end."

This, then, is the end, this is the purpose in physiology and in experimental medicine : to make one's self master of life in order to be able to direct it. Let us suppose that science advances and that the conquest of the unknown is finally completed; the scientific age which Claude Bernard saw in his dreams will then be realized. When that time comes the doctor will be the master of maladies ; he will cure without fail ; his influence upon the human body will conduce to the welfare and strength of the species. We shall enter upon a century in which man, grown more powerful, will make use of nature and will utilize its laws to produce upon the earth the greatest possible amount of justice and freedom. There is no nobler, higher, nor grander end. Here is our rôle as intelligent beings : to penetrate to the wherefore of things, to become superior to these things, and to reduce them to a condition of subservient machinery.

Well, this dream of the physiologist and the experimental doctor is also that of the novelist, who employs the experimental method in his study of man as a simple individual and as a social animal. Their object is ours ; we also desire to master certain phenomena of an intellectual and personal order, to be able to direct them. We are, in a word, experimental moralists, showing by experiment in what way a passion acts in a certain social condition. The day in which we gain control of the mechanism of this passion we can treat it and reduce it, or at least make it as inoffensive as possible. And in this consists the practical utility and high morality of our naturalistic works, which experiment on man, and which dissect piece by piece this human machinery in order to set it going through the influence of the environment.   When things have advanced further, when we are in possession of the different laws, it will only be necessary to work upon the individuals and the surroundings if we wish to find the best social condition.   In this way we shall construct a practical sociology, and our work will be a help to political and economical sciences.   I do not know, I repeat, of a more noble work, nor of a grander application.   To be the master of good and evil, to regulate life, to regulate society, to solve in time all the problems of socialism, above all, to give justice a solid foundation by solving through experiment the questions of criminality—is not this being the most useful and the most moral workers in the human workshop ?

Let us compare, for one instant, the work of the idealistic novelists to ours; and here this word idealistic refers to writers who cast aside observation and experiment, and base their works on the supernatural and the irrational, who admit, in a word, the power of mysterious forces outside of the determinism of the phenomena.   Claude Bernard shall reply to this for me : " What distinguishes experimental reasoning from scholastic is the fecundity of the one and the sterility of the other.   It is precisely the scholastic, who believes he has absolute certitude, who attains to no results. This is easily understood, since by his belief in an absolute principle he puts himself outside of nature, in which everything is relative.   It is, on the contrary, the experimenter, who is always in doubt, who does not think he possesses absolute certainty about anything, who succeeds in mastering the phenomena which surround him, and in increasing his power over nature."   By and by I shall return to this question of the ideal, which is in truth but the question of indeterminism. Claude Bernard says truly : " The intellectual conquest of man consists in diminishing and driving back indeterminism, and so, gradually, by the aid of the experimental method, gaining ground for determinism." We experimental novelists have the same task ; our work is to go from the known to the unknown, to make ourselves masters of nature ; while the idealistic novelists deliberately remain in the unknown, through all sorts of religious and philosophical prejudices, under the astounding pretense that the unknown is nobler and more beautiful than the known. If our work, often cruel, if our terrible pictures needed justification, I should find, indeed, with Claude Bernard this argument conclusive : " You will never reach really fruitful and luminous generalizations on the phenomena of life until you have experimented yourself and stirred up in the hospital, the amphitheater, and the laboratory the fetid or palpitating sources of life. If it were necessary for me to give a comparison which would explain my sentiments on the science of life, I should say that it is a superb salon, flooded with light, which you can only reach by passing through a long and nauseating kitchen."

I insist upon the word which I have employed, that of experimental novelists as applied to naturalistic novelists. One page of " L'Introduction " struck me as being very forcible, that in which the author speaks of the vital " circulus." " The muscular and nervous organs preserve the activity of the organs which make the blood ; but the blood, in its turn, nourishes the organs which produce it. There is in this a social or

organic solidarity, which keeps up a perpetual movement, until the derangement or cessation of the action
of a necessary and vital element has broken the equilibrium or brought about some trouble or stoppage in
the play of the animal machinery. The problem of
the experimentalist doctor consists in finding the cause
of any organic disarrangement, that is to say, in seizing
the initial phenomenon. We shall see how a disloca-
tion of the organism, or a disarrangement the most
complex in appearance, can be traced to a simple initial
cause, which calls forth immediately the most complex
effects." All that is necessary here is to change the
words experimental doctor to experimental novelist,
and this passage is exactly applicable to our naturalistic literature.   The social circulus is identical with the
vital circulus ; in society, as in human beings, a solidarity exists which unites the different members and the
different organisms in such a way that if one organ
becomes rotten many others are tainted and a very
complicated disease results. Hence, in our novels,
when we experiment on a dangerous wound which
poisons society, we proceed in the same way as the
experimentalist doctor ; we try to find the simple initial
cause in order to reach the complex causes of which
the action is the result.   Go back once more to the
example of *Baron Hulot* in " Cousine Bette." See the
final result, the dénouement of the novel : an entire
family is destroyed, all sorts of secondary dramas are
produced, under the action of *Hulot's* amorous temperament. It is there, in this temperament, that the
initial cause is found. One member, *Hulot,* becomes
rotten, and immediately all around him are tainted, the
social circulus is interrupted, the health of that society

is compromised. What emphasis Balzac lays on the character of *Baron Hulot ;* with what scrupulous care he analyzes him! The experiment deals with him chiefly, because its object is to master the symptoms of this passion in order to govern it. Suppose that *Hulot* is cured, or at least restrained and rendered inoffensive, immediately the drama ceases to have any longer any *raison d'être ;* the equilibrium, or more truly the health, of the social body is again established. Thus the naturalistic novelists are really experimental moralists.

And I reach thus the great reproach with which they think to crush the naturalistic novelists, by treating them as fatalists. How many times have they wished to prove to us that as soon as we did not accept free will, that as soon as man was no more to us than a living machine, acting under the influence of heredity and surroundings, we should fall into gross fatalism, we should debase humanity to the rank of a troop marching under the baton of destiny. It is necessary to define our terms : we are not fatalists, we are determinists, which is not at all the same thing. Claude Bernard explains the two terms very plainly : " We have given the name of determinism to the nearest or determining cause of phenomena. We never act upon the essence of phenomena in nature, but only on their determinism, and by this very fact, that we act upon it, determinism differs from fatalism, upon which we could not act at all. Fatalism assumes that the appearance of any phenomenon is necessary apart from its conditions, while determinism is just the condition essential for the appearance of any phenomenon, and such appearance is never forced. Once the search for the determinism of phenomena is placed as a fundamental principle of the experimental method, there is no longer either materialism, or spiritualism, or inanimate matter, or living matter; there remain but phenomena of which it is necessary to determine the conditions, that is to say, the circumstances which play, by their proximity to these phenomena, the rôle of nearest cause." This is decisive. All we do is to apply this method in our novels, and we are the determinists who experimentally try to determine the condition of the phenomena, without departing in our investigations from the laws of nature. As Claude Bernard very truly says, the moment that we can act, and that we do act, on the determining cause of phenomena—by modifying their surroundings, for example—we cease to be fatalists.

Here you have, then, the moral purpose of the experimental novelist clearly defined. I have often said that we do not have to draw a conclusion from our works; and this means that our works carry their conclusion with them. An experimentalist has no need to conclude, because, in truth, experiment concludes for him. A hundred times, if necessary, he will repeat the experiment before the public; he will explain it; but he need neither become indignant nor approve of it personally; such is the truth, such is the way phenomena work; it is for society to produce or not to produce these phenomena, according as the result is useful or dangerous. You cannot imagine, as I have said elsewhere, a savant being provoked with azote because azote is dangerous to life; he suppresses azote when it is harmful, and not otherwise. As our power is not the same as that of a savant, as we are experimentalists without being practitioners, we ought to content ourselves with searching out the determinism of social phenomena, and leaving to legislators and to men of affairs the care of controlling sooner or later these phenomena in such a way as to develop the good and reject the bad, from the point of view of their utility to man.

In our rôle as experimental moralists we show the mechanism of the useful and the useless, we disengage the determinism of the human and social phenomena so that, in their turn, the legislators can one day dominate and control these phenomena. In a word, we are working with the whole country toward that great object, the conquest of nature and the increase of man's power a hundredfold. Compare with ours the work of the idealistic writers, who rely upon the irrational and the supernatural, and whose every flight upward is followed by a deeper fall into metaphysical chaos. We are the ones who possess strength and morality.

IV.

I HAVE said before that I chose " L'Introduction " because medicine is still looked upon by many as an art. Claude Bernard proves that it ought to be a science, and in his book we see the birth of a science, a very instructive spectacle in itself, and which shows us that the scientific domain is extending and conquering all the manifestations of human intelligence. Since medicine, which was an art, is becoming a science, why should not literature also become a science by means of the experimental method?

It must be remarked that all things hang together: If the territory of the experimental doctor is the body of man, as shown in the phenomena of his different organs both in their normal and pathological condition, our territory is equally the body of man, as shown by his sensory and cerebral phenomena, both in their normal and pathological condition. If we are not satisfied with the metaphysical man of the classical age we must, perforce, take into consideration the new ideas on nature and on life, with which our age has become imbued. We continue necessarily, I repeat, the work of the physiologist and the doctor, who have continued, in their turn, that of the physician and the chemist. Hence we enter into the domain of science. I will not touch on the question of sentiment and form, but will reserve that for another time.

Let us see first what Claude Bernard says about

medicine : " Certain doctors contend that medicine can only be conjectural, and they conclude that a doctor is an artist, who ought to make up for the indeterminism in particular cases by his genius and his personal tact. All sciences have necessarily commenced by being conjectural ; there are still to-day in every science conjectural parts. Medicine is still nearly all conjecture. I do not deny that ; but I only want to say that modern science should make an effort to come out of this provisionary state, which does not constitute a definite scientific condition—not any more for medicine than for the other sciences. The scientific condition will be longer in taking shape and more difficult to obtain in medicine by reason of the complexities of its phenomena ; but the end of the medical savant is to reduce in his science, as in all the others, the indeterminate to the determinate." The mechanism of the birth and the development of a science is here clearly defined. Men still look upon the doctor as an artist, because there is in medicine an enormous place still left to conjecture. Naturally, the novelist merits still more the name of artist, as he finds himself buried still deeper in the indeterminate. If Claude Bernard confesses that the complexity of its phenomena will prevent medicine, for a long time yet, from arriving at a scientific state, what shall we say of the experimental novel, in which the phenomena are much more complicated still ? But this does not prevent the novel from entering upon the scientific pathway, obedient to the general evolution of the century.

Moreover, Claude Bernard himself has indicated the evolutions of the human mind. " The human mind," he says, " at various periods of its progress has passed

successively through feeling, reason, and experiment.
First, feeling alone, dominating reason, created the
truths of faith, that is to say, theology.   Reason, or
philosophy, becoming afterward the mistress, brought
forth scholasticism.   Finally, experiment, that is to
say, the study of natural phenomena, taught man that
the truths of the exterior world were to be found
formulated, in the first place, neither in reason nor in
feeling.   These last are, indeed, our indispensable
guides, but to obtain the truth it is necessary to
descend into the objective reality of things, where they
lie concealed under their phenomenal form.   Thus it is
that in the natural progress of things the experimental
method appears, which sums up the whole, and which
supports itself successfully on the three branches of
this immovable tripod : feeling, reason, and experiment.
In the search after truth by means of this method,
feeling has always the initiative ; it engenders the idea
a priori or intuition ; reason, or the reasoning power,
immediately develops the idea and deduces its logical
consequences.   But if feeling must be guided by the
light of reason, reason in its turn must be guided by
experiment."

I have given this passage entire, as it is of the greatest importance.   It shows clearly the rôle that the
personality of the novelist should play, apart from the
style.   Since feeling is the starting point of the experimental method, since reason subsequently intervenes to
end in experiment, and to be controlled by it, the genius
of the experimentalist dominates everything, and this
is what has made the experimental method, so inert in
other hands, such a powerful tool in the hands of
Claude Bernard.   I have said the word : method is but

the tool; it is the workman, it is the idea, which he
brings, which makes the *chef-d'œuvre.* I have already
quoted these lines: " It is a particular feeling, a *quid
proprium,* which constitutes the originality, the invention, or the genius of each one." This, then, is the part
taken by genius in the experimental novel. As Claude
Bernard says again : " The idea is the seed; the
method is the soil which furnishes the conditions for
developing and prospering it, and bringing forth its
best fruits, according to nature." Thus everything is
reduced to a question of method. If you are content
to remain in the *a priori* idea, and enjoy your own
feelings without finding any basis for it in reason or
any verification in experiment, you are a poet ; you
venture upon hypotheses which you cannot prove ; you
are struggling vainly in a painful indeterminism, and in
a way that is often injurious. Listen to these lines of
" L'Introduction ": " Man is naturally a metaphysician
and proud ; he believes that the idealistic creations of
his brain, which coincide with his feelings, represent
the reality. Thus it follows that the experimental
method is not innate and natural to man, for it is only
after having wandered for a long time among theological and scholastical discussions that he ends by recognizing the sterility of his efforts in this path. Man
then perceives that he cannot dictate laws to nature,
because he does not possess in himself the knowledge
and the criterion of exterior things ; he realizes
that in order to arrive at the truth he must, on
the contrary, study the natural laws and submit his
ideas, if not his reason, to experiment, that is to say,
to the criterion of facts." What becomes of the genius
of the experimental novelist ? The genius, the idea

a priori, remains, only it is controlled by experiment. The experiment naturally cannot destroy his
genius; on the contrary, it confirms it. To take the
case of a poet, for example: To show he has genius is
it necessary that his feeling, his idea, *a priori*, should
be false? Evidently not, for the genius of a man will
be so much the greater when experiment has proved
the truth of his personal idea. Our age of lyricism,
our romantic disease, was alone capable of measuring
a man's genius by the quantity of nonsense and folly
which he put in circulation. I conclude by saying
that in our scientific century experiment must prove
genius.

This is the drift of our quarrel with the idealistic
writers. They always start out from an irrational
source of some kind, such as a revelation, a tradition,
or conventional authority. As Claude Bernard declares: "We must admit nothing occult; there are
but phenomena and the conditions of phenomena."
We naturalistic novelists submit each fact to the test
of observation and experiment, while the idealistic
writers admit mysterious elements which escape analysis, and therefore remain in the unknown, outside of
the influence of the laws governing nature. This
question of the ideal, from the scientific point of view,
reduces itself to a question of indeterminate or determinate. All that we do not know, all that escapes us
still, that is truly the ideal, and the aim of our human
efforts is each day to reduce the ideal, to conquer
truth from the unknown. We are all idealists, if we
mean by this that we busy ourselves with the ideal.
But I dub those idealists who take refuge in the
unknown for the pleasure of being there, who have

a taste but for the most risky hypotheses, who disdain to submit them to the test of experiment under the pretext that the truth is in themselves and not in the things. These writers, I repeat, accomplish a vain and harmful task, while the observer and the experimentalist are the only ones who work for the strength and happiness of man, making him more and more the master of nature. There is neither nobility, nor dignity, nor beauty, nor morality in not knowing, in lying, in pretending that you are greater according as you advance in error and confusion. The only great and moral works are those of truth.

What we alone must accept is what I will call the stimulus of the ideal. Certainly our science is very limited as yet, beside the enormous mass of things of which we are ignorant. This great unknown which surrounds us ought to inspire us with the desire to pierce it, to explain it by means of scientific methods. And this does not refer only to scientific men ; all the manifestations of human intelligence are connected together, all our efforts have their birth in the need we feel of making ourselves masters of the truth. Claude Bernard explains this very clearly when he writes : " The sciences each possess, if not a special method, at least special processes, and, moreover, they reciprocally serve as tools for one another. Mathematics serves as a tool to physics, to chemistry, and to biology in very different measure ; physics and chemistry serve as powerful tools to physiology and medicine. In this mutual help which the sciences are to each other, you must distinguish clearly the savant who advances each science and he who makes use of it. The physician and the chemist are not mathematicians because they

employ calculation; the physiologist is not a chemist
or a physician because he uses chemical reactions or
medical instruments, any more than the chemist and
the physician are physiologists because they study the
compositions or the properties of certain liquids and
certain animal or vegetable tissues." This is the reply
which Claude Bernard can be said to make for us naturalists to the critics who taunt us with making pretensions to science. We are neither chemists nor physicians nor physiologists; we are simply novelists who
depend upon the sciences for support. We certainly
do not pretend to have made discoveries in physiology which we do not practice; only, being obliged
to make a study of man, we feel we cannot deny the
efficacy of the new physiological truths. And I will
add that the novelists are certainly the workers who
rely at once upon the greatest number of sciences,
for they treat of them all and must know them all,
as the novel has become a general inquiry on nature
and on man. This is why we have been led to apply
to our work the experimental method as soon as this
method had become the most powerful tool of investigation. We sum up investigation, we throw ourselves
anew into the conquest of the ideal, employing all
forms of knowledge.

Let it be well understood that I am speaking of the
"how" of things and not of the "why." For an
experimental savant, the ideal which he is endeavoring
to reduce, the indeterminate, is always restricted to
the "how." He leaves to philosophers the other ideal,
that of the "why," which he despairs of determining. I think that the experimental novelists equally
ought not to occupy themselves with this unknown

quality, unless they wish to lose themselves in the follies of the poets and the philosophers. It is surely an object large enough to try to know the entire mechanism of nature, without troubling one's self for the time being with the origin of the mechanism. If we some day succeed in knowing it, we shall doubtless owe our knowledge to method, and it is better then to begin at the beginning with the study of phenomena, instead of hoping that a sudden revelation will reveal to us the secret of the world. We are the workmen; we will leave to the metaphysicians this great unknown of the " why " they have struggled with so vainly for centuries, in order to confine our efforts to that other unknown of the " how," which is cleared away more and more every day by our investigation. The only ideal which ought to exist for us, the naturalistic novelists, should be one which we can conquer.

Besides, in the slow conquest which we can make over this unknown which surrounds us, we humbly confess the ignorant condition in which we are. We are beginning to march forward, nothing more; and our only real strength lies in our method. Claude Bernard, after acknowledging that experimental medicine is in its infancy still, does not hesitate to give great credit to empirical medicine. " In reality," he says, " empiricism, that is to say, observation or accidental experiment, has been the origin of all science. In the complex sciences dealing with man empiricism necessarily governs the practice much longer than in those of the more simple sciences." And he is willing to admit that at the crisis of a disease, when the determinism or nearest cause of the pathological phenomena has not been found, the best thing to do is to act empirically ; as, moreover, happens in the growth of knowledge, since empiricism invariably precedes the scientific condition of any branch of knowledge. Certainly if doctors must resort to empiricism in nearly every case, we have much greater reasons for using it, we novelists whose science is more complicated and less determined. I say once more, it is not a question of creating the science of man, as an individual and as a social being, out of the whole cloth ; it is only a question of emerging little by little and with all the inevitable struggles from the obscurity in which we lie concerning our own natures, happy if, amid so many errors, we can determine one truth. We experiment, that is to say that, for a long time still, we must use the false to reach the true.

Such is the feeling among strong men. Claude Bernard argues fiercely against those who persist in seeing only an artist in a doctor. He knows the habitual objection of those who pretend to look upon experimental medicine " as a theoretical conception of which nothing for the moment justifies the practical reality, because no fact demonstrates the attainment in medicine of the scientific precision of the experimental sciences." But he does not let this worry him ; he shows that " experimental medicine is but the natural outcome of practical medical investigation directed by a scientific mind." And here is his conclusion : " Without doubt it will be a long time before medicine becomes truly scientific ; but that does not prevent us from conceiving the possibility of such a thing, and doing all that we can to help it by trying daily to introduce into medicine the method which is to lead us to it."

All this, which I will not tire you by repeating, applies perfectly to the experimental novel. Put the word " novel " in place of " medicine," and the passage remains equally true.

I will address to the young literary generation which is growing up around me these grand and strong words of Claude Bernard. I know none more manly. " Medicine is destined to escape little by little from empiricism, and she will escape, as have all the other sciences, by the experimental method. This profound conviction sustains and controls my scientific life. I am deaf to the voices of those doctors who demand that the causes of scarlatina and measles shall be experimentally shown to them, and who think by that to draw forth an argument against the use of the experimental method in medicine. These discouraging objections and denials generally come from systematic or lazy minds, those who prefer to rest on their systems or to sleep in darkness instead of making an effort to become enlightened. The experimental direction which medicine is taking to-day is definitely defined. And it is no longer the ephemeral influence of a personal system of any kind ; it is the result of the scientific evolution of medicine itself. My convictions in this respect are so strong that I endeavor to impress them clearly upon the minds of the young medical students who are following my course at the Collège de France. The students must be inspired before all else with the scientific spirit, and initiated into the ideas and the tendencies of modern science."

Though I have frequently written the same words and given the same advice, I will repeat them here : " The experimental method alone can bring the novel out of the atmosphere of lies and errors in which it is plunged. All my literary life has been controlled by this conviction. I am deaf to the voices of the critics who demand that I shall formulate the laws of heredity and the influence of surroundings in my characters; those who make these discouraging objections and denials but speak from slothfulness of mind, from an infatuation for tradition, from an attachment more or less conscious to philosophical and religious beliefs. The experimental direction which the novel is taking to-day is a definite one. And it is no longer the ephemeral influence of a personal system of any kind, it is the result of the scientific evolution, of the study of man himself. My convictions in this respect are so strong that I endeavor to impress them clearly upon the minds of the young writers who read my works; for I think it necessary, above all things else, to inspire them with the scientific spirit, and to initiate them into the ideas and the tendencies of modern science."

V.

BEFORE concluding it is necessary for me to touch upon several secondary points.

If it is necessary to state the facts precisely on any one subject, it is on that of the impersonal character of the method. Some have accused Claude Bernard of wishing to pose as an innovator; and he has replied to these attacks as follows: "I have certainly not pretended to be the first to propose the application of physiology to medicine. That was recommended a long time ago, and numerous attempts have been made in this direction. In my works, and in my lectures at the Collège de France, I have only followed out an idea which has already borne fruit in its application to medicine." This is what I myself have replied when they have accused me of wishing to pose as an innovator and the leader of a new school. I have said that I introduce nothing, that I simply endeavor to apply in my novels and critical essays the scientific method which has been in use for a long time. But naturally they have pretended not to hear me, and they still continue to talk of my vanity and my ignorance.

I have already repeated twenty times that naturalism is not a personal fantasy, but that it is the intellectual movement of the century. Perhaps they will believe Claude Bernard, who speaks with greater authority on this subject than I can lay claim to; he declares that: "The revolution which the experi-

mental method has caused in science consists mainly
in the substitution of a scientific criterion for a
personal authority. It is the characteristic of the
experimental method to depend only on itself, as it
carries within itself its criterion, which is experiment.
It recognizes no authority but that of facts, and it
frees itself from personal authority." Consequently, it
no longer admits the authority of any theory either.
"The idea should always remain independent; it must
be enchained neither by scientific, nor philosophical,
nor religious beliefs. Man must be strong and free in
the manifestation of his ideas, must follow his instinct,
and not dwell upon the puerile fears of the contradiction of any theories; . . . he must modify theory by
adapting it to nature, and not nature by adapting it to
theory." From this there results an incomparable
breadth. " The experimental method is the scientific
method which proclaims the liberty of thought. It not
only throws off the philosophical and theological yoke,
but it no longer admits scientific personal authority.
This is not said from pride or boastfulness. The experimentalist, on the contrary, shows his humility in
denying personal authority, for he doubts his own
knowledge, and he submits the authority of men to
that of experiment and the laws which govern nature."

This is why I have said so many times that naturalism is not a school, as it is not embodied in the genius
of one man, nor in the ravings of a group of men, as was
romanticism ; that it consists simply in the application
of the experimental method to the study of nature
and of man. Hence it is nothing but a vast movement, a march forward in which everyone is a workman,
according to his genius. All theories are admitted,

and the theory which carries the most weight is the one which explains the most. There does not appear to me to be a literary or scientific path larger or more direct. Everyone, the great and the small, moves freely, working and investigating together, each one in his own specialty, and recognizing no other authority than that of facts proved by experiment. Therefore in naturalism there could be neither innovators nor leaders; there are simply workmen, some more skillful than others.

Claude Bernard explains the defiance which we should assume toward theories thus: " You must have a strong faith and yet not believe; I will explain myself by saying that it is necessary in science to believe firmly in the principles and to doubt the formulas; in fact, on one side we are sure that determinism exists, but we are never certain of possessing it. We must be immovable on the principles of experimental science (determinism), and yet not believe in the theories absolutely." I will quote the following passage, in which he announces the end of systems: " Experimental medicine is not a new system of medicine, but, on the contrary, the negation of all systems. In fact, the coming of experimental medicine will result in dispersing from science all individual views, to replace them by impersonal and general theories, which will be, as in other sciences, but a regular co-ordination deduced from the facts furnished by experiment."

If Claude Bérnard repels the charge of being an innovator, or rather, an inventor, who brings a personal theory with him, he refers also several times to the danger there would be in a savant's meddling with philosophical systems. " The experimental doctor," he says, " should neither be a spiritualist nor a materialist. These names belong to an old school of natural philosophy which has fallen into disuse in the progress of science. We shall never fully understand either mind or matter; and, if this were the proper place, I could easily show that on one side as on the other you soon reach scientific negation, from which it follows that all considerations of this kind are idle and useless. It is for us to study only phenomena, to know the material conditions of their manifestations, and to determine the laws of these manifestations." I have said that in the experimental novel it is best for us to hold to the strictly scientific point of view if we wish to base our studies on solid ground; not to go out from the " how," not to attach ourselves to the " why." However, it is very certain that we cannot always escape this need of our intelligence, this restless curiosity which makes us desire to know the essence of things. I think that it is best for us to accept the philosophical system, which adapts itself the best to the actual condition of the sciences, but simply from a speculative point of view. For example, transformism is actually the most rational system, and is the one which is based most directly upon our knowledge of nature. Behind a science, behind a manifestation of any kind of the human intelligence, there always lies more or less clearly what Claude Bernard calls a philosophical system. To this system it is not well to attach one's self devotedly, but 'to hold tenaciously to the facts, free to modify the system if the facts call for it. But the system exists none the less, and it exists so much the more as science is less advanced and less firm. For us naturalistic novelists, who are still in the lisping stage, hypothesis is fatal. By and by I will take up the rôle of hypothesis in literature.

Nevertheless, if in practice Claude Bernard thrusts aside philosophical system, he recognizes the necessity of philosophy. " From a scientific point of view, philosophy represents the eternal desire of the human reason after knowledge of the unknown. Hence philosophers always confine themselves to questions that are in dispute, and to those lofty regions that lie beyond the boundaries of science. In this way they communicate to science a certain inspiration which animates and ennobles it. They strengthen the mind—developing it by an intellectual gymnastics— at the same time that they ever carry it toward the never-completed solution of great problems. Thus they keep up a cult of the unknown, and quicken the sacred fire of investigation, which ought never to be extinguished in the heart of a savant." This passage is very fine, but the philosophers have never been told in better terms that their hypotheses are pure poetry. Claude Bernard evidently looks upon the philosophers, among whom he believes he has a great many friends, as musicians often gifted with genius, whose music encourages the savants while they work and inspires the sacred fire of their great discoveries. But the philosophers, left to themselves, will sing forever and never discover a single truth.

I have neglected until now the question of form in the naturalistic novel, because it is precisely there that individuality shows in literature. Not only is a writer's genius to be found in the feeling and in the idea *a priori* but also in the form and style. But the question of method and the question of rhetoric are distinct from each other. And by naturalism, I say again, is meant the experimental method, the introduction of observation and experiment into literature. Rhetoric, for the moment, has no place here. Let us first fix upon the method, on which there should be agreement, and after that accept all the different styles in letters which may be produced, looking upon them as the expressions of the literary temperament of the writers.

If you wish my true opinion upon this subject, it is this : that to-day an exaggerated importance is given to form. I have a great deal to say on this subject, but it would carry me beyond the limits of this essay. In reality, I think that the form of expression depends upon the method; that language is only one kind of logic, and its construction natural and scientific. He who writes the best will not be the one who gallops madly among hypotheses, but the one who walks straight ahead in the midst of truths. We are actually rotten with lyricism ; we are very much mistaken when we think that the characteristic of a good style is a sublime confusion with just a dash of madness added ; in reality, the excellence of a style depends upon its logic and clearness.

Claude Bernard considers that philosophers are really musicians who play a sort of Marseillaise made up of hypotheses, and swell the hearts of the savants as they rush to attack the unknown ; and he has much the same idea of artists and writers. I have remarked that a great many of the most intelligent savants, jealous of the scientific certainty which they enjoy, would very willingly confine literature to the ideal. They themselves seem to feel the need of taking little recreations in the world of lies after the fatigue of their exact labors, and they are fond of amusing themselves with the most daring hypotheses, and with fictions which they know perfectly well to be false and ridiculous. Claude Bernard was right when he said: " Literary and artistic productions will never grow old in the sense that they are the expressions of sentiments as unchangeable as human nature." In fact, form is sufficient to immortalize a work ; the spectacle of a powerful individuality reproducing nature in superb language will interest all ages ; only the works of a savant, from this same point of view, will be read always, for the reason that the thought of a great savant who knows how to write is much more interesting than that of a poet. However far astray the savant may be in his hypothesis, he still remains the equal of the poet, who is certain to have been equally mistaken. The point to be emphasized is this, that our domain is not limited to the expression of sentiments as unchangeable as human nature because it is essential also to exhibit the working of these sentiments.

We have not exhausted our matter when we have depicted anger, avarice, and love ; all nature and all of man belong to us, not only in their phenomena, but in the causes of these phenomena. I well know that this is an immense field, the entrance to which they would willingly have refused us ; but we have broken down the barriers and have entered it in triumph. This is why I do not accept the following words of Claude Bernard : " In art and letters personality dominates everything. There one is dealing with a spontaneous creation of the mind that has nothing in common with the verification of natural phenomena, in which

our minds can create nothing." I have here detected
one of our most illustrious savants sharing in the
attempt to refuse to letters the *entrée* to the scientific
field. I do not know what letters he refers to in this
definition of a literary work: "A spontaneous creation
of the mind that has nothing in common with the
verification of natural phenomena." Doubtless he has
lyrical poetry in his mind, for he never could have
written that phrase had he understood the experimental novel as shown in the works of Balzac and
Stendhal. I can only repeat what I have said before,
that apart from the matter of form and style, the
experimental novelist is only one special kind of
savant, who makes use of the tools of all other savants,
observation and analysis. Our field is the same as the
physiologist's, only that it is greater. We operate, like
him, on man; and Claude Bernard recognizes this
fact himself, that the cerebral phenomena can be determined the same as other phenomena. It is true that
Claude Bernard can tell us that we are lost in hypotheses; but to conclude from this that we shall never
arrive at the truth sits very badly on him, as he has
struggled all his life to make a science of medicine,
which the great majority of his contemporaries look
upon as an art.

Let us clearly define now what is meant by an
experimental novelist. Claude Bernard gives the following definition of an artist: "What is an artist? He
is a man who realizes in a work of art an idea or a sentiment which is personal to him." I absolutely reject
this definition. On this basis if I represented a man
as walking on his head, I should have made a work of
art, if such happened to be my personal sentiments.

But in that case I should be a fool and nothing else. So one must add that the personal feeling of the artist is always subject to the higher law of truth and nature. We now come to the question of hypothesis. The artist starts out from the same point as the savant; he places himself before nature, has an idea *a priori*, and works according to this idea. Here alone he separates himself from the savant, if he carries out his idea to the end without verifying its truth by the means of observation and experiment. Those who make use of experiment might well be called experimental artists; but then people will tell us that they are no longer artists, since such people regard art as the burden of personal error which the artist has put into his study of nature. I contend that the personality of the writer should only appear in the idea *a priori* and in the form, not in the infatuation for the false. I see no objection, besides, to its showing in the hypothesis, but it 'is necessary to clearly understand what you mean by these words.

It has often been said that writers ought to open the way for savants. This is true, for we have seen in "L'Introduction" that hypothesis and empiricism precede and prepare for the scientific state which is established finally by the experimental method. Man commenced by venturing certain explanations of phenomena, the poets gave expression to their emotions, and the savants ended by mastering hypotheses and fixing the truth. Claude Bernard always assigns the rôle of pioneers to the philosophers. It is a very noble rôle, and to-day it is the writers who should assume it and who should endeavor to fill it worthily. Only let it be well understood that each time that a truth is

established by the savants the writers should immediately abandon their hypothesis to adopt this truth;
otherwise they will remain deliberately in error without
benefiting anyone.   It is thus that science, as it advances, furnishes to us writers a solid ground upon
which we should lean for support, to better enable us to
shoot into new hypotheses.   In a word, every phenomenon, once clearly determined, destroys the hypothesis
which it replaces, and it is then necessary to trans-
port your hypothesis one step further into the
new unknown which arises.   I will take a very simple example in order to make myself better understood : it has been proved that the earth revolves
around the sun ; what would you think of a poet who
should adopt the old belief that the sun revolves
around the earth?   Evidently the poet, if he wishes
to risk a personal explanation of any fact, should
choose a fact whose cause is not already known.   This,
then, illustrates the position hypothesis should occupy for experimental novelists ; we must accept determined facts, and not attempt to risk about them our
personal sentiments, which would be ridiculous, building throughout on the territory that science has conquered ; then before the unknown, but only then,
exercising our intuition and suggesting the way to
science, free to make mistakes, happy if we produce
any data toward the solution of the problem.   Here
I stand at Claude Bernard's practical programme, who
is forced to accept empiricism as a necessary forerunner.   In our experimental novel we can easily risk
a few hypotheses on the questions of heredity and
surroundings, after having respected all that science
knows to-day about the matter.   We can prepare the

ways, we can furnish the results of observation, human data which may prove very useful. A great lyrical poet has written lately that our century is a century of prophets. Yes, if you wish it; only let it be well understood that these prophets rely neither upon the irrational nor the supernatural. If the prophets thought best to bring up again the most elementary notions, to serve up nature with a strange religious and philosophical sauce, to hold fast to the metaphysical man, to confound and obscure everything, the prophets, notwithstanding their genius in the matter of style, would never be anything but great gooses ignorant whether they would get wet if they jumped into the water. In our scientific age it is a very delicate thing to be a prophet, as we no longer believe in the truths of revelation, and in order to be able to foresee the unknown we must begin by studying the known.

The conclusion to which I wish to come is this: If I were to define the experimental novel I should not say, as Claude Bernard says, that a literary work lies entirely in the personal feeling, for the reason that in my opinion the personal feeling is but the first impulse. Later nature, being there, makes itself felt, or at least that part of nature of which science has given us the secret, and about which we have no longer any right to romance. The experimental novelist is therefore the one who accepts proven facts, who points out in man and in society the mechanism of the phenomena over which science is mistress, and who does not interpose his personal sentiments, except in the phenomena whose determinism is not yet settled, and who tries to test, as much as he can, this personal sentiment, this idea *a priori,* by observation and experiment.

I cannot understand how our naturalistic literature can mean anything else. I have only spoken of the experimental novel, but I am fairly convinced that the same method, after having triumphed in history and in criticism, will triumph everywhere, on the stage and in poetry even. It is an inevitable evolution. Literature, in spite of all that can be said, does not depend merely upon the author; it is influenced by the nature it depicts and by the man whom it studies. Now if the savants change their ideas of nature, if they find the true mechanism of life, they force us to follow them, to precede them even, so as to play our rôle in the new hypotheses. The metaphysical man is dead; our whole territory is transformed by the advent of the physiological man. No doubt "Achilles' Anger," "Dido's Love," will last forever on account of their beauty; but to-day we feel the necessity of analyzing anger and love, of discovering exactly how such passions work in the human being. This view of the matter is a new one; we have become experimentalists instead of philosophers. In short, everything is summed up in this great fact: the experimental method in letters, as in the sciences, is in the way to explain the natural phenomena, both individual and social, of which metaphysics, until now, has given only irrational and supernatural explanations.

A LETTER TO THE YOUNG
PEOPLE OF FRANCE.

A LETTER TO THE YOUNG
PEOPLE OF FRANCE.

I DEDICATE this article to the young people of
France, this youth who to-day have seen only
twenty years, but who will be the society of to-morrow.
Two events of great importance have just occurred:
the representation of " Ruy Blas" at the Comédie
Française, and the public reception of M. Renan at the
Academy. Great noise and wild enthusiasm have
burst forth, the public press has rolled out high-sound-
ing phrases in honor of the nation's genius, and it has
been said that like events should console us in our
disasters and assure us of future triumphs. There has
been a flight into the ideal, an escape from the earth
and a soaring in mid-air, a sort of counter charge on
the part of poetry against the scientific spirit.

I find the question distinctly defined in the *Répub-
lique Française*: " Paris has just witnessed and given to
the world the spectacle of two great intellectual feasts,
which will remain an honor and a crown to this enlightened and liberal France, of which our great and glorious
city is the chief representative. The reception of M.
Ernest Renan at the Academy, the revival of ' Ruy
Blas' at the Comédie Française, may, in truth, be regarded as two events of which we have a right to be

proud. There are among us some young people who are searching for their path in life ; they go straight ahead, pushing forward, hungry for novelties, and they boast, with the *naïveté* of inexperience, to be further advanced than their predecessors in the limitless domain of the art which is striving to do battle with nature. Yes, that is true; some among them who have mistaken their strength have declared war against the ideal, but they will be conquered ; their defeat can be safely predicted after what took place night before last at the Comédie Française." To understand my meaning the flowery phrases of the journalist must be explained. It means that these young people are the writers of the naturalistic school—those whose spirit is in sympathy with the scientific movement of the century, and whose useful tools are observation and analysis. The journalist states that these writers have declared war against the ideal, and he predicts that they will be vanquished by lyricism and romantic rhetoric. Nothing could be truer; the other evening, when Victor Hugo's beautiful verses were applauded, it gave the scientific movement of the century a set-back, it was the suppression of observation and analysis.

I will quote some other testimony, in order to explain more clearly the question which I wish to examine. M. Renan, at the commencement of his speech at the reception, wishing to flatter the Academy, and forgetting his old-time admiration for Germany, spoke as follows: "You are mistrustful of a culture which makes men neither more amiable nor better. I very much fear that these people, given to great seriousness, no doubt, while reproaching us for our levity, may experience some disappointment with regard to the hopes which they entertain of gaining the world's favor by other means than those which have so far been successful. A science pedantic in its solitude, a literature without humor, an ill-tempered government, a fashionable society without any sparkle, a spiritless nobility, gentlemen lacking in politeness, great generals with barbarous speech, will not easily or soon overthrow the remembrance of our old French society, so brilliant, so polished, so eager to please." To this the Berlin *Gazette Nationale* replied: "The nations of Europe are in a struggle which admits of no truce; the one which does not push ahead will be overthrown. Any nation which thinks to rest content with laurels already won is instantly condemned to decadence and death. This is the true state of affairs, which so great a nation as the French should learn to know. But to attain this end men of serious natures and not flatterers are needed. We shall look upon as our true friend the oné who teaches us to guard ourselves from that which we most fear in the world: empty vagueness, and the insufficient appreciation of our competitors in the material and intellectual domain. We know the inevitable consequence by experience."

Now I say that it is the duty of every patriotic Frenchman to reflect on these two documents. I do not speak of the patriotism which wraps itself in a flag, which gives itself vent in odes and cantatas; but of the patriotism of men of science and thought, who desire the nation's greatness by practical means. Yes, M. Renan is right: we have had and we still have a great deal of glory; but ponder on these terrible words: "The one who does not push ahead will be overthrown." Do you not hear in them that knell of the past ages which the new movement is sounding? To-morrow—that means this twentieth century, whose slow birth is brought about by this scientific evolution; to-morrow—that means universal inquiry, the spirit of truth transforming society; and if we wish to-morrow to belong to us we must be new men, marching toward the future by method, by logic, by study, and a full appreciation of reality. To applaud a burst of rhetoric, to become enthusiastic for the ideal, are but the nervous emotions of women, who weep as they listen to beauti ful music. To-day we have need of the manliness of truth to enable us to be as great in the future as we were in the past.

This is what I am going to try to demonstrate to the youth of France. I wish to breathe into their hearts a dislike for fine words, a distrust for these flights into the ethereal. We others, who confine our-selves to facts, who take up all problems, we are accused, in our study of the facts, of filthiness; we hear ourselves branded as corrupters every day. The time has come in which to prove to the new generation that the real corrupters are these word-mongers, and that there is a fatal fall in the mud after each flight into the ideal.

I.

ALL nations honor their great men. Above all, they render homage to their illustrious writers who have left imperishable monuments behind them. Homer and Vergil have survived the ruins of Greece and Rome. Thus it is that Victor Hugo's poetical monument will remain indestructible, and our century has a right to be proud of this superb work which is the glory of the French language, and will live through future ages. We cannot proclaim the poet's glory too loudly. He is great among the greatest. He was an admirable master of words, and he will live the undisputed king of lyrical poets. But we must make a distinction. Besides the form, the rhythm of the words, besides the purely linguistic monument, there stand the principles of the work. They carry with them truth or falsehood. They are the product of a method and become a fatal force, which advances or retards the century. If I applaud Victor Hugo as a poet, I dislike him as a thinker and a teacher. Not only does his philosophy appear to me as obscure, contradictory, and made up of emotions and not of truths, but, above all, I find it dangerous, exercising a harmful influence on the public, leading young men into the lies of poesy and all the mental derangements of romantic exaltation.

And all this we can easily see in this representation of " Ruy Blas," which has caused such a *furore*. It is the poet, the superb master of style, whom we applaud.

He has uplifted the language ; he has written verses which have the glitter of gold and the sonorousness of bronze. In no literature do I know poetry that is grander or more skillful, of a purer lyrical tone, of a more intense life. But no one could truthfully applaud the philosophy or the truthfulness of the work. If you set aside the clique of fierce admirers who strive to make Victor Hugo a universal man, as great a thinker as he is a poet, the world shrugs its shoulders before the incongruities of "Ruy Blas." One is obliged to look upon this drama as a fairy story, around which the author has woven a marvelous poetry. When once you examine it from a historical or a logical point of view, when once you endeavor to find practical truths, facts, data, you are entangled in a bewildering chaos of errors and misrepresentations; you fall into the nothingness of lyrical madness. The most peculiar thing of all is that Victor Hugo made pretensions to hiding a parable under the poetry of " Ruy Blas."

Read the preface, and see how in Victor Hugo's conception this lackey amorous of a queen represents the people desiring liberty, while *Don Salluste* and *Don César de Bazan* typify the nobility of a dying monarchy. Everyone knows how complaisant symbols usually are ; you can put them where you will and make them signify what you please. But this one carries the thing too far. Look at the characters in "Ruy Blas," at this imaginary lackey, who had been to college, who had written verses before he donned a livery, who never handled a tool, and who, instead of learning a trade, warmed himself in the sun's rays and fell madly in love with duchesses and queens. *Ruy Blas* is a Bohemian, an outcast, a worthless fellow. In

no sense is he one of the people. But, admitting for an
instant that he represents the people, let us see how he
behaves, and let us try to see what he signifies. From
this point of view everything becomes topsy-turvy.
The people, urged on by the nobility, love a queen;
the people become grand ministers, and waste their
time in fine speeches; the people kill the nobility, then
take poison immediately; what is the meaning of this
gibberish? What becomes of the famous symbol? If
the people kill themselves without cause, after having
suppressed the nobility, society is at an end. The
wretchedness of this extravagant intrigue is felt, and
becomes absolute folly as soon as the poet attempts
to make it signify anything serious. I will not point
out any further the incongruities of " Ruy Blas," as far
as good sense and simple logic are concerned. As a
lyrical poem, I repeat, the work is a marvel; but one
must not for a moment hope to find any human nature,
clearly defined ideas, an analytical method or a true
philosophy. It is a piece of beautiful music, nothing
else.

Then, again : " Ruy Blas," they say, is a flight into
the ideal, from whence radiates all manner of beautiful
ideas; it elevates the soul, it urges one forward to
great actions, it is refreshing and comforting. What
matter if it is but a lie! It takes us out of our everyday life and carries us to the heights. We breathe
freely, leaving the unclean works of the naturalistic
school behind us. Here we come to the delicate point
of the quarrel. Though we have not the time to
discuss the subject to its bottom, let us see what
" Ruy Blas " contains of honor and virtue. First
we must set aside *Don Salluste* and *Don César*. The

former is Satan, as Victor Hugo justly says; as to the
latter, notwithstanding his chivalric respect for women,
he shows a doubtful morality.   Now as to the queen.
This queen behaves badly in taking a lover; I know
very well that she is weary, and that her husband
makes a mistake in his too close watch of her ; but
truly, if all the women who were weary took to themselves lovers, it would cause a revolution in every
family.   Then as to *Ruy Blas*, he is a swindler, who
in real life would find his way to jail.   What do we
find ?   This lackey accepts the queen from *Don Salluste's* hands; he consents to enter into a deceit which
must appear all the more shameful to the spectator,
because *Don César*, the vagabond, the friend of robbers,
has just branded its infamy in two superb tirades; he
does more, he steals a name which is not his.   Fur-
thermore, he carries this name for a year, he deceives
a queen, an entire court, and the people, and he com-
mits these villainies for the sake of an intrigue; in the
end he understands his trickery and filthiness so well
that he poisons himself.   And all this time this man is
but a scamp and a debaucher.   My soul is not uplifted
in his company.   I would rather say my soul is filled
with disgust, because I go, in spite of myself, behind the
poet's verses, and I try to establish the facts and to
demonstrate to myself what does not appear on the
surface.   In reality, *Ruy Blas* is but an unprincipled
adventurer, who carries his kitchen manners into the
boudoir.   It is no use for Victor Hugo to carry his
drama into the higher atmosphere of poetry ; the reality which underlies it is infamous.   Notwithstanding
the beauty of the verses, the facts presented by this
drama are not only silly, they are unclean ; they do

not urge one on to good deeds, because the people
concerned in it are but scamps and rogues; they are
neither refreshing nor elevating, because they start in
the mud and the mire and end in blood. These are the
facts. Now to the verses. It is true that they often
express the most beautiful sentiments in the world. *Don
César* speaks words on the respect due to women; the
queen speaks words on the sublimity of love; *Ruy Blas*
speaks words about ministers who steal the state.
Always words! oh, as many words as you please. Can
it be that they expect to uplift people's souls merely
by a lot of words? *Mon Dieu !* yes, and this is the
point I am anxious to reach; that it is simply a
question of rhetorical virtue and honor. The romantic and lyric school depended entirely upon words.
They are inflated words, hypertrophies startling under
the uncouth exaggeration of the idea. Is not the
example striking? In the facts madness and coarseness,
in the expressions a noble passion, a proud virtue, and
a superior honesty. But it is all built on nothing; it
is a construction of language aimlessly beating the air.
This is romanticism.

I have criticised at different intervals the romantic
evolution, and it is useless for me to take up the history of this movement again. But I must insist upon
the fact that it was purely an uprising of rhetoricians.
Victor Hugo's rôle, which is a considerable one, has for
its object a reburnishing of the poetic language, the
creation of a new rhetoric. In 1830 the battle was
really a fight over the dictionary. The classical language was dying of inertia; the romanticists had in-
fused new blood into it by putting into circulation an
unknown and despised vocabulary, by employing a

host of sparkling images, by a livelier and more enlarged manner of feeling and rendering. But, putting aside this question of language, you can see that the romanticists did not separate themselves from the classical school ; for like it they remained deists, idealists, and symbolists ; like it they costumed beings and acts ; they placed them in an orthodox heaven ; they had the same dogmas, the same measures, the same rules. But it must be added that lyricism carried the new school much further into the realm of absurdity than did the old classical. The poets of 1830 had done much to enlarge the literary field by striving to reproduce man, in his entirety, with his smiles and his tears, by giving nature a part to play, an idea originated by Rousseau long before. But they spoiled these conquered liberties, they abused them in a strange manner by throwing themselves at once outside the pale of humanity and the natural order of events. For example, if they dealt with nature, if they painted it, instead of studying it as a definite environment, completing the characters, they animated it with their own dreams, peopled it with legends and nightmares ; in the same way in their characters, they boasted that they accepted the whole man, body and soul, and their first care was to lift him into the clouds and make him a lie. Thus, inevitably, it came to pass that the classical school, with its rigid and dead world, was still more humane, nearer to the truth, more logical and complete, than the romanticists with their vast horizon and the new elements of life which they employed. An evolution accomplished by these lyrical poets was bound to produce this result ; and this is what we briefly explain now. Lyricism in a literary school is a poetical exaltation eluding all analysis, and bordering on folly. Victor Hugo is but a lyrical poet, then; he is essentially a rhetorician of genius in his language, his philosophy, and his morality. But do not look beneath his words nor his rhymes, for I tell you again you will find an inconceivable chaos of errors, contradictions, solemn child's play, and pompous abominations.

To-day when we study the literary movements since the commencement of the century, the romantic movement seems to be the logical forerunner of the great naturalistic evolution. It was not without a reason that the lyric poets were produced first. Their coming can be explained as the outcome of the social conditions of the time, and as a result of the shocks of the Revolution and the Empire; after these massacres the poets found consolation in dreams. But they came, more than for any other reason, because in literature they had a great mission to accomplish. This was the renewing of the language. It was necessary to throw the old dictionary into the ditch, to recast the language, to invent new words and figures, to create a new style for the use of the new society; and the lyrical poets seemed the only fit ones to lead in such a work. They came with revolutionary ideas in color, with a passion for figures, with rhythm as their dominating concern. They were painters, sculptors, musicians, who depended upon sound, form, and light more than anything else. For them the idea was but a secondary consideration, and we remember this school of "art for art's sake" as an absolute triumph for style. The essential characteristic of the lyrical school is a song in which human thought frees itself from the shackles of method and envelopes itself in sonorous words. We can acknowledge also the glory which our language acquired in passing through this poetical flame. We find at the commencement of the century a literature of learned men, ponderous, exact, logical ; and their language, weakened by three centuries of classical usage, was like a tarnished, useless tool. A generation of lyrical poets, I repeat, was necessary to adorn the language, to reburnish the tool and make it of use again. This " Canticle of Canticles " of the dictionary, this pile of silly words flinging themselves at and dancing upon the idea, were perhaps necessary. The romanticists came in their time, they forged the tool which the century needed. It is thus that all great states are founded on a battle.

We shall see, a little further on, what state was to be founded, thanks to the romantic battle. Rhetoric had conquered ; the idea could arise and formulate itself, thanks to the new language. We must greet Victor Hugo as the powerful fabricator of this language. If in him the dramatic author, the novelist, the critic, the philosopher are subjects of debate; if lyricism, the sublime madness, always comes forth to upset in a moment his judgments and his conceptions—he is above all and always the rhetorician of genius of whom I have just spoken. This is the reason for the sovereignty which he has exercised and which he will exercise again. He has created a style, he holds sway over the century, not by his ideas, but by his words; the ideas of the century, those that rule, are scientific method, experimental analysis, and naturalism; the words are the rich novelties of exhumed or invented terms, those magnificent images, those superb roundings of the phrases which usage has rendered common. At the commencement of the movement the words always crushed the idea, because they struck one more forcibly. Victor Hugo since his early youth has royally draped himself in the mantle of form. Beside him stands Balzac, who carries the idea of the century—analysis and observation; but he seems naked, and is hardly noticed. Happily, later, the idea disengages itself from rhetoric, asserts itself, reigns with a sovereign strength. Here is where we stand. Victor Hugo remains a great poet—the greatest of lyrical poets. But the century has torn itself from him, the scientific idea pushes itself to the front. In "Ruy Blas" it is the rhetorician whom we applaud. The philosopher and the moralist causes us to smile.

II.

LET us now turn to the reception of M. Ernest Renan at the Académie Française. This reception was also a great literary festival. It was a great triumph for liberty of thought; that must be admitted before everything else. To make myself better understood I shall distinguish between the Renan of the legend and the Renan of reality. I must call to mind the publication of the "Vie de Jésus." It was a thunderclap. M. Renan was unknown to the general public. He enjoyed the reputation of being an erudite writer, a distinguished linguist, who did not go beyond the limits of a certain coterie. And all at once, in one day, his figure stood out before all France, with the terrifying profile of Antichrist. He committed the sacrilege of disturbing Jesus on his cross. He was pictured in the likeness of Satan, with two horns and a tail. The fright was greatest among the clergy; all the country curates ordered the bells rung, and excommunicated him in their sermons; the bishops sent forth charges and pamphlets, the Pope paled under his triple crown. It was said that the Jesuits burned the editions of "The Life of Jesus" as soon as the publisher put them on the market, which assured for the book an inexhaustible sale. As for the public, the feeling became greater and greater, fed by the fright of the clergy. The devotees made the sign of the cross, and terrified bad children by threatening them with

M. Renan; while the indifferent ones became interested in this audacious author, and endowed him with gigantic proportions. He became the spirit that denied; he symbolized science killing faith. In a word, our century of scientific inquiry became incarnate in him. If you add that he passed for an unfrocked priest, you complete the picture of this rebel archangel, modern Satan, conqueror of God, suppressing the Creator with the weapon of the century.

Such was the legendary Renan, and such he has remained for certain people. If we pass to the true Renan we are surprised. The savant remains an erudite, but he has also become a poet. Picture to yourself a man with the temperament of a believer, a contemplative creature growing up to manhood in a Breton fog. He had been brought up as a strict Catholic; his first desire had been to become a priest, and his whole education had tended toward the sacerdotal office. He comes to Paris, he enters the seminary steeped in the deep religious teachings of the country from whence he came. Then a corner in his brain, silent until that day, began to work. Was it a breath of Paris which had wafted over him in passing? Was it a far-away predisposition which awakened in the man, that had had its first germs in the child? He alone could tell us in confessing the sins of his boyhood. Whatever it was, a dissenting voice arose in him. From that moment the priest was dead. It is always the same story: the first shiver of doubt, then the sad combat followed by the final overflow. M. Renan quitted the seminary, and commenced the study of languages. But that which was not dead in him was the ideal and the spiritual. All the beliefs of his youth which he had battled with and crushed had returned upon him and found another vent, and were given expression in a burst of beautiful poetry. It is a curious instance of the tyrannical force that a man's nature has over him. Since he could not be a priest, he would be a poet; with nothing else would his temperament be satisfied. Without doubt, a nature less steeped in religious fantasy, brought up in a less misty country, would have gone to the end of the scientific research. But M. Renan stops halfway, carrying in his breast an eternal regret for his lost faith and the vague happiness of doubting his own doubts. This transformation of faith into poetry is characteristic of him. He is no longer a believer, but he is not a savant. I see in him a man of transition. The spirit of romanticism has gone along the same path.

Yes, M. Renan is a pantheist of the romantic school. It has been advanced that though he replaces God by the worship of humanity, he has not exactly denied the divinity of Christ, as he has made him the most perfect, the most lovable of men. I have no desire to lose myself in the intricacies of this philosophical question; I shall not examine his theories of the slow formation of a superior humanity, of a group of intellectual Messiahs, reigning on earth by the power of their faculties. It is sufficient for me that he, like Victor Hugo, is a deist, and that his beliefs, though possessed of more equilibrium, are not less the imaginations of the lyrical poet, as far away from the affirmations of dogma, as from the affirmations of science. Being neither a believer nor a savant, he remains a poet. He hovers in the vagueness dear to contemplative souls. His thought has no firm simplicity. You perceive what very possibly his opinions may be; but does he really believe them? This is something no one can tell, for he dislikes any definite conclusion. And if, leaving the philosopher, we pass to the writer, we find the romanticist in all his charm and greatness. I do not mean that it is the superb bewilderment of Victor Hugo, his magnificent antithesis, his piling up of grand words and images. It is rather Lamartine's flowing honey, a beatific and religious reverie, a style which has the voluptuousness of a caress and the unction of a prayer. The phrase kneels and swoons away in a vapor of incense, in the mystical light of the stained glass windows. You immediately conclude that M. Renan has entered into the Gothic cathedral of romanticism, and that he has remained there not as a believer, but as a writer. We find the poet still lingering midway between the erudite and the savant, as he had remained midway in the formulas of philosophy.

This is the difference between the M. Renan of the legend and the M. Renan of reality. I must add that the stubborn ones, the bigoted Catholics and fools, who cleave to a once conceived idea, continue to look upon M. Renan as Antichrist. Years have passed since its publication, and the majority of the reading public have come to look upon "The Life of Jesus" as a beautiful poem, hiding under its flowery language a few of the modern exegetical affirmations. All the truths are not touched upon; only a choice is made by an artistic hand, and embellished by the most loving imagination. To fully understand M. Renan's process you need only compare his book with that of the German writer Strauss, with his harsh discussions and his tedious demonstrations; in him we find but the erudite and learned writer, whose style is devoid of ornament, and whose sole thought is the truth. Thus, at the present day, for the greater number of readers, M. Renan, the terrible, has become the charming M. Renan. He is accepted as a melodist, who certainly committed a wrong in choosing so sacred a subject to sing to his music; but, truth to tell, he has written some very beautiful music. And it is the melodist to whom the Académie Française has opened its doors. I have reached my point now; I contend that the Académie has fêted the rhetorician and not the savant. This literary *fête* was again given in honor of a lyric poet.

But we must be severe, for in our complaisant and hypocritical century severity alone can make the nation virile. I do not dispute the fact that the Académie has made a good choice in opening its arms to M. Renan, and that the opportunity very rarely offers for them to make as good a one. M. Renan, whose erudition is very extended, is, besides, one of our most refined prose writers. Literally, his little finger is worth more than ten academicians taken haphazard from the benches of the learned company. Only his election must not be looked upon as a triumph of the modern scientific formula in this institution. There is under this famous cupola only another poet. The true courage consisted in naming M. Renan after the resounding success of his " Life of Jesus." To-day he has forced open the doors by his charming personality; he is not seated in his chair with his horns and his tail, but crowned by the hands of ladies. Nobody fears him any longer, he has even become the refuge of religious souls, torn by and restless under the dry and naked science of to-day. Therefore let them not make such a fuss over the liberalism of the Académie. It has welcomed a writer; that is as it should be. Modern science has had no reason to cry out " Victory !" as at the solemn receptions of Claude Bernard and M. Littré.

What appears to me most characteristic in M. Renan's discourse is the manner in which he accepts the discoveries of science—as a versatile idealist who utilizes everything in order to continue and enlarge his dreams. A quotation from the speech made at his reception will explain what I mean: " The sky, as we see it by means of modern astronomy, is vastly superior to that solid vault studded by brilliant stars, supported by columns some distance away in the clouds, with which the past centuries were content. . . . If I sometimes have melancholy remembrances of the nine choirs of angels who surrounded the seven planets, and of that crystalline sea which rolled at the feet of the Eternal One, I console myself by thinking that the infinite into which our eyes plunge is a real infinite, a thousand times more sublime to the true thinker than all the azure circles of the paradise of Angelo da Fiesole. How much do the profound views of the chemist and crystallographer on the atom exceed the vague notion possessed by the scholastic philosophers about matter! The triumph of science is really the triumph of idealism!" Listen to this cry; it is typical; it is the wail of the poet who, each time that you force the regions of the unknown to a further distance, willingly consents to move with you, but only for the privilege of installing himself to dream in a mysterious corner, to whose depths you have not yet descended.   As M. Renan himself states in his speech, a savant does not admit the unknown, the ideal, but as a problem whose solution he is trying to find.   A fresh proof that M. Renan is not a savant is that he must have his mysterious corner, and the more you contract this corner, the further you carry it to the depth of the infinite, the more he seems to be enchanted ; because, as he will tell you, his dream becomes more distant and sublime.   Thus: " The triumph of science is really the triumph of idealism."   I already knew this phrase from having heard it used so often as conclusive argument.   It is the refuge of those idealists who do not deny modern science.   As they believe that there will always be an ultimate mystery about the nature of matter and life that can never be solved, they move their ideal further away at each new discovery, saying that even though hunted from belief to belief they always have this final point as an unassailable refuge. This is a very elastic faith in the ideal.   I have a very slight philosophical esteem for these dreamers who at each step of science ask for a rest to indulge in a dream, and leave it but to move on further and to find a more retired corner for their reveries.   M. Renan is one of these poets of the ideal who follow the savants with faltering steps, and who profit by each halt to gather fresh flowers.

His great success—I speak of his widespread and popular success—is due to his style.   In Germany Strauss, wrapped up in the terseness of his argument, had simply stirred a small portion of the public, the erudites and the theologians ; the great crowd of worldly people were simply indifferent.   With us, on the contrary, M. Renan, much less frank in his negation, but treating the subject with armfuls of rhetorical flowers, had infatuated the whole public. It is only another proof of the omnipotence of form. The success of " The Life of Jesus " is but the success of " Ruy Blas "; it is the language, the sound, the color, the odor, which takes captive through the senses a keenly artistic people. In all this there is a nervous, a material effect. When a master of style is a genius, he is the undisputed master of the multitude; he takes them boldly and leads them where he will. A savant creates a vacuum in his audience, while a poet arouses enthusiasm even among his adversaries. This is the explanation of that outburst of romanticism in the first half of the century. In the same way to-day we applaud vociferously as a breath of lyrical poetry passes by us.

However, it must be admitted that this *furore* about form is transitory. People admit the power of the writer, then shrug their shoulders when he poses as a thinker or savant. And this is the punishment of those timid ones who dared not carry their thought out to its true end, of those clever fellows who tried to win over each one by flattering all. Yes, this artifice of ambitious souls, this process of letting fall only pleasing, well-clothed truths, this skillfully balanced way of writing which is not lying, yet is not the truth, all these hypocritical tactics rebound against those who use them, either from their temperament or through shrewd calculation. One day, after having been greeted with acclamations, they find themselves alone, celebrated, it is true, filled with honors and recompenses, but they enjoy the reputation of being only flute players when they were eager for the fadeless glory of great thinkers and famous savants.

I will not conclude in my own words. I read a severe criticism which struck me as very forcible, and I give it without comment: "A man like M. Renan ought to have some influence over his times, and he has none. He has never been taken seriously. In vain he approaches the deepest problems; no one admits his solutions; only levity and laughter have been seen where the philosopher, the savant, has looked for an entire and austere attention. The writer alone will live; the future will admit that he has fathomed all the subtleties of language, and that in spite of the crowd of to-day's musicians and the clash of the brass, the sweet notes of his oboe swell out, rising above everything else. Posterity will class him among the illustrious failures, among those who, in a time of change and awakening, chose the part of sweet leisure and flowery dreams."

III.

BY a species of irony it almost always happens that the newly elected academician is obliged to pronounce a eulogy on a dead member whose style and temperament are directly opposite to his. This is just what has happened, and you can easily understand how strange it seems to hear M. Renan scattering his flowery phrases over the life and work of Claude Bernard, the savant, who had put his life and the whole force of his powerful intellect into the experimental method. The spectacle is one curious enough to startle you. I wish to place the haughty and stern form of Claude Bernard face to face with Victor Hugo and M. Renan. It will be science facing rhetoric, naturalism facing idealism.

The pleasant side to this task lies in this fact, that I shall not myself have to interfere at all. M. Renan himself will furnish me with all the comparisons I need in his discourse at the reception. I find there a number of decisive arguments in favor of naturalism. It will be sufficient to quote some passages and add a few lines of comment.

In the first place, I will make a brief *résumé* of the life of Claude Bernard. " He was born in the little village of Saint Julien, near Villefranche, in a tiny house surrounded by vineyards, which was always the dearest spot on earth to him." He lost his father when very young, was brought up by his mother, and received his first lessons from the village priest: later he went to the college of Villefranche; afterward he started out in life as an apothecary's clerk. Even then he dreamed of attaining literary glory. " He tried everything: obtained a moderate success in a theater at Lyons with a little comedy, the title of which he would never divulge; afterward he started for Paris, with a tragedy in five acts in his valise, and a letter." This letter was addressed to Marc Girardin, who persuaded him to abandon literature. From that moment Claude Bernard set out to find his vocation. He met Magendie, whose favorite pupil he became. His struggles were long and terrible. His marvelous works are well known; his great discoveries which did so much for physiology. Now I will let M. Renan speak of him: "Recompenses came slowly to this great career, which, one might truly say, could afford to pass them by, because it was itself its own recompense. Your companion had a hard road to travel in the commencement of his life as a savant; and his reward came to him late. The Academy of Sciences, The Sorbonne, The College of France, The Museum, desired the fame of possessing him. Your assembly added the final crown to these honors by conferring on him the highest title to which a man devoted to intellectual work can aspire. A personal wish of the Emperor Napoleon III. called him to the senate."

Here I will stop. This little bit of biography is sufficient to establish a parallel between Claude Bernard and M. Renan. Notice the similarity of their start in life; both were educated by a priest, only the first grew to manhood on a sunny hillside, while the other was steeped from his childhood in the ocean's mist. At once the differences in temperament showed themselves. M. Renan, by nature poetical and religious, dreamed of being a priest, and later, notwithstanding his great erudition, notwithstanding his skepticism, could not rid himself of the cloudiest spiritualism; Claude Bernard, with his exact mind, went straight to experimental science, and had but one end, to track the truth from unknown to unknown. What I find most characteristic in him are his first literary attempts. His tragedy is miserable, its style is distressing. You feel he is entangled in a kind of literature where his observation, his analysis, his logic, are of no use to him. He makes a mess of classical literature, as he had made a mess of romantic literature, and after that his only refuge is in science. M. Renan says himself: "The period was more favorable to a literature of a commonplace character than to deep researches which are not adapted to pretty phrases." These lines amuse me; they remind you that M. Renan has succeeded in writing pretty phrases upon researches hardly susceptible of poetical treatment. But you see plainly the reasons which threw Claude Bernard into science.

But let us take up at once this question of style. M. Renan touches on this point in several places, and in excellent words. For instance: "The true method of investigation, presupposing a firm and sound judgment, carries with it solid qualities of style. The memoirs of Letronne and Eugène Burnouf, apparently without any kind of form, is a *chef-d'œuvre* in its way. The rule of good scientific style is clearness, perfect adaptation to the subject, a complete forgetfulness of self, in fact, absolute abnegation. It is also the rule for writing well on any subject. The best writer is the one who treats a great subject and forgets himself in thinking of his subject." Then again : "A writer of course he was, and an excellent writer, because he never thought of being one. He had the first qualities of a writer, which is not to think about the writing itself. His style, it was his own thoughts ; and as these thoughts were always great and strong, his style, in consequence, was also great and strong. His mode of expression was excellent for a scientific man, because based upon the fundamental principles of a style true, temperate, appropriate to what it wished to explain, or rather upon logic, the only eternal basis of good style." And then again, further on : "We must look up to our masters of the Port-Royal to find a like sobriety, an absence of all desire to shine, a disdain for the arts of an unworthy literature which seeks to relieve the austerity of the subject by insipid adornment."

I could never have brought myself to the point of condemning romantic rhetoric in such severe terms. M. Renan, carried away by the truth, forgets the "insipid adornment" with which he has relieved the "austerity" of "The Life of Jesus." How far away are the tirades of "Ruy Blas" from logic, "the only eternal basis of good style." The latter is the weapon of truth, the weapon of the century. Lyricism, with its pile of great words, its resounding epithets, is only an outburst of madness, only the insanity of ecstatic souls who kneel before the ideal, trembling lest the last little mysterious closet in which they enshrine their dreams be torn from them.

Now I come to the pith of the quarrel, to the war waged by science against the ideal, against the unknown

This was Claude Bernard's grand rôle. He started at the beginning, taking nature at its fountain head, solving problems by experiment, taking his stand on facts, and at each step forcing the unknown to recoil before him. Listen to what M. Renan says: "The highest philosophy was the result of this gathering together of facts set forth with an inflexible rigor. Bernard recognizes what we call 'determinism' as the supreme law of the universe; that is to say, the inflexible connection of phenomena which prevents any supernatural agent from interfering to modify the result. There are not, as it has often been stated, two orders of science: these absolutely precise, and those fearful of derangement by mysterious forces. That great mystery of physiology which Bichat admits still, that capricious power which some people pretend can offer a resistance to matter and makes life a sort of miracle, Bernard rejects entirely. 'The obscure idea of cause,' he says, 'should be relegated to the origin of things; it should give place in science to the idea of the connection of conditions.'" And then, further on, M. Renan adds: "Claude Bernard did not pretend to be ignorant of the fact that the problems which he stirred up touched upon the gravest philosophical questions. This did not move him. He did not think it was the rôle of the savant to worry himself over the consequences which might come out of his researches. He belonged to no sect. He was searching after the truth, and that was all." Here we have the very spirit of modern science. We have given up the problems in question; actual science has ordered a revision of the pretended truths which the past laid down under the name of certain dogmas. We study nature and man, we classify data, we advance step by step, employing the experimental and analytical method; but we take good care not to draw conclusions, because the inquiry still continues, and none can flatter themselves as yet to know the last word. We do not deny God; we endeavor to mount up to him by making an analysis of the world. If he is at the head of it all we shall find it out, science will reveal it to us. For the moment we put him to one side, we do not want a supernatural element, a superhuman axiom which will distract us in our observations. Those who begin by assuming an Absolute introduce into their observations of men and things a purely imaginative conception, a subjective dream, more or less attractive in its æsthetic charm, but utterly futile as far as truth and morality are concerned.

At this point I leave the scientific and enter the literary field. The naturalistic formula in literature, such as I shall now define it, is identical with the naturalistic formula in the sciences, and particularly in physiology. It is the same inquiry lifted from physiological phenomena up to passionate and social facts; the spirit of the century gives an impulse to all intellectual manifestations, the novelist who studies manners completes the work of the physiologist who studies the organisms. I quote M. Renan again: "Though Claude Bernard speaks but little on social questions, his was too great a mind not to apply to them his general principles. This conquering character of science he admits even in the sciences of humanity." "The active rôle of the experimental sciences," he says, "does not stop at the physical, chemical, and physiological sciences, it extends to the active and moral sciences. We begin to understand that it is not sufficient to remain an inert spectator of good and evil, enjoying the one and guarding one's self from the other. Modern morals aspire to a much grander rôle; they search out the causes, endeavor to explain and act upon them, to master good and evil, to bring the former forth and develop it, to do battle with the latter and destroy it." These words are strong; they contain all the high and severe morality of the contemporaneous novelists of the naturalistic school, which people are imbecile enough to accuse of obscenity and depravity. Enlarge the rôle of the experimental sciences, extend them to the study of the passions, the painting of manners, and you obtain romances which search out the causes, which explain them, which gather together human data in order to be the master of the surroundings and of man, so as to develop the good elements and exterminate the bad. We are doing a work identical with that of the savants. It is impossible to base any legislation whatsoever on the lies of the idealists. On the contrary, from the true data, which the naturalists bring forth, a better society can some day be established, which will live by logic and method. From the moment that we are truthful, we become moral.

This is the picture which M. Renan draws of the labors of the savant: " He passes his life in an obscure laboratory in the Collège de France; and there, in the midst of the most repulsive sights, breathing the atmosphere of the dead, his hands steeped in blood, he discovers the inmost secrets of life; and the truths which come out from this gloomy room dazzle those who are able to appreciate them. Claude Bernard himself says: ' The physiologist is not a man of the world, he is a savant, he is a man absorbed in a scientific idea which he is following up; he no longer hears the cries of the animals, he no longer sees the flowing blood—he sees but his idea, and perceives only the organisms which hide the problems from him which he wishes to discover. In the same manner the surgeon is not stopped by the cries and sobs of his patient, because he sees but his idea and the object of the operation before him. Still, again, the anatomist does not feel that he is in a horrible charnel house; under the influence of a scientific idea he delightedly follows a nervous thread in the swelling and putrid flesh which for another man would be an object of horror and disgust.'" In face of such a picture will you not pardon some audacities to novelists of the naturalistic school, who, for love of the truth, follow with delight the derangements produced by a passion in a person bad to the marrow of his bones? Will you reproach us with our horrible charnel houses, the blood which we cause to flow, the sobs which we force on our readers? Nevertheless we hope that our gloomy rooms may send forth some truths which will dazzle those who are able to appreciate them.

Such is the grand figure of Claude Bernard. He represents modern science in his disdain for mere excellence of form, in his vigorous and methodical examination free from any concession to mystery and reverie. He admits no irrational source such as a revelation, a tradition, a conventional and arbitrary authority. He asserts that in the problem of man everything ought to be studied and explained through the sole tool of experiment and analysis. In a word, this man is the incarnation of truth vouched for and proved. And besides, what a decisive influence he has had on his times. Each one of his discoveries has broadened human intelligence. His scholars crowded around him. He left data behind him over which future savants will work. And now turn back to M. Renan's solitude, the fine writer who idealized his borrowed ideas and his scholarly discoveries. Evidently he is but a charmer, a late dreamer; the strength of the century belongs to Claude Bernard. That magnificent flight of poetry, Victor Hugo's lyricism, is but a superb piece of music beside Claude Bernard's virile conquests of the mystery of life. While the lyrical poet mixes everything up, enlarges the unknown into a wider field in which to parade the follies of his imagination, the physiologist diminishes the field of lies, restricts human ignorance, honors reason and justice. Here is where I find the only true morality; it is from this spectacle that great lessons and great thoughts should spring.

IV.

LET us now see how this formula of modern science is applicable to literature. In the first place I am well aware of the argument which the lyric poets advance: that there is science and that there is poetry. Certainly there is no idea of suppressing the poets. We are merely trying to put them in their proper place, and to establish the fact that they are not the ones who, walking at the head of the century, preach to us of morality and patriotism.

In the first days of the world poetry was the dream of science with this newborn race. Of the two faculties belonging to man, to feel and to understand, the first brought forth poets, the second savants. Take man in his cradle : his senses are simply awakening, he is in ecstasy over everything ; he sees not the reality, he lives in a land of dreams. But as he grows older a curiosity to find out the meaning of things takes possession of him ; his awakening intelligence gropes about; he puts forth hypothesis upon hypothesis; he reaches a condition in which he discovers ideas of a certain breadth and with a certain reasonableness to them. At this age he is a poet ; the universe is but an immense mystery in which he parades his conceptions of its nature. In a little while certain more exact conceptions demand recognition ; his mystery, his ideal is narrowed, he ends by lodging it in the distant horizon, and in the obscure causes of life. The history of humanity is parallel to that of this man. The ideal is the outcome of our first ignorance. As science advances the ideal recedes. M. Renan transforms it, which comes to the same thing. I do not wish to enter upon a philosophical discussion, nor to affirm that one day science will completely suppress the unknown. It is not necessary for us to trouble ourselves about that; all we have to do is to go straight ahead in the conquest of the true, ready to accept the last conclusions. Our quarrel with the idealists lies simply in the fact that we start from observation and experiment, while they start from an absolute. Science is, then, to speak truly, but explained poetry; the savant is a poet who replaces imaginary theories by the exact study of men and things. In our time it is but a question of temperament; the brains of some are so constituted that it appears to them grander and more sensible to take up again the old dreams, to look at the world with blind madness and through the medium of their deranged nerves; others feel that the only state that savors of sanity or offers any possibility of real greatness for an individual, as for a nation, is by taking firm hold of realities, and by placing our intelligence and our human affairs on the solid foundation of truth. The former are the lyric poets, the romanticists; the latter are the naturalists. And the future depends upon the choice which coming generations will make between the two schools. It remains for the young people to determine which it shall be.

For some time past a great many senseless things have been said about the naturalistic formula. The press has put forth some very foolish theories, which concern me personally. For three years I have vainly tried to explain that I am not an innovator, that I am not trying to boom an invention. My only rôle has been that of a critic who studies his times, and who tries to show, supported by strong proofs, in what direction the century appears to be moving. I find the naturalistic formula in the eighteenth century; in fact, to my way of thinking, it seems to have started with the beginning of the world. I have shown how splendidly it has been developed in our national literature by such men as Stendhal and Balzac; I have said that our present novels but follow the works of these masters, and I have mentioned as in the first rank MM. Gustave Flaubert, Edmond and Jules Goncourt, and Alphonse Daudet. With such examples before them how can anyone say that I have invented a theory for my own particular use? What fools some men are to represent me to the public as a man puffed out with pride, who wishes to impose his form of expression as the only true style, and who bases upon his works all the past and the future of French literature!

In truth, this statement is the height of blindness and bad faith. Do they hear me to-day? Do they understand that the scientific formula of Claude Bernard is but the formula of the naturalistic writers? This formula belongs to the entire century. It is in no sense mine; I am not a fool to the extent of wishing to substitute my books for the ages of travail, for the long labor of human genius. My humble ambition goes no further than the desire to state precisely the nature of the present evolution, to separate it from the romantic period, to clear away the ground, in short, so as to make room for the fatal struggle now in progress between idealists and naturalists, and to predict victory ultimately for the latter. Outside of these theoretical discussions I have never posed save as the most determined follower of the truth.

Yes, our naturalistic formula is identical with that of the physiologists, the chemists, and the physicians. The use of this formula in our literature dates from the last century, from the first awakenings of our modern science. The ball has been set going and the inquiry will become universal. Several times already I have written the story of this vast movement which is sweeping us into the future. It has remodeled history and criticism, freeing them from the scholastic formulas that were based on haphazard observation; it has transformed the novel and the drama, beginning with Diderot and Rousseau down to Balzac and his followers. Can anyone deny these facts? and do they not include some hundred years in our history in which we see the scientific spirit throwing all the beautiful classical rules aside, and after taking its first steps in the romantic movement, enjoying its final triumph in the works of the naturalistic writers? Then, again, I am not the naturalistic school: that includes every writer who, willingly or not, employs the scientific formula, and taking up the study of the world by observation and analysis, denies the absolute, or any revealed or irrational ideal. The naturalistic school boasts of such men as Diderot, Rousseau, Balzac, and Stendhal, and twenty others besides. They make a grotesque caricature of me when they put me forward as a pope, as the chief of a new school. We have no religion, therefore no one can be a pope with us. As to our school, it is too large to be obedient to one chief. It is not like the romantic school, which is incarnate in one individual fantasy, in the genius of one poet. It does not live by its mode of expression; it exists, on the contrary, by a formula; and on this ground the day we elect a chief we will choose, above anyone else, a savant like Claude Bernard. If but a short time ago I devoted so much time to M. Renan, it was but to establish, on positive proofs taken from an idealist, that the strength of the century lies in science and naturalism. Look at Claude Bernard; he is our man, the man of the scientific formula, freed from all jingling of words, and such as the author of " The Life of Jesus " has depicted him.

Permit me here to illustrate my meaning by a personal anecdote. One day I had been talking to a very intelligent journalist, and had given him, at great length, the foregoing explanations, and repeated most strenuously that I had never had the wild ambition to play the rôle of "founder of a new school." I added that, without mentioning Balzac, there were in contemporaneous literature older names than mine, who were much better entitled to the name of "master." Finally I made the remark that the mistake on the subject of my pretensions doubtless came from the fact that I was the standard bearer of the scientific idea. While I was speaking the journalist became very grave; he looked disappointed and bored. He, who up to that time had been so very much interested in naturalism, interrupted me, crying out: "What! Is that all it is? Why, then, it's not even remarkable." That word means a great deal. The moment that I became reasonable, that I no longer preached a ridiculous religion, the thing ceased to be remarkable; as soon as naturalism, instead of being confined to the works of one writer on the obscene, was widened so as to include the intellectual movement of the century, it was no longer worthy of notice.

This is the height of nonsense; they preferred, and they still prefer, to consider naturalism the literature of obscenity. It is no use for me to protest and say that my individual efforts involve only myself and leave the formula intact; they cease not to repeat that naturalism is an invention of mine, which was launched in order to pass " L'Assommoir " off as a Bible. These people notice only the word. Words, always words! They cannot imagine anything back of the words. I am naturally a peaceful man, but I am seized with a ferocious desire to strangle those who say before me: " Ah, yes! naturalism—that is, nasty words! "

And who ever said that? I have almost worn myself out repeating that naturalism is not in the words; that its strength lies in the fact that it is a scientific formula. How many times shall I be obliged to say again that it is simply the study of men and things by observation and analysis, entirely free from any preconceived idea of the absolute? The question of style comes afterward. We will discuss it now, if you are willing.

I have explained at length how, according to my way of thinking, the romanticists came to do especially the work of stylists in our language. This revision of the dictionary was a necessity. Personally I often have regretted that the lyrical poets were necessarily charged with this work when I see what wildness and tinsel they have put in the style; we have the work of years before us to tone down these materials, and to reach a language as solid as it is rich. All of the writers of the second half of the century are, in question of style, but the children of the romanticists. This is undeniable. They have forged a tool which they have bequeathed to us, and of which we make use daily. The best of us owe our language to the poets and prose writers of 1830.

But who does not understand to-day that the reign of the word-mongers is over? Now that they have given us the tools, they have disappeared of necessity. And we in our turn come to do our work. The ground has been cleared; the question of language no longer stops us; we have complete liberty, and every facility for proceeding to the grand inquiry. It is a time of clear vision in which the idea is separated from the form. The romanticists bequeathed to us the form which we need to adjust after strictly logical methods, while retaining its richness. As to the idea, it is acquiring more and more influence, and is made manifest in the application of the scientific formula to everything, to politics as well as to literature.

Therefore, once more, naturalism means simply a formula, the analytical and experimental method namely. You are a naturalist if you make use of this method, whatever the character of your style. Stendhal is a naturalist as much as Balzac, though the dryness of his style in no way resembles Balzac's almost epic grandeur; but both proceed by analysis and experiment. I can call to mind in our own times writers whose literary temperament appears to be entirely opposed, and yet who meet and join hands in the naturalistic formula. This is why naturalism is not a school in the narrow sense of the word, and that is why there is no distinct head, because it leaves the field free to all individualities. Unlike the romantic school, it is not confined to the style of one man nor to the folly of a group. It is a literature open to all personal efforts, incarnate in the evolution of the human intelligence of our times. You are not commanded to write in a certain style nor to copy a certain master. You are asked to hunt out and classify your share of human data, and discover your corner of truth, thanks to the aid of method.

Here the writer is but a man of science. His artistic personality is subsequently shown in his style. Here, too, is where his skill comes in. They repeat this stupid argument to us, that we shall never reproduce nature in its exactness. Doubtless we shall always intermingle with our work our individuality and our way of rendering facts. But there is an abyss between the naturalistic writer who goes from the known to the unknown, and the idealist who aspires to go from the unknown to the known. If we do not give you nature in its entirety we at least give you truthful nature as we see it through our individuality, while the others complicate the deviations of their own sight with the errors of an imagined nature, which they accept in a haphazard way as being true. All we ask of them is to take up the study of the world in its first analysis, without abandoning any of their writer's temperament.

Does there exist a school with a more extended field? I know very well that the thought affects the form. And this is why I think that the language is becoming calmer and solider since the great hullabaloo of 1830. If we are condemned to repeat this music our sons will tear themselves away from it. I only wish we could attain this scientific style of which

M. Renan speaks in such praise. This would be a truly strong style, such as suits a literature founded on truth ; it would be a style free from any fashionable jargon, and embodying solidity and a classical breadth. Until that time we shall put flourishes at the end of our phrases, since our romantic education so wills it ; only we will prepare for the future by gathering together all the human data we can, and by making as much use of analysis as our tool will permit. This is naturalism, or if the word frightens you, and paraphrase would make it clear, the formula of modern science as applied to literature.

V.

I ADDRESS myself now to the young people of France. I conjure them to reflect before choosing either the path of idealism or that of naturalism; for the greatness of the nation, the welfare of the country, depend to-day upon their choice.

Young people of to-day are taught to applaud the sonorous verses of " Ruy Blas "; they have the chant of M. Renan given to them as a correct solution of modern science and philosophy; and from both sides they are made drunk with lyricism; their heads are filled with words; their nervous systems are distracted with this music to such an extent that they come to believe that morality and patriotism only consist of the well-turned phrases of the word-mongers. A republican journal has just written the following: " Some few writers, who have mistaken their strength, have declared war on the ideal; but they will be vanquished." But it is not we who have declared war against idealism; it is the century, it is the science of these last hundred years. So it is the century which will be vanquished, science will be vanquished, Claude Bernard, all those who came before him, and all his followers will be vanquished. Truly, one might almost think one's self dreaming when one reads such childish affirmations in a paper which prides itself on its seriousness, and which seems to have no suspicion that the French republic exists to-day by the force of a scientific formula. By all means let them applaud Victor Hugo's grand poetry and M. Renan's exquisite prose; nothing can be more desirable. But let them not say to young people: "This is the bread which you must eat in order to be strong; nourish yourself on the ideal and fine words in order to be great." This is disastrous counsel; the ideal and fine words will kill them; they can but live by science. It is science which forces idealism to flee before it; it is science which is preparing us for the twentieth century. We should be a great deal happier if science had further reduced the ideal, the absolute, the unknown, or by whatever other name they choose to call their formula.

I will go still further. This is a severe and frankly critical work. M. Renan has stirred up an unfortunate question, that of our defeats in 1870. He puts us ahead of our conquerors; he accuses them of mere mind culture; he exalts the polished gay culture of the old-time Frenchman. We should find this suggestion very clever if it were only a piece of flattery addressed to the Academy. But we have evidently heard M. Renan's convictions, who in a long letter has returned to the parallel of the two nations: one whose charm has conquered the world; the other whose military discipline and surly temperament have turned away those who love grace. It is not my intention to examine what is passing in Germany to-day, and I hope that we shall never change our temperament, which, truth to tell, would be rather a difficult thing to do. If M. Renan means to say that we should remain polished and happy, good talkers, and good company, he is right. But if he means to insinuate that fine talk and the ideal remain the only weapons by which we can conquer the world, that we shall be so much stronger, so much greater, as we remain blindly submissive to the old French culture, represented by the Academy, I say that he expresses a very dangerous opinion for the nation. What we must confess is that in 1870 we were beaten by science. Undoubtedly we were thrown into a war for which we were. unprepared by the imbecility of the Empire. But is it not true that under more disadvantageous circumstances France formerly was not conquered, when she lacked everything, even troops and money? It is evident, then, that at that time the old-fashioned French culture, her gay way of fighting, her fine dare-devil spirit, were sufficient to assure her victory. In 1870, on the contrary, we were crushed under the military method of a more phlegmatic people, less brave than we; we were overwhelmed by an army maneuvered by logical rules; we were disbanded by an application of the scientific formula to the art of war, without speaking of a more powerful artillery than our own, of a better equipped army, of a better disciplined one, and a more intelligent knowledge of the art of warfare. Again, I repeat, in spite of these disasters, from which we are still suffering, the true patriotism is to see that new times have come upon us, and to accept the scientific formula instead of dreaming of some mythical return into the literary quagmires of the ideal. Scientific principles conquered us; let us employ science if we would conquer others. Great commanders using sonorous words are not to be regretted if it so happens that sonorous words cannot bring about victory.

This is why the idealists accuse us of being unpatri-

otic, we naturalists, men of science. It is because we
rhyme no odes, neither do we make use of sonorous
words. The romantic school has reduced patriotism
to a simple question of rhetoric. To be patriotic it is
sufficient to write a drama or literary work of any kind,
bringing in the work *patrie* as often as possible, to
wave flags, and to write long tirades on acts of courage.
By these means they pretend that you uplift souls and
prepare them for revenge. It is always the same old
idea of music which produces only a sensory excitement to fine actions. It works on the nervous system ;
there is no thought of appealing to the intelligence, to
the faculty of comprehension, and to the power of
practical application. The rôle which these theoretical
patriots fill can be aptly compared to a military band
playing martial music while the soldiers are fighting ;
this excites them, intoxicates them, gives them more
or less contempt for danger. But this nervous excitement has but a momentary and relative influence on
the victory. Victory depends more and more in our
modern days upon the technical genius of the com-
mander-in-chief, upon the hand which applies the
scientific formula of the period to the tactics of
war. Look at the history of all great generals. Put
your youths under the savants, and not under the
poets, if you would have strong, vigorous young men.
The folly of lyricism can but bring forth heroic fools ;
and what we want are soldiers brave, healthy in mind
and body, marching mathematically to victory. Retain the music of the rhetoricians ; but let it be well
understood that it is simply music. We are the true
patriots—we who wish to see France scientific, rid of
lyrical declamations, strengthened by the culture of

truth, applying the scientific formula in all things, in politics as in literature, in social economy as in the art of war.

And now let us consider the moral side of the question. I have already demonstrated that honest men would not receive one of the characters who play so prominent a part in " Ruy Blas " in their *salons*. They are nothing but rogues and swindlers and adulterous women. The whole romantic repertoire covers itself with filth and blood, without having the excuse of being able to draw forth any true data from its exposed corpses. The morality of the idealists lives in the clouds far above the facts. It is made up of maxims which it attempts to apply to abstractions. The ideal is the common standard expressed in some dogma about virtue, and this is why so many people are virtuous, as they are Catholics without being practical ones. I do not wish to be personal ; but I have often remarked that the greatest *roués* pretend to the most rigid moral principles. Behind their grand-sounding words what perverted minds ! Women full of infatuation for the ideal, affecting the utmost refinements of delicacy, and falling at each step into the pitfall of adultery. Or it is the politicians defending family ties in their journals so strenuously as not to admit of a risky word, and yet speculating in all the latest financial jobbery, stealing from some, ruining others, giving free rein to their greed for fortune and ambition. For these people the ideal is a veil behind which any crime can be committed. When the curtain is drawn before the ideal, when the candle of truth is blown out, they are sure of being no longer seen, and the night is made hideous with their revelries. In the name of the ideal they pretend to impose silence on all truth which confuses them ; the ideal becomes a sort of police, a prohibition against touching on certain subjects, a tie which shall bind the common people in order to keep them good, while the wicked ones smile in a skeptical manner, and permit to themselves what they forbid to others. One feels all the misery of this dogmatic morality which beats the bass drum so loudly in the rhetorical outbursts of the poets, and which, like a ballet dancer, is furiously applauded and then forgotten as soon as the back is turned. It is but a breaking out on the skin, a grand wave of musical honesty which they listen to *en masse* in the theater, but which individually interests no one. People are neither better nor worse after coming away ; they take up their vices again, and the world goes on in its same old way. All that is not based on facts, all that is not demonstrated by experiment, has no practical value.

They accuse us of immorality, we writers of the naturalistic school ; and they are right : we lack the morality of mere words. Our morality is what Claude Bernard has so precisely defined : " The modern morality searches out the causes, desires to explain and act upon them ; in a word, to master the good and the evil ; to bring forth the one and develop it ; to battle against the other, extirpate and destroy it." The high and stern philosophy of our naturalistic works is admirably summed up in those few lines. We are looking for the causes of social evil ; we study the anatomy of classes and individuals to explain the derangements which are produced in society and in man. This often necessitates our working on tainted subjects, our descending into the midst of human follies and miseries. But we obtain the necessary data so that by knowing them one may be able to master the good and the evil. Lo! here is what we have seen, observed, and explained in all sincerity. Now it remains for the legislators to bring the good and develop it; to battle against the bad, to extirpate and destroy it. No work can be more moralizing than ours, then, because it is upon it that law should be based. How far are we from the tirades in favor of virtue which interests no one? Our virtue does not consist of words, but of acts; we are the active laborers who examine the building, point out the rotten girders, the interior crevices, the loosened stones, all the ravages which are not seen from the outside, and which can at any moment undermine the entire edifice. Is not this a work more truly useful, more serious, and more worthy than that of placing one's self on a rock, a lyre in one's hand, and striving to encourage men by a hullabaloo of deep-sounding words? Ah! what a parallel I could draw between the works of the romanticists and those of the naturalists! The ideal is the root of all dangerous reveries. The moment that you leave the solid ground of truth you are thrown into all kinds of monstrosities. Take the novels and dramas of the romantic school; study them from this point of view; you will find there the most shameful subtleties of the *debauché*, the most stupefying insanities of mind and body. Without doubt these bad places are magnificently draped; they are infamous alcoves before which is drawn a silken curtain; but I maintain that these veils, these hidden infamies, offer a much greater peril, in so much that the reader may dream over them at his ease, enlarge upon them, and abandon himself to them as a delicious and permissible recreation. With the naturalistic writings this hypoc- risy is impossible. These works may frighten, but they do not corrupt. Truth misleads no one. If it is forbid- den to children it is the prerogative of men, and who- ever makes himself familiar with it derives a certain profit therefrom. All this is a simple and irrefutable matter upon which all the world should agree. They call us corrupters ; nothing can be more foolish. The corrupters are the idealists who lie.

In truth, if they criticise us with so much asperity it is because we derange so many people in the enjoy- ment of their secret sins. It is hard to renounce this ideal, this sensual paradise, the windows of which are hermetically closed. The entrance is effected by a little door, and you find yourself in the midst of black chambers lighted by candles. We demolish this wicked place, and they are angered. Then there was such a clatter in the big words of the rhetoricians, so pleasant a shiver in the lyricism of the romantic poets ! Youth abandoned itself to it as it abandons itself to easy pleasures. To take up science, to enter into the austere laboratory of the savant, to renounce the sweet dreams for terrible truths, caused the newly escaped collegians to tremble. They wish to enjoy their years of attract- ive waywardness. And this is why one part of the youth of to-day is still entangled in lyrical bewilder- ments. But the movement is started, the scientific formula is imperative, and many young writers have accepted it already. It is to-morrow for which all things are making preparation. The children born to-day will be, they must not forget, the men of the twentieth century. Let the idealistic poet sing of the unknown, if they but leave us, the naturalistic writers, the privilege of driving back this unknown as much as we can. I do not push my reasonings, as do certain positivists, to the extent of predicting the approaching end of poetry. I simply assign to poetry the part of orchestra; the poets can continue to make sweet music for us while we work.

It now remains but for me to conclude. I will finish by telling what ought to be, according to my ideas, the place and the work of France in modern Europe. We reigned for a long time over all nations. Why is it that to-day our influence seems to be on the wane? It is because, after the thunderclap of our Revolution, we did not set ourselves to the hard scientific labor which the new epoch demanded. We certainly have in our race the genius which finds and asserts the truth through a sudden inspiration. Where we lack is in the next step, in patient method and the carrying out of the law that has been energetically formulated in the crisis. We are capable of planting a beacon which will illuminate the whole world, and the next day of flying off into poetry, of disburdening ourselves of lyrical declarations, of ignoring facts so as to plunge into I know not what ideal. This is why we, who should be at the summit, after the seeds of truth, which we have ceaselessly brought to light, find ourselves at this moment shorn of some of our former power, crushed by heavier and more methodical races. But our path is marked out for us if we would reign once more. We have but to put ourselves resolutely under the schooling of science. No more lyricism, no more empty words, but facts and information. The empire of the world will belong to the nation who pos-

sesses most strongly the power of clear observation
and of minute analysis. And remember that all the
qualities of race of which M. Renan speaks can be
retained; there is no need to be sullen, lacking in wit
and gayety, or to mar our conquests by pedantry and
military formality; we shall be just so much the
stronger as we use science in our warfare, as we employ
it to the triumph of liberty, keeping at the same time
that frankness of character that belongs naturally to us.
Young men of France, listen to me—this is patriotism:
It is by the use of the scientific formula that we shall
one day retake Alsace and Lorraine.

NATURALISM ON THE STAGE.

NATURALISM ON THE STAGE.

I.

IN the first place, is it necessary to explain what I understand by " naturalism " ? I have been found fault with on account of this word ; some pretend to this day not to understand what I mean by it. It is easy to cut jokes about this subject. However, I will explain it again, as one cannot be too clear in criticism.

My great crime, it would seem, has been to have invented and given to the public a new word in order to designate a literary school as old as the world. In the first place, I cannot claim the invention of this word, which has been in use in several foreign literatures ; I have at the most only applied it to the actual evolution in our own literature. Further, naturalism, they assure us, dates from the first written works. Who has ever said to the contrary ? This simply proves that it comes from the heart of humanity. All the critics, they add, from Aristotle to Boileau, have promulgated this principle, that a work must be based on truth. All this delights me and furnishes me with new arguments. The naturalistic school, by the mouth even of those who deride and attack it, is thus built on an indestructible foundation. It is not one man's caprice, the mad folly of a group of writers; it is born in the eternal depth of things, it started from the necessity which each writer found of taking nature for his basis. Very well, so far we are agreed. Let us start from this point.

Well, they say to me, why all this noise? why do you pose as an innovator and revealer of new doctrines? It is here the misunderstanding commences. I am simply an observer, who states facts. The empiricists alone put forth invented formulas. The savants are content to advance step by step, relying on the experimental method. One thing is certain, I have no new religion in my pocket. I reveal nothing, for the simple reason that I do not believe in revelation; I invent nothing, because I think it more useful to obey the impulses of humanity, the continuous evolutions which carry us along. My rôle as critic consists in studying from whence we come and our present state. When I venture to foretell where we are going it is purely speculation on my part, a purely logical conclusion. By what has been, and by what is, I think I am able to say what will be. That is my whole endeavor. It is ridiculous to assign me any other rôle; to place me on a rock, as pope and prophet; to represent me as the head of a school and on familiar terms with God.

But as to this new word, this terrible word of naturalism? I should have pleased my critics better had I used the words of Aristotle. He spoke of the true in art, and that ought to be sufficient for me. Since I accept the eternal basis of things and do not seek to create the world a second time, I no longer have need of a new term. Truly, are they mocking me? Does not the eternal basis of things take upon itself divers forms, according to the times and the degree of civilization ? Is it possible that for six thousand years each race has not interpreted and named, according to its own fashion, the things coming from a common source? Homer is a naturalistic poet—I admit that at once; but our romanticists are not naturalists after his style; between the two literary epochs there is an abyss. This is to judge from an absolute point of view, to efface all history at one stroke; it is to huddle all things together and keep no account of the constant evolution of the human mind. One thing is certain, that any piece of work will always be only a corner of nature as seen through a certain temperament. Only we cannot be content with this truth and go no further. As we approach the history of literature, we must necessarily come upon strange elements, upon manners, events, and intellectual movements which modify, arrest, or precipitate literatures. My personal opinion is that naturalism dates from the first line ever written by man. From that day truth was laid down as the necessary foundation of all art. If we look upon humanity as an army marching through the ages, bent upon the conquest of the true, in spite of every form of wretchedness and infirmity, we must place writers and savants in the van. It is from this point of view that we should write the history of a universal literature, and not from that of an absolute ideal or a common æsthetical measure, which is perfectly ridiculous. But it must be understood that I cannot go as far back as that, nor undertake so colossal a work; I cannot examine the marches and countermarches of the writers of all nations, and set down through what darkness and what lights they passed.

I must set myself a limit, therefore I go no further
back than the last century, where we find that marvelous expansion of intelligence, that wonderful movement from whence came our society of to-day. And it
is just there that I discover a triumphant affirmation
of naturalism, ·it is there that I meet with the word.
The long thread is lost in the darkness of the ages; it
answers my purpose to take it in hand at the eighteenth
century and follow it to our day.   Putting aside Aristotle and Boileau, a particular word was necessary to
designate an evolution which evidently starts from the
first days of the world, but which finally arrives at a
decisive development in the midst of circumstances
especially favorable to it.

Let us start, then, at the eighteenth century. We have
at that period a superb outburst.   One fact dominates
all, the creation of a method.   Until then the savants
had worked as the poets did, from individual fantasy,
by strokes of genius.   A few discovered truths, but
they were scattered truths; no tie held them together,
and mixed with them were the grossest errors.   They
wished to create science at one bound the way you
write a poem; they joined it on to nature by quack
formulas, by metaphysical considerations which would
astound us to-day. All at once a little circumstance
revolutionized this sterile field in which nothing grew.
One day a savant proposed, before concluding, to experiment. He abandoned supposed truths, he returned
to first causes, to the study of bodies, the observation
of facts. Like a schoolboy he consented to become
humble, to learn to spell nature before reading it
fluently. It was a revolution: science detached itself
from empiricism, its method consisted in marching

from the known to the unknown. They started from
an observed fact, they advanced from observation to
observation, hesitating to conclude before being in
possession of the necessary elements. In one word,
instead of setting out with synthesis, they commenced
with analysis; they no longer tried to draw the truth
from nature by means of divination or revelation; they
studied it long and patiently, passing from the simple
to the complex, until they were acquainted with its
mechanism. The tool was found; such a way of working was to consolidate and extend all the sciences.

Indeed, the benefit was soon apparent. The natural
sciences were established, thanks to the minute and
thorough exactitude of observation; in anatomy alone
an entirely new world was opened up; each day it
revealed a little more of the secret of life. Other
sciences were created—chemistry and natural philosophy. To-day they are still young, but they are
growing, and they are bringing truth to light in a
manner harassing from its rapidity. I cannot examine
each science thus. It is sufficient to name in addition
cosmography and geology, two sciences which have
dealt so terrible a blow to religious fables. The outburst was general, and it continues.

But everything holds together in civilization. When
one side of the human mind is set working other parts
are affected, and ere long you have a complete evolution. The sciences, which until then had borrowed
their share of imagination from letters, were the first
to cut free from fantastic dreams and return to nature;
next letters were seen in their turn to follow the
sciences, and to adopt also the experimental method.
The great philosophical movement of the eighteenth

century was a vast inquiry, often hesitating, it is true, but which ended by bringing into question again all human problems and offering new solutions of them. In history, in criticism, the study of facts and surroundings replaces the old scholastic rules. In the purely literary works nature intervenes and reigns with Rousseau and his school; the trees, the waters, the mountains, the great forests, obtain recognition and take once more their place in the mechanism of the world; man is no longer an intellectual abstraction; nature determines and completes him. Diderot remains beyond question the grand figure of the century; he foresees all the truths, he is in advance of his time, waging a continual war against the worm-eaten edifice of conventions and rules. Magnificent outburst of an epoch, colossal labor from which our society has come forth, new era from which will date the centuries into which humanity is entering, with nature for a basis, method for a tool!

This is the evolution which I have called naturalism, and I contend that you can use no better word. Naturalism, that is, a return to nature; it is this operation which the savants performed on the day when they decided to set out from the study of bodies and phenomena, to build on experiment, and to proceed by analysis. Naturalism in letters is equally the return to nature and to man, direct observation, exact anatomy, the acceptance and depicting of what is. The task was the same for the writer as for the savant. One and the other replaced abstractions by realities, empirical formulas by rigorous analysis. Thus, no more abstract characters in books, no more lying inventions, no more of the absolute; but real characters, the true history

of each one, the story of daily life. It was a question
of commencing all over again; of knowing man down
to the sources of his being before coming to such conclusions as the idealists reached, who invented types of
character out of the whole cloth; and writers had only
to start the edifice at the foundation, bringing together
the greatest number of human data arranged in their
logical order. This is naturalism; starting in the first
thinking brain, if you wish; but whose greatest evolution, the definite evolution, without doubt took place
in the last century.

So great an evolution in the human mind could not
take place without bringing on a social overthrow.
The French Revolution was this overthrow, this tempest which was to wipe out the old world, to give place
to the new. We are the beginning of this new world,
we are the direct children of naturalism in all things,
in politics as in philosophy, in science as in literature
and in art. I extend the bounds of this word naturalism because in reality it includes the entire century,
the movement of contemporaneous intelligence, the
force which is sweeping us onward, and which is working toward the molding of future centuries. The history of these last óne hundred and fifty years proves
it, and one of the most typical phenomena is the
momentary rebound of the minds which succeeded to
Rousseau and Chateaubriand; that singular outburst
of romanticism on the very threshold of a scientific age.
I will stop here for an instant, for there are some very
important observations to make on this subject.

It is rarely the case that a revolution breaks out
calmly and sensibly. Brains become deranged, imaginations become frightened, gloomy, and peopled with

phantoms. After the rude shocks of the last century, and under the tender and restless influence of Rousseau, we find poets adopting a melancholy and fatal style. They know not where they are going. They throw themselves into bitterness, into contemplation, into the most extraordinary dreams. However, they also have been breathed upon by the spirit of the Revolution. They also are rebels. They bring about a rebellion of color, of passion, of fantasy; they talk of breaking outright with rules, and they renew the language by a burst of lyrical poetry, sparkling and superb. Moreover, truth has touched them, they exact local coloring, they believe in resurrecting the dead ages. This is romanticism. It is a violent reaction against classical literature, it is the first revolutionary use which the writers make of the reconquered literary liberty. They smash windows, they become intoxicated ; maddened with their cries they rush into every extreme from the mere necessity of protesting. The movement is so irresistible that it carries everything with it, not only the flamboyant literature, but painting, sculpture, music, even ; they all become romantic ; romanticism triumphs and stamps itself everywhere. For one moment, in view of so powerful and so general a manifestation, one could almost believe that this literary and artistic formula had come to remain for a long time. The classical style had lasted at least two centuries; why should not the romantic style, which had taken its place, remain an equal length of time ? And people were surprised when, at the end of a quarter of a century, they found romanticism in its last agony, slowly dying a beautiful death. Then truth came forth into the light. The romantic movement was without question but a skirmish. Poets, novelists of great talents, a whole generation full of magnificent enthusiasm had been able to start a wrong scent. But the century did not belong to these overexcited dreamers, to these children of the dawn, blinded by the light of the rising sun. They represented nothing definite ; they were but the advance guard, charged with clearing away the *débris*, and insuring the future conquest by their excesses. The century belongs to the naturalists, to the direct sons of Diderot, whose solid battalions followed, and who will finally found a true state. The ends of the chain came together once more ; naturalism triumphed with Balzac. After the violent catastrophes of its infancy, the century at last took the broad path marked out for it. This romantic crisis was bound to be produced, because it corresponded to the social catastrophe of the French Revolution in the same manner that I willingly compare triumphant naturalism to our actual republic, which bids fair to be founded by science and reason.

This is where we stand to-day. Romanticism, which corresponded to nothing durable, which was simply the restless regret of the old world and the bugle call to battle, gave away before naturalism, which rose up stronger and more powerful, leading the century of which it is in reality the breath. Is it necessary to exhibit it everywhere? It arises from the earth on which we walk ; it grows every hour, penetrates and animates all things. It is the strength of our productions, the pivot upon which our society turns. It is found in the sciences, which continued on their tranquil way during the folly of romanticism ; it is found in all the manifestations of human intelligence, disengaging itself more and more from the influences of romanticism which once for a moment seemed to have submerged it. It renews the arts, sculpture, and, above all, painting; it extends the field of criticism and history ; it makes itself felt in the novel; and it is by means of the novel, by means of Balzac and Stendhal, that it lifts itself above romanticism, thus visibly relinking the chain with the eighteenth century. The novel is its domain, its field of battle and of victory. It seems to have chosen the novel in order to demonstrate the power of its method, the glory of the truth, the inexhaustible novelty of human data. To-day it takes possession of the stage, it has commenced to transform the theater, which is the last fortress of conventionality. When it shall triumph there its evolution will be complete; the classical formulas will find themselves definitely and solidly replaced by the naturalistic formula, which should by right be the formula of the new social condition.

It seemed to me necessary to insist upon and to explain at length the meaning of this word naturalism, as a great many pretend not to understand me. But I will drop the question now; I simply wish to study the naturalistic movement on the stage. But I must at the same time speak of the contemporaneous novel, for a point of comparison is indispensable to me. We will see where the novel stands and where the stage stands. The conclusion will thus be easier to reach.

II.

I HAVE often talked with foreign writers, and I have found the same astonishment expressed by them all. They are better able than we are to judge of the drift of our literature, for they see us from a distance, and they are outside and away from our daily quarrels. They express great astonishment that there are two distinct literatures with us, cut adrift from each other completely: the novel and the stage. No parallel exists among our neighbors. In France it seems that for half a century literature has been divided in two; the novel has passed to one side, the stage remains on the other; and between is dug a deeper and deeper ditch. Let us examine this situation for a moment; it is very curious and very instructive. Our current criticism—I speak of newspaper critics, whose hard task is to judge from day to day new pieces—our criticism lays down the principle that there is nothing in common between a novel and a dramatic work, neither the frame nor the development; it even goes so far as to say that there are two distinct styles, the theatrical style and the novelist's style, and a subject which could be put in a book could not be placed upon the stage. Why not say at once, as strangers do, that we have two literatures? It is but too true; such criticism has but stated a fact. It only remains to be seen if it does not aid in the detestable task of transforming this fact into a law by saying that this is so, because it cannot be

otherwise. Our continual tendency is to draw up
rules and codify everything. The worst of it is that,
after we have bound ourselves hand and foot with
rules and conventions, we have to use superhuman
efforts to break the fetters.

In fact, we have two literatures entirely dissimilar in
all things. Once a novelist wishes to write for the
stage they mistrust him; they shrug their shoulders.
Did not Balzac strand himself? It is true that M.
Octave Feuillet has succeeded. I am going to take
up this question at the beginning in order to solve it
logically. But first let us study the contemporaneous
novel.

Victor Hugo wrote poems, even when he descended
to prose; Alexander Dumas, *père*, was but a prolific
story-teller; George Sand gave us the dreams of her
imagination in an easy and happy flow of language. I
will not go back to those writers who belong to that
superb outburst of romanticism, and who have left us
no direct descendants. I mean to say that their influence is felt to-day only by our rebound from it, and in
a manner of which I will speak later. The sources of
our contemporaneous novel are found in Balzac and in
Stendhal. We must look for them and consult them
there. Both escaped from the craze of romanticism:
Balzac because he could not help himself; and Stendhal from his superiority as a man. While the whole
world was proclaiming the triumphs of the lyrics, while
Victor Hugo was noisily crowned king of literature,
both died almost in obscurity, in the midst of the
neglect and disdain of the public. But they left behind
them in their works the naturalistic formula of the
century; and the future was to show their descendants

pressing to their tombs, while the romantic school was dying from bloodlessness, and survived only in one illustrious old man, respect for whom prevented the telling of the truth. This is but a rapid review. There is no need of explaining the new formula which Balzac and Stendhal introduced. They made the inquiry with the novel that the savants made with science. They no longer imagined nor told pretty stories. Their task was to take man and dissect him, to analyze him in his flesh and in his brain. Stendhal remained above all else a psychologist. Balzac studied more particularly the temperaments, reconstructed the surroundings, gathered together human data, and assumed the title of doctor of social sciences. Compare "Père Goriot" or "Cousine Bette" to preceding novels, to those of the seventeenth century as to those of the eighteenth, and you will better understand what the naturalistic evolution accomplished. The name "romance" alone has been kept, which is wrong, for it has lost all significance.

I must now choose among the descendants of Balzac and Stendhal. First, there is M. Gustave Flaubert, and it is he who will complete the actual formula. We shall see in him the reaction from the romantic influence of which I have spoken to you. One of Balzac's most bitter disappointments was that he did not possess Victor Hugo's brilliant form. He was accused of writing badly, and that made him very unhappy. He sometimes tried to compete with the ringing lyrics, as for instance when he wrote "La Femme de Trente Ans," and "Le Lis dans la Vallée"; but in this he did not succeed; this great writer never wrote better prose than when he kept his own strong and fluent style. In

passing to M. Gustave Flaubert the naturalistic formula
was given into the hands of a perfect artist. It was
solidified, and became hard and shining as marble. M.
Gustave Flaubert had grown up in the midst of romanticism. All his leanings were toward the movement of
1830. When he published "Mme. Bovary" it was as
a defiance to the realism of that time, which prided
itself on writing badly. He intended to prove that you
could talk of the little provincial *bourgeoisie* with the
same ampleness and power which Homer has employed
in speaking of the Greek heroes. But happily the
work had another result. Whether M. Gustave Flaubert intended it or not, he had brought to naturalism
the only strength which was lacking to it, that of that
perfect and imperishable style which keeps works alive.
From that time the formula was firmly established.
There was nothing for the newcomers to do but to
walk in this broad path of truth aided by art. The
novelists went on and continued M. Balzac's inquiry,
advancing more and more in the analysis of man as
affected by the action of his surroundings; only they
were at the same time artists, they had the originality
and the science of form, they seemed to have raised
truth from the dead by the intense life of their style.

At the same time as M. Gustave Flaubert, MM.
Edmond and Jules de Goncourt were laboring also for
this brilliancy of form. They did not come from the
romantic school. They possessed no Latin, no classical
aids; they invented their own language; they jotted
down, with an incredible intensity, their feelings as
artists weary of their art. In "Germinie Lacertéaux"
they were the first to study the people of Paris, painting the faubourgs, the desolate landscapes of the

suburbs, daring to tell everything in a refined language which gave beings and things their proper life. They had a great influence over the groups of naturalistic novelists. If we found our solidity, our exact method, in M. Gustave Flaubert, we must add that we were very much stirred by this new language of the MM. Goncourt: as penetrating as a symphony, giving that nervous shiver of our age to all objects, going further than the written phrase, and adding to the words of the dictionary a color, a sound, and a subtle perfume. I do not judge, I but state my facts. My only end is to establish the source of the contemporaneous novel, and to explain what it is and why it is.

These, then, are the sources clearly indicated. First, Balzac and Stendhal, a physiologist and a psychologist, weaned from the rhetoric of romanticism, which was nothing but an uprising of word-lovers. Then, between us and these two ancestors, we find M. Gustave Flaubert on one side, and MM. Edmond and Jules de Goncourt on the other, giving us the science of style, fixing the formula in new modes of expression. In these names you have the naturalistic novel. I will not speak of its actual representatives. It will suffice to indicate the distinctive characteristics of this novel.

I have said that the naturalistic novel is simply an inquiry into nature, beings, and things. It no longer interests itself in the ingenuity of a well-invented story, developed according to certain rules. Imagination has no longer place, plot matters little to the novelist, who bothers himself with neither development, mystery, nor *dénouement ;* I mean that he does not intervene to take away from or add to reality; he does not construct a framework out of the whole cloth, according to the needs of a preconceived idea. You start from the point that nature is sufficient, that you must accept it as it is, without modification or pruning; it is grand enough, beautiful enough to supply its own beginning, its middle, and its end. Instead of imagining an adventure, of complicating it, of arranging stage effects, which scene by scene will lead to a final conclusion, you simply take the life study of a person or a group of persons, whose actions you faithfully depict. The work becomes a report, nothing more; it has but the merit of exact observation, of more or less profound penetration and analysis, of the logical connection of facts. Sometimes, even, it is not an entire life, with a commencement and an ending, of which you tell; it is only a scrap of an existence, a few years in the life of a man or a woman, a single page in a human history, which has attracted the novelist in the same way that the special study of a mineral can attract a chemist. The novel is no longer confined to one special sphere; it has invaded and taken possession of all spheres. Like science, it is the master of the world. It touches on all subjects: writes history; treats of physiology and psychology; rises to the highest flights of poetry; studies the most diverse subjects—politics, social economy, religion, and manners. Entire nature is its domain. It adopts the form which pleases it, taking the tone which seems best, feeling no longer bounded by any limit. In this we are far distant from the novel that our fathers were acquainted with. It was a purely imaginative work, whose sole end was to charm and distract its readers. In ancient rhetorics the novel is placed at the bottom, between the fables and light poetry. Serious men disdained novels, abandoned them to women, as a frivolous and compromising recreation. This opinion is still held in the country and certain academical centers. The truth is that the masterpieces of modern fiction say more on the subject of man and nature than do the graver works of philosophy, history, and criticism. In them lies the modern tool.

I pass to another characteristic of the naturalistic novel. It is impersonal; I mean to say by that that the novelist is but a recorder who is forbidden to judge and to conclude. The strict rôle of a savant is to expose the facts, to go to the end of analysis without venturing into synthesis; the facts are thus: experiment tried in such and such conditions gives such and such results; and he stops there, for if he wishes to go beyond the phenomena he will enter into hypothesis; we shall have probabilities, not science. Well! the novelist should equally keep to known facts, to the scrupulous study of nature, if he does not wish to stray among lying conclusions. He himself disappears, he keeps his emotion well in hand, he simply shows what he has seen. Here is the truth; shiver or laugh before it, draw from it whatever lesson you please, the only task of the author has been to put before you true data. There is, besides, for this moral impersonality of the work a reason in art. The passionate or tender intervention of the writer weakens a novel, because it ruins the clearness of its lines, and introduces a strange element into the facts which destroys their scientific value. One cannot well imagine a chemist becoming incensed with azote, because this body is injurious to life, or sympathizing with oxygen for the contrary reason. In the same way, a novelist who feels the need of becoming indignant with vice, or applauding virtue, not only spoils the data he produces, for his intervention is as trying as it is useless, but the work loses its strength; it is no longer a marble page, hewn from the block of reality; it is matter worked up, kneaded by the emotions of the author, and such emotions are always subject to prejudices and errors. A true work will be eternal, while an impressionable work can at best tickle only the sentiment of a certain age.

Thus the naturalistic novelist never interferes, any more than the savant. This moral impersonality of a work is all-important, for it raises the question of morality in a novel. They reproach us for being immoral, because we put rogues and honest men in our books, and are as impartial to one as to the other. This is the whole quarrel. Rogues are permissible, but they must be punished in the wind-up, or at least we must crush them under our anger and contempt. As to the honest men, they deserve here and there a few words of praise and encouragement. Our impassability, our tranquillity in our analysis in the face of the good and bad, is altogether wrong. And they end by saying that we lie when we are most true. What! nothing but rogues, not one attractive character? This is where the theory of attractive characters comes in. There must be attractive characters in order to give a kindly touch to nature. They not only demand that we should have a preference for virtue, but they exact that we should embellish virtue and make it lovable. Thus, in a character, we ought to make a selection, take the good sentiments and pass the wicked by in silence; indeed, we would be more commendable still if we invented a person out of the whole cloth; if we would mold one on the conventional form demanded by propriety and good manners. For this purpose there are ready-made types which writers introduce into a story without any trouble. These are attractive characters, ideal conceptions of men and women, destined to compensate for the sorry impression of true characters taken from nature. As you can see, our only mistake in all this is that we accept only nature, and that we are not willing to correct what is by what should be. Absolute honesty no more exists than perfect healthfulness. There is a tinge of the human beast in all of us, as there is a tinge of illness. These young girls so pure, these young men so loyal, represented to us in certain novels, do not belong to earth; to make them mortal everything must be told. We tell everything, we do not make a choice, neither do we idealize; and this is why they accuse us of taking pleasure in obscenity. To sum up, the question of morality in novels reduces itself to two opinions: the idealists pretend that it is necessary to lie to be moral; the naturalists affirm that there is no morality outside of the truth. Moreover, nothing is so dangerous as a romantic novel; such a work, in painting the world under false colors, confuses the imagination, throws us in the midst of hair-breadth escapes; and I do not speak of the hypocrisies of fashionable society, the abominations which are hidden under a bed of flowers. With us these perils disappear. We teach the bitter science of life, we give the high lesson of reality. Here is what exists; endeavor to repair it. We are but savants, analyzers, anatomists; and our works have the certainty, the solidity, and the practical applications of scientific works. I know of no school more moral or more austere.

Such to-day is the naturalistic novel. It has triumphed; all the novelists accept it, even those who attempted at first to crush it in the egg. It is the same old story; they deride, and then they praise and finally imitate it. Success is sufficient to turn the source of the current. Besides, now that the impetus has been given, we shall see the movement spreading more and more. A new literary century is beginning for us.

III.

I PASS now to our contemporaneous stage. We have just seen to what place the novel has risen; we must now endeavor to define the present position of dramatic literature. But before entering upon it I will rapidly recall to the reader's mind the great evolutions of the stage in France.

In the beginning we find unformed pieces, dialogues for two characters, or for three at the most, which were given in the public square. Then halls were built, tragedy and comedy were born, under the influence of the classical renaissance. Great geniuses consecrated this movement — Corneille, Molière, Racine. They were the product of the age in which they lived. The tragedy and comedy of that time, with their unalterable rules, their etiquette of the court, their grand and noble air, their philosophical dissertations and oratorical eloquence are the exact reproduction of contemporaneous society. And this identity, this close affinity of the dramatic formula and the social surroundings, is so strong that for two centuries the formula remains almost the same. It only loses its stiffness, it merely bends in the eighteenth century with Voltaire and Beaumarchais. The ancient society is then profoundly disturbed; the excitement which agitates it even touches the stage. There is a need for greater action, there is a sullen revolt against the rules, a vague return to nature. Even at this period Diderot and Mercier laid down squarely the basis of the naturalistic theater; unfortunately, neither one nor the other produced a masterpiece, and this is necessary to establish a new formula. Besides, the classical style was so solidly planted in the soil of the ancient monarchy that it was not carried away entirely by the tempest of the Revolution. It persisted for some time longer, weakened, degenerated, gliding into insipidity and imbecility. Then the romantic insurrection, which had been hatching for years, burst forth. The romantic drama killed the expiring tragedy; Victor Hugo gave it its death-blow, and reaped the benefits of a victory for which many others had labored. It is worth noticing that through the necessities of the struggle the romantic drama became the antithesis of the tragedy; it opposed passion to duty, action to words, coloring to psychological analysis, the Middle Ages to antiquity. It was this sparkling contrast which assured its triumph. Tragedy must disappear, its knell had sounded; for it was no longer the product of social surroundings; and the drama brought in its train the liberty that was necessary in order boldly to clear away the *débris*. But it seems to-day as though that should have been the limit of its rôle. It was but a superb affirmation of the nothingness of rules, of the necessity of life. Notwithstanding all this uproar, it remained the rebellious child of tragedy; in a similar fashion it lied; it costumed facts and characters with an exaggeration which makes us smile nowadays; in a similar fashion it had its rules and its effects—effects much more irritating, as they were falser. In fact, there was but one more rhetoric on the stage. The romantic drama, however, was not to have as long a reign as tragedy. After performing its revolutionary task it died out, suddenly exhausted, leaving the place clear for reconstruction. Thus the history is the same on the stage as in the novel. As a result of this inevitable crisis in romanticism, the traditions of naturalism reappear, the ideas of Diderot and Mercier come more and more to the surface. It is the new social state, born of the Revolution, which fixes little by little a new dramatic formula in spite of many fruitless attempts and of advancing and retreating footsteps. This work was inevitable. It produced itself and it will be produced again by the force of things, and it will never stop until the evolution shall be complete. The naturalistic formula will be to our century what the classical formula has been to past centuries.

Now we have arrived at our own period. Here I find a considerable activity, an extraordinary outlay of talent. It is an immense workroom in which each one works with feverish energy. All is confusion as yet, there is a great deal of lost labor, very few blows strike out direct and strong; still the spectacle is none the less marvelous. One thing is certain, that each laborer is working toward the definite triumph of naturalism, even those who appear to fight against it. They are, in spite of everything, borne along by the current of the time ; they go of necessity where it goes. As none in the theater has been of large enough caliber to establish the formula at a stroke by the sheer force of his genius, it would almost seem as if they had divided the task, each one giving in turn, and with reference to a definite point, the necessary shove onward. Let us now see who are the best known workers among them.

In the first place, there is M. Victorien Sardou. He

is the actual representative of the comedy with a plot. The true heir of M. Scribe, he has renovated the old tricks and pushed scenic art to the point of prestidigitation. This kind of play is a continuous and ever more strongly emphasized reaction against the old-time classical stage. The moment that facts are opposed to words, that action is placed above character, the sure tendency is to a complicated plot, to marionettes led by a thread, to sudden changes, to unexpected *dénouements.* The reign of Scribe was a notable event in dramatic literature. He exaggerated this new principle of action, making it the principle thing, and he also displayed great ability in producing extraordinary effects, inventing a code of laws and recipes all his own. This was inevitable; reactions are always extreme. What has been for a long time called the fashionable stage had then no other source than an exaggerated principle of action at the expense of the delineation of character and the analysis of emotion. The truth escaped them in their effort to grasp it. They broke one set of rules to invent others, which were falser and more ridiculous. The well-written play—I mean by that the play written on a symmetrical and even pattern—has become a curious and amusing plaything, which diverts the whole of Europe. From this dates the popularity of our *repertoire* with foreigners. To-day it has **undergone** a slight change; M. Victorien Sardou thinks less of the cabinetwork, but though he has enlarged the frame and laid more stress on legerdemain, he still remains the great representative in the theater of action, of amorous action, this quality dominating and overpowering everything else. His great quality is movement; he has no life, he has only movement, which carries away the characters, and which often throws an illusive glamour over them; you could almost believe them to be living, breathing beings; but they are in reality only well-staged puppets, coming and going like pieces of perfect mechanism. Ingenuity, dexterity, just a suspicion of actuality, a great knowledge of the stage, a particular talent for episode, the smallest details prodigally and vividly brought forward—such are M. Sardou's principal qualities. But his observation is superficial; the human data which he produces have dragged about everywhere and are only patched up skillfully; the world into which he leads us is a pasteboard world, peopled by puppets. In each one of his works you feel the solid earth giving way beneath your feet; there is always some far-fetched plot, a false emotion carried to the last extremity, which serves as a pivot for the whole play, or else an extraordinary complication of facts, which a magical word is supposed to unravel at the end. Real life is entirely different. Even in accepting the necessary exaggerations of a farce, one looks for and wants more breadth and more simplicity in the means. These plays are never anything more than vaudevilles unnecessarily exaggerated, whose comic strength partakes altogether of caricature. I mean by that that the laughter evoked is not spontaneous, but is called forth by the grimaces of the actors. It is useless to cite examples. Everyone has seen the village which M. Victorien Sardou depicts in " Les Bourgeois de Pont-Arcy"; the character of his observation is here clearly revealed—silhouettes hardly rejuvenated, the stale jokes of the day, which are in everyone's mouth. Compared with Balzac, for instance, of how low an

order are these plays. " Rabagas," for instance, the
satire in which is excellent, is spoiled by a very inferior
amorous intrigue. "La Famille Benoiton" in which
certain caricatures are very amusing, has also its faults
—the famous letters, these letters which are to be
found throughout M. Sardou's writings, and which are
as necessary to him as the jugglery and the presto-
change to the conjurer. He has had immense success,
a fact easy of explanation, and I am very glad he has.
Remark one thing, that, though he very often runs
counter to the truth, he has nevertheless been of great
service to naturalism. He is one of the workmen of
whom I spoke a short time ago, who are of their period,
who work according to their strength for a formula
which they have not the genius to carry out in its
entirety. His personal rôle is exactness in the stage
setting, the most perfect material representation possible of everyday existence. If he falsifies in filling
out the frames, at least he has the frames themselves,
and that is already something gained. To me his
reason for being is that above all things. He has come
in his hour, he has given the public a taste for life and
tableaux hewn from reality.

I now turn to M. Alexander Dumas, *fils.* Truly, he
has done better work still. He is one of the most
skillful workmen in the naturalistic workroom. Little
remains for him but to find the complete formula, and
then let him realize it. To him we owe the physiological studies on the stage; he alone, up to the present time, has been brave enough to show us the sex
in the young girl, the beast in the man. "La Visite
de Noces," and certain scenes in the " Demi-Monde "
and the " Fils Naturel," possess analysis which is abso-

lutely remarkable and rigorously truthful. Here are
human data which are new and excellent; and that is
certainly very rare in our modern *repertoire*. You see
I do not make any bones about praising M. Dumas,
fils. But I admire him with reference to a group of
ideas which later will cause me to appear very severe
upon him. According to my way of thinking, he has
had a crisis in his life, he has developed a philosophic
vein, he manifests a deplorable desire for legislation,
preaching, and conversion. He has made himself God's
substitute on this earth, and as a result the strangest
freaks of imagination spoil his faculties of observation.
He no longer makes use of human observation save to
reach superhuman results and astonishing situations,
dressed out in full-blown fantasy. Look at " La Femme
de Claude," " L'Étrangère," and other pieces still.
This is not all : cleverness has spoiled M. Dumas. A
man of genius is not clever, and a man of genius is
necessary to establish the naturalistic formula in a
masterly fashion. M. Dumas has imbued all his characters with his wit ; the men, the women, even the children in his plays make witty remarks, these famous
witticisms which so often give a play success. Nothing can be falser or more fatiguing ; it destroys all
the truth of the dialogue. Again, M. Dumas, who
before everything is a thorough playwriter, never
hesitates between reality and a scenic exigency ;
he sacrifices the reality. His theory is that truth
is of little consequence provided he can be logical.
A play becomes with him a problem to be solved ;
he starts out from a given point, he must reach
another point without tiring his public ; and the
victory is gained if you have been agile enough to

jump over the breakneck places, and have forced the public to follow you in spite of itself. The spectators may protest later, cry out against the want of the reality, fight against it; but nevertheless they have belonged to the anthor during the evening. All M. Dumas' plays are written on this theory. He wins a triumph in spite of paradox, unreality, the most useless and *risque* thesis, through the mere strength of his wrists. He who has been touched by the breath of naturalism, who has written such clearly defined scenes, never recoils, however, before a fiction when he needs it for the sake of argument or simply as a matter of construction. It is the most pitiable mixture of imperfect reality and whimsical invention. None of his plays escape this double current. Do you remember in the " Fils Naturel " the incredible story of *Clara Vignot*, and in " L'Étrangère," the extraordinary story of *La Vierge du Mal?* I cite at haphazard. It would seem as though M. Dumas never made use of truth but as a springboard with which to jump into emptiness. He never leads us into a world that we know; the surroundings are always false and painful; the characters lose all their natural accent, and no longer seem to belong to the earth. It is no longer life, with its breadth, its shades, ànd its good nature; it is a debate, an argument, something cold, dry, and rasping in which thére is no air. The philosopher has killed the observer—such is my conclusion, and the dramatic writer has finished the philosopher. It is to be deeply regretted.

Now I come to Émile Augier. He is the real master of our French stage. His was the most constant, the most sincere, and the most regular effort. It must be remembered how fiercely he was attacked by the romanticists; they called him the poet of good sense, they ridiculed certain of his verses, though they did not dare to ridicule verses of a similiar character in Molière. The truth was that M. Augier worried the romanticists, for they feared in him a powerful adversary, a writer who took up anew the old French traditions, ignoring the insurrection of 1830. The new formula grew greater with him; exact observation, real life, true pictures of our society in correct and quiet language, were introduced. M. Émile Augier's first works, dramas and comedies in verse, had the great merit of appearing at our classical theater; they had the same simplicity of plot as the best classical plays, as in "Philiberte," for example, where the story of an ugly girl who became charming, and whom all the world courted, was sufficient to fill three acts, without the slightest complication; their main point was the elucidating of character, and they possessed also a spirit of genial good nature and the strong, quiet movement that would naturally arise among people who drew apart and then came together again as their emotions impelled them. My conviction is that the naturalistic formula will be but the development of this classical formula, enlarged and adapted to our surroundings. Later M. Émile Augier made his own personality more strongly felt. He could not help employing the naturalistic formula when he began to write in prose, and depicted our contemporaneous society more freely. I mention more particularly "Les Lionnes Pauvres," "Le Mariage d'Olympe," "Maître Guerin," "Le Gendre de M. Poirier," and those two comedies which created the most talk, "Les Effrontés," and "Le

Fils de Giboyer." These are very remarkable works, which all, more or less, in some scenes, realize the new theater, the stage of our time. The bold, unrepentant effrontery, for instance, with which *Guerin*, the notary, dies, so novel and true in its effect; the excellent picture of the newly enriched *bourgeois* in the "Gendre de M. Poirer"; both of these are admirable studies of human nature; *Giboyer*, again, is a curious creation, quite true to life, living in the midst of a society depicted with a great deal of excellent sarcasm. M. Augier's strength, and what makes him really superior to M. Dumas, *fils*, is his more human quality. This human side places him on solid ground; we have no fear that he will take those wild leaps into space ; he remains well balanced, not so brilliant, perhaps, but much more sure. What is there to prevent M. Augier from being the genius waited for, the genius destined to make the naturalistic formula a fixture ? Why, I ask, does he only remain the wisest and the strongest of the workmen of the present hour? In my opinion it is because he has not known how to disengage himself from conventions, from stereotyped ideas, from made-up characters. His stage is constantly belittled by figures. "*executés de chic*," as they say in the studio. Thus it is rarely that you do not find, in his comedies, the pure young girl who is very rich and who does not wish to marry, because she scorns to be married for her money. His young men are equally heroes of honor and loyalty, sobbing when they learn that their fathers made their money unscrupulously. In a word, the interesting character predominates ; I mean the ideal type of good and beautiful sentiments always cast in the same mold, that mere symbol, that hieratic personification outside of all true observation. This commandant *Guerin*, this model of military men, whose uniform aids in the *dénouement ; Giboyer's* son, that archangel of delicacy, born of a man of ill repute, and *Giboyer* himself, so tender in his baseness ; *Henri*, the son of *Charrier* in " Les Effrontés," who goes bond for his father when he has dabbled in an equivocal affair, and who finally induces the latter to reimburse the men whom he has wronged—all these are very beautiful, very touching ; only as human data very unlikely. Nature is not so unmixed, neither in the good nor in the evil. You cannot accept these interesting characters except as a contrast and a consolation. This is not all ; M. Augier often modifies a character by a stroke of his wand. His reason is easily seen ; he wants a *dénouement*, and he changes a character after an effective scene. For instance, the climax in the " Gendre de M. Poirier." Really it is very accommodating ; you do not make a light man out of a dark one so easily. Considered from the point of genuine observation these brusque changes are to be deplored ; a temperament is the same to the end, or at least is only changed by slowly working causes, apparent only to a very minute analysis. M. Augier's best characters, those which will remain longest, because they are the most complete and logical, to my thinking, are *Guerin* the notary, and *Pommeau* in "Les Lionnes Pauvres." The climax in both plays is very good. Reading "Les Lionnes Pauvres" over I bethought me of *Mme. Marneffé*, married to an honest man. Compare *Seraphine* to *Mme. Marneffé*, place M. Émile Augier and Balzac face to face for one instant, and you will understand why, notwithstanding his good qualities, M. Émile Augier has not firmly established the new formula on the stage. His hand was not bold enough to rid himself of the conventionalities which encumber the stage. His plays are too much of a mixture ; not one of them stands out with the decisive originality of genius. He softens his lines too much ; still he will remain in our dramatic literature as a pioneer, who possessed great and strong intelligence.

I would like to have spoken of M. Eugène Labiche, whose comic vein is very refreshing ; of M. Meilhac and M. Halévy, these sharp observers of Parisian life ; of M. Goudinet, who by his witty scenes, depicted without any action, has given the last blow to the downfall of the formula of Scribe.

But it must be sufficient for me to explain myself by means of the three dramatic authors whose work I have just analyzed and who are really the most celebrated. Their talent and their different gifts I greatly admire. Only I must say, once more, I judge them from the point of view of a group of ideas and the place which their works will hold in the literary movement of the century.

IV.

NOW that all the elements are known I have in my hands all the data which I need for argument and conclusion. On one side, we have seen what the naturalistic novel is at the present time; on the other, we have just ascertained what the first dramatic authors have made of our stage. It remains but to establish a parallel.

No one contests the point that all the different forms of literary expression hold together and advance at the same time. When they have been stirred up, when the ball is once set rolling, there is a general push toward the same goal. The romantic insurrection is a striking example of this unity of movement under a definite influence. I have shown that the force of the current of the age is toward naturalism. To-day this force is making itself felt more and more; it is rushing on us, and everything must obey it. The novel and the stage are carried away by it. Only it has happened that the evolution has been much more rapid in the novel; it triumphs there while it is just beginning to put in an appearance on the stage. This was bound to be. The theater has always been the stronghold of convention for a multiplicity of reasons, which I will explain later. I simply wish, then, to come down to this: The naturalistic formula, however complete and defined in the novel, is very far from being so on the stage, and I conclude from that that it will be com-

pleted, that it will assume sooner or later there its
scientific rigor, or else the stage will become flat, and
more and more inferior.

Some people are very much irritated with me; they
cry out: "But what do you ask? what evolution do
you want? Is the evolution not an accomplished fact?
Have not M. Émile Augier, M. Dumas, *fils*, and M.
Victorien Sardou pushed the study and the painting of
our society to the farthest possible lengths? Let us
stop where we are. We have already too much of the
realities of this world." In the first place, it is very
naïve in these people to wish to stop; nothing is
stable in a society, everything is borne along by a continuous movement. Things go in spite of everything
where they ought to go. I contend that the evolution,
far from being an accomplished fact on the stage, is
hardly commenced. Up to the present time we have
taken only the first steps. We must wait until certain
ideas have wedged their way in, and until the public
becomes accustomed to them, and until the force of
things abolishes the obstacles one by one. I have
tried, in rapidly glancing over MM. Victorien Sardou,
Dumas, *fils*, and Émile Augier, to tell for what reasons
I look upon them as simply laborers who are clearing
the paths of *débris*, and not as creators, not as geniuses
who are building a monument. Then after them I am
waiting for something else.

This something else which arouses so much indignation and draws forth so many pleasantries is, however,
very simple. We have only to read Balzac, M. Gustave Flaubert, and MM. de Goncourt again—in a word,
the naturalistic novelists—to discover what it is. I am
waiting for them, in the first place, to put a man of

flesh and bones on the stage, taken from reality, scientifically analyzed, without one lie. I am waiting for them to rid us of fictitious characters, of conventional symbols of virtue and vice, which possess no value as human data. I am waiting for the surroundings to determine the characters, and for characters to act according to the logic of facts, combined with the logic of their own temperament. I am waiting until there is no more jugglery of any kind, no more strokes of a magical wand, changing in one minute persons and things. I am waiting for the time to come when they will tell us no more incredible stories, when they will no longer spoil the effects of just observations by romantic incidents, the result being to destroy even the good parts of a play. I am waiting for them to abandon the cut and dried rules, the worked-out formulas, the tears and cheap laughs. I am waiting until a dramatic work free from declamations, big words, 'and grand sentiments has the high morality of truth, teaches the terrible lesson that belongs to all sincere inquiry. I am waiting, finally, until the evolution accomplished in the novel takes place on the stage ; until they return to the source of science and modern arts, to the study of nature, to the anatomy of man, to the painting of life, in an exact reproduction, more original and powerful than anyone has so far dared to place upon the boards.

This is what I am waiting for. They shrug their shoulders and reply to me that I shall wait forever. Their decisive argument is that you must not expect these things on the stage. The stage is not the novel. It has given us what it could give us. That ends it ; we must be satisfied.

Now we are at the pith of the quarrel. I am trying to uproot the very conditions of existence on the stage. What I ask is impossible, which amounts to saying that fictions are necessary on the stage; a play must have some romantic corners, it must turn in equilibrium round certain situations, which must unravel themselves at the proper time. They take up the business side; first, any analysis is wearisome; the public demands facts, always facts; then there is the perspective of the stage; an act must be played in three hours, no matter what its length is; then the characters are endowed with a particular value, which necessitates setting up fictions. I will not put forth all the arguments. I arrive at the intervention of the public, which is really considerable; the public wishes this, the public will not have that; it will not tolerate too much truth; it exacts four attractive puppets to one real character taken from life. In a word, the stage is the domain of conventionality; everything is conventional, from the decorations to the footlights which illuminate the actors, even down to the characters, who are led by a string. Truth can only enter by little doses adroitly distributed. They even go so far as to swear that the theater will cease to exist the day that it ceases to be an amusing lie, destined to console the spectators in the evening for the sad realities of the day.

I know all these reasonings, and I shall try to respond to them presently, when I reach my conclusion. It is evident that each kind of literature has its own conditions of existence. A novel, which one reads alone in his room, with his feet on his andirons, is not a play which is acted before two thousand spectators. The novelist has time and space before him; all sorts of liberties are permitted him; he can use one hundred pages, if it pleases him, to analyze at his leisure a certain character; he can describe his surroundings as much as he pleases; he can cut his story short, can retrace his steps, changing places twenty times—in one word, he is absolute master of his matter. The dramatic author, on the contrary, is inclosed in a rigid frame; he must heed all sorts of necessities. He moves only in the midst of obstacles. Then, above all, there is the question of the isolated reader and the spectators taken *en masse;* the solitary reader tolerates everything, goes where he is led, even when he is disgusted; while the spectators, taken *en masse*, are seized with prudishness, with frights, with sensibilities of which the author must take notice under pain of a certain fall. All this is true, and it is precisely for this reason that the stage is the last citadel of conventionality, as I stated further back. If the naturalistic movement had not encountered on the boards a difficult ground, filled with obstacles, it would already have taken root there with the intensity and with the success which have attended the novel. The stage, under its conditions of existence, must be the last, the most laborious, and the most bitterly disputed conquest of the spirit of truth.

I will remark here that the evolution of each century is of necessity incarnated in a particular form of literature. Thus the seventeenth century evidently incarnated itself in the dramatic formula. Our theater threw forth then an incomparable glitter, to the detriment of lyrical poetry and the novel. The reason was that the stage then exactly responded to the spirit of the period. It abstracted man from nature, studied him with the philosophical tool of the time; it has the swing of a pompous rhetoric, the polite manners of a society which had reached perfect maturity. It is the fruit of the ground; its formula is written from that point where the then civilization flowed with the greatest ease and perfection. Compare our epoch to that, and you will understand the decisive reasons which made Balzac a great novelist instead of a great dramatist. The spirit of the nineteenth century, with its return to nature, with its need of exact inquiry, quitted the stage, where too much conventionality hampered it, in order to stamp itself indelibly on the novel, whose field is limitless. And thus it is that scientifically the novel has become the form, *par excellence*, of our age, the first path in which naturalism was to triumph. To-day it is the novelists who are the literary princes of the period; they possess the language, they hold the method, they walk in the front rank, side by side with science. If the seventeenth century was the century of the stage, the nineteenth will belong to the novel.

Let us admit for one moment that criticism has some show of reason when it asserts that naturalism is impossible on the stage. Here is what they assert. Conventionality is inevitable on the stage; there must always be lying there. We are condemned to a continuance of M. Sardou's juggling; to the theories and witticisms of M. Dumas, *fils;* to the sentimental characters of M. Émile Augier. We shall produce nothing finer than the genius of these authors; we must accept them as the glory of our time on the stage. They are what they are because the theater wishes them to be such. If they have not advanced further to the front, if they have not obeyed more implicitly the grand current of truth which is carrying us onward, it is the theater which forbids them. That is a wall which shuts the way, even to the strongest. Very well! But then it is the theater which you condemn; it is to the stage that you have given the mortal blow. You crush it under the novel, you assign it an inferior place, you make it despicable and useless in the eyes of future generations. What do you wish us to do with the stage, we other seekers after truth, anatomists, analysts, searchers of life, compilers of human data, if you prove to us that there we cannot make use of our tools and our methods? Really! The theater lives only on conventionalities; it must lie; it refuses our experimental literature! Oh, well, then, the century will put the stage to one side, it will abandon it to the hands of the public amusers, while it will perform elsewhere its great and glorious work. You yourselves pronounce the verdict and kill the stage. It is very evident that the naturalistic evolution will extend itself more and more, as it possesses the intelligence of the age. While the novelists are digging always further forward, producing newer and more exact data, the stage will flounder deeper every day in the midst of its romantic fictions, its worn-out plots, and its skillfulness of handicraft. The situation will be the more sad because the public will certainly acquire a taste for reality in reading novels. The movement is making itself forcibly felt even now. There will come a time when the public will shrug its shoulders and demand an innovation. Either the theater will be naturalistic or it will not be at all; such is the formal conclusion.

And even now, to-day, is not this becoming the situation? All of the new literary generation turn their backs on the theater. Question the young men of twenty-five years—I speak of those who possess a real literary temperament; they will show great contempt for the theater; they will speak of its successful authors with such faint approval that you will become indignant. They look upon the stage as being of an inferior rank. That comes solely from the fact that it does not offer them the soil of which they have need; they find neither enough liberty nor enough truth there. They all veer toward the novel. Should the stage be conquered by a stroke of genius to-morrow you would see what an outpouring would take place. When I wrote elsewhere that the boards were empty I merely meant they had not yet produced a Balzac. You could not, in good faith, compare M. Sardou, Dumas, or Augier to Balzac; all the dramatic authors, put one on top of the other, do not equal him in stature. The boards will remain empty, from this point of view, so long as a master hand has not, by embodying the formula in a work of undying genius, drawn after him to-morrow's generations.

V.

I HAVE perfect faith in the future of our stage. I will not admit that the critics are right in saying that naturalism is impossible on the stage, and I am going to explain under what conditions the movement will without question be brought about.

It is not true that the stage must remain stationary; it is not true that its actual conventionalities are the fundamental conditions of its existence.

Everything marches, I repeat; everything marches forward. The authors of to-day will be overridden; they cannot have the presumption to settle dramatic literature forever. What they have lisped forth others will cry from the house top; but the stage will not be shaken to its foundations on that account; it will enter, on the contrary, on a wider, straighter path. People have always denied the march forward; they have denied to the newcomers the power and the right to accomplish what has not been performed by their elders. The social and literary evolutions have an irresistible force; they traverse with a slight bound the enormous obstacles which were reputed impassable. The theater may well be what it is to-day; to-morrow it will be what it should be. And when the event takes place all the world will think it perfectly natural.

At this point I enter into mere probabilities, and I no longer pretend to the same scientific rigor. So long as I have reasoned on facts I have demonstrated the

truth of my position. At present I am content to fore-
tell.   The evolution will take place, that is certain.
But will it pass to the left? will it pass to the right?
I do not know.   One can reason, and that is all.

In the first place, it is certain that the conditions
existing on the stage will always be different. The
novel, thanks to its freedom, will remain perhaps the
tool, *par excellence*, of the century, while the stage will
but follow it and complete the action.   The wonderful
power of the stage must not be forgotten, and its
immediate effect on the spectators.   There is no better
instrument for propagating anything.   If the novel,
then, is read by the fireside, in several instances, with a
patience tolerating the longest details, the naturalistic
drama should proclaim before all else that it has no
connection with this isolated reader, but with a crowd
who cry out for clearness and conciseness.   I do not
see that the naturalistic formula is antagonistic to this
conciseness and this clearness.   It is simply a question
of changing the composition and the body of the work.
The novel analyzes at great length and with a minute-
ness of detail which overlooks nothing; the stage can
analyze as briefly as it wishes by actions and words.
A word, a cry, in Balzac's works is often sufficient to
present the entire character.   This cry belongs essentially to the stage.   As to the acts, they are consistent
with analysis in action, which is the most striking form
of action one can make.   When we have gotten rid of
the child's play of a plot, the infantile game of tying
up complicated threads in order to have the pleasure
of untying them again; when a play shall be nothing
more than a real and logical story—we shall then enter
into perfect analysis; we shall analyze necessarily the

double influence of characters over facts, of facts over characters. This is what has led me to say so often that the naturalistic formula carries us back to the source of our national stage, the classical formula. We find this continuous analysis of character, which I consider so necessary, in Corneille's tragedies and Molière's comedies; plot takes a secondary place, the work is a long dissertation in dialogue on man. Only instead of an abstract man I would make a natural man, put him in his proper surroundings, and analyze all the physical and social causes which make him what he is. In a word, the classical formula is to me a good one, on condition that the scientific method is employed in the study of actual society, in the same way that the chemist studies minerals and their properties.

As to the long descriptions of the novelist, they cannot be put upon the stage; that is evident. The naturalistic novelists describe a great deal, not for the pleasure of describing, as some reproach them with doing, but because it is part of their formula to be circumstantial, and to complete the character by means of his surroundings. Man is no longer an intellectual abstraction for them, as he was looked upon in the seventeenth century; he is a thinking beast, who forms part of nature, and who is subject to the multiplicity of influences of the soil on which he grows and where he lives. This is why a climate, a country, a horizon, a room, are often of decisive importance. The novelist no longer separates his character from the air which he breathes; he does not describe him in order to exercise his rhetorical powers, as the didactic poets did, as Delille does, for example; he simply notes the material conditions in which he finds his characters at each

hour, and in which the facts are produced, in order to
be absolutely thorough in order that his inquiry may
belong to the world's great whole and reproduce the
reality in its entirety.   But it is not necessary to carry
descriptions to the stage; they are found there naturally.   Are not the stage settings a continual description,
which can be made much more exact and startling
than the descriptions in a novel?   It is only painted
pasteboard, some say ; that may be so, but in a novel it is
less than painted pasteboard—it is but blackened paper,
notwithstanding which the illusion is produced. After
the scenery, so surprisingly true, that we have recently
seen in our theaters, no one can deny the possibility of
producing on the stage the reality of surroundings.   It
now remains for dramatic authors to utilize this reality,
they furnishing the characters and the facts, the scene
painters, under their directions, furnishing the descriptions, as exact as shall be necessary.   It but remains
for a dramatic author to make use of his surroundings
as the novelists do, since the latter know how to introduce them and make them real.

I will add that the theater, being a material reproduction of life, external surroundings have always been
a necessity there.   In the seventeenth century, however, as nature was not taken into consideration, as
man was looked upon only as a purely intellectual
being, the scenery was vague—a peristyle of a temple,
any kind of a room, or a public place.   To-day the
naturalistic movement has brought about a more and
more perfect exactness in the stage settings.   This was
produced little by little, almost inevitably.   I even find
here a proof of the secret work that naturalism has
accomplished in the stage since the commencement of

the century. I have not time to study any more deeply this question of decorations and accessories; I must content myself by stating that description is not only possible on the stage, but it is, moreover, a necessity which is imposed as an essential condition of existence.

There is no necessity for me to expatiate on the change of place. For a long time the unity of place has not been observed. The dramatic authors do not hesitate to cover an entire existence, to take the spectators to both ends of the world. Here conventionality remains mistress, as it is also in the novel. It is the same as to the question of time. It is necessary to cheat. A play which calls for fifteen days, for example, must be acted in the three hours which we set apart for reading a novel or seeing it played at the theater. We are not the creative force which governs the world; our power of creation is of a second-hand sort; we only analyze, sum up in a nearly always groping fashion, happy and proclaimed as geniuses when we can disengage one ray of the truth.

I now come to the language. They pretend to say that there is a special style for the stage. They want it to be a style altogether different from the ordinary style of speaking, more sonorous, more nervous, written in a higher key, cut in facets, no doubt to make the chandelier jets sparkle. In our time, for example, M. Dumas, *fils*, has the reputation of being a great dramatic author. His "mots" are famous. They go off like sky rockets, falling again in showers to the applause of the spectators. Besides, all his characters speak the same language, the language of witty Paris, cutting in its pardoxes, having a good hit always in view, and sharp and hard. I do not deny the sparkle of this language—not a very solid sparkle, it is true—but I deny its truth. Nothing is so fatiguing as these continual sneering sentences. I would rather see more elasticity, greater naturalness. They are at one and the same time too well and not well enough written. The true style-setters of the epoch are the novelists; to find the infallible, living, original style you must turn to M. Gustave Flaubert and to MM. de Goncourt. When you compare M. Dumas' style to that of these great prose writers you find it is no longer correct— it has no color, no movement. What I want to hear on the stage is the language as it is spoken every day; if we cannot produce on the stage a conversation with its repetitions, its length, and its useless words, at least the movement and the tone of the conversation could be kept; the particular turn of mind of each talker, the reality, in a word, reproduced to the necessary extent. MM. Goncourt have made a curious attempt at this in " Henriette Maréchal," that play which no one would listen to, and which no one knows anything about. The Grecian actors spoke through a brass tube; under Louis XIV. the comedians sang their rôles in a chanting tone to give them more pomp; to-day we are content to say that there is a particular language belonging to the stage, more sonorous and explosive. You can see by this that we are progressing. One day they will perceive that the best style on the stage is that which best sets forth the spoken conversation, which puts the proper word in the right place, giving it its just value. The naturalistic novelists have already written excellent models of dialogue, reduced to strictly useful words.

There now remains but the question of sentimental characters. I do not disguise the fact that it is of prime importance. The public remain cold and irresponsive when their passion for an ideal character, for some combination of loyalty and honor, is not satisfied. A play which presents to them but living characters taken from real life looks black and austere to them, when it does not exasperate them. It is on this point that the battle of naturalism rages most fiercely. We must learn to be patient. At the present moment a secret change is taking place in the public feeling; people are coming little by little, urged onward by the spirit of the century, to admit the bold reproduction of real life, and are even beginning to acquire a taste for it. When they can no longer stand certain falsehoods we shall very nearly have gained our point. Already the novelists' work is preparing the soil in accustoming them to the idea. An hour will strike when it will be sufficient for a master to reveal himself on the stage to find a public ready to become enthusiastic in favor of the truth. It will be a question of tact and strength. They will see then that the highest and most useful lessons will be taught by depicting what is, and not by oft-dinned generalities, nor by airs of bravado, which are chanted merely to tickle our ears.

The two formulas are before us: the naturalistic formula, which makes the stage a study and a picture of real life; and the conventional formula, which makes it purely an amusement for the mind, an intellectual speculation, an art of adjustment and symmetry regulated after a certain code. In fact, it all depends upon the idea one has of literature, and of dramatic literature in particular. If we admit that literature is but an inquiry about men and things entered into by original minds, we are naturalists; if we pretend that literature is a framework superimposed upon the truth, that a writer must make use of observation merely in order to exhibit his power of invention and arrangement, we are idealists, and proclaim the necessity of conventionality. I have just been very much struck by an example. They have just revived, at the Comédie Française, " Le Fils Naturel " of M. Dumas, *fils*. A critic immediately jumps into enthusiasm. Here is what he says: "*Mon Dieu !* but that is well put together ! How polished, dove-tailed, and compact ! Is not this machinery pretty ? And this one, it comes just in time to work itself into this other trick, which sets all the machinery in motion." Then he becomes exhausted, he cannot find words eulogistic enough in which to speak of the pleasure he experiences in this piece of mechanism. Would you not think he was speaking of a plaything, of a puzzle, with which he amused himself by upsetting and then putting all the pieces in order again ? As for me, " Le Fils Naturel " does not affect me in the least. And why is that ? Am I a greater fool than the critic ? I do not think so. Only I have no taste for clockwork, and I have a great deal for truth. Yes, truly, it is a pretty piece of mechanism. But I would rather it had been a picture of life. I yearn for life with its shiver, its breath, and its strength ; I long for life as it is.

We shall yet have life on the stage as we already have it in the novel. This pretended logic of actual plays, this equality and symmetry obtained by processes of reasoning, which come from ancient metaphysics, will fall before the natural logic of facts and beings such as reality presents to us. Instead of a stage of fabrication we shall have a stage of observation. How will the evolution be brought about? To-morrow will tell us. I have tried to foresee, but I leave to genius the realization. I have already given my conclusion: Our stage will be naturalistic, or it will cease to exist.

Now that I have tried to gather my ideas together, may I hope that they will no longer put words into my mouth which I have never spoken? Will they still continue to see, in my critical opinions, I know not what ridiculous inflations of vanity or odious retaliations? I am but the most earnest soldier of truth. If I am mistaken, my judgments are there in print; and fifty years from now I shall be judged, in my turn; I may perhaps be accused of injustice, blindness, and useless violence. I accept the verdict of the future.

THE INFLUENCE OF MONEY
IN LITERATURE.

THE INFLUENCE OF MONEY
IN LITERATURE.

I OFTEN hear the following complaint uttered around me : " The literary instinct is dying out, letters are pushed to one side by commerce, money is destroying talent." And there are many other accusations uttered against the democracy which is invading our *salons* and our academies, which detracts from the beauty of our language, which makes the writer a merchant, disposing or not of his merchandise according to the trademark it bears, and as a result of the transaction amassing a fortune or dying in misery.

These complaints and accusations enrage me. It is certain, in the first place, that the literary spirit of the seventeenth and eighteenth centuries is no longer that of our nineteenth century. An intellectual movement has little by little brought about a transformation which to-day is complete. First, let us see what this transformation really is. Then it will be easy for us to determine the place which money holds in our literature.

I.

LATELY I have been re-reading Sainte-Beuve's critical essays, that interminable series of volumes, in which he confesses himself at such great length. And it was ·during this reading that I was struck with the profound modifications that have taken place in our feelings about literature. Sainte-Beuve, whose intelligence is so flexible and so great, and so well able to appreciate modern works, had nevertheless a tender preference for those of the past. He expresses a continual regret, a sort of homesickness, for the dead ages, for the seventeenth century above all ; it escapes him, in a page, or in a phrase, on no matter what subject. He acknowledges the present time, he flatters himself that he knows and comprehends all its productions ; but his temperament carries him away, and he goes back to the past and lives more at his ease with his melancholy joys and mid his memories as a scholar and a man of letters. He was born two hundred years too late. I have never understood the charm of the literary temperament better, as it was cultivated by old France. Sainte-Beuve was certainly one of the last to feel and weep with this old world, and its echo vibrates the more strongly in him because he has one foot in each of the two epochs, the past and the present, and because he is more of an actor than a judge. His true confessions were written in his hours of trouble, and they sound like a cry of personal sorrow.

Here is the picture Sainte-Beuve draws of the writer when he turns back to that past about which he dreams. The writer is an erudite and lettered man, who, above all else, needs leisure. He lives in the depths of a library, far from the noise of the street, in a sweet companionship with the Muses. It is a condition of luxury, of spiritual refinement, with just enough mental stimulus, and the soft soothing of one's entire nature. Literature was the pastime of a chosen society, which charmed the poet first, before it contributed to the happiness of a select circle. No hypothesis of forced labor, of prolonged vigils, of work anxiously awaited and accomplished in a hurry; on the contrary, there was a smiling politeness toward inspiration, works were written in favorable hours, in entire ease of heart and mind. Men of the upper classes were alone capable of producing anything under such circumstances; I mean by that, rich and well-conditioned men, to whom a god had given the necessary leisure. And the idea of gain never entered into this work; the writer made phrases as the bird pours forth trills, for his pleasure and the pleasure of others. There was no question of paying him any more than there was of paying the nightingale. He was simply fed. They agreed that money was a gross thing which debased the dignity of letters; at least there is no example presented to us of a man gaining a fortune by writing; and this being accepted, the writers draped themselves in their poverty, and for the necessities of life looked to some prince's charity. Writers were an ornament, a luxury, something lifted out of common life, something that could not be openly bought and sold like other commodities; the great ones alone could pay for this fantasy, as they paid for the privilege of having buffoons and ballet dancers.

I emphasize particularly the characteristics of the literary sense of that age. The writer of those times had in him nothing of the savant, full of zeal for truth, and finding his whole pleasure in making discoveries. He was, before all else, a skillful musician who played beautiful airs with the words and expressions current in that day; even those writers who had some sense for human nature were content to deliver long dissertations on the subject of man, an abstract, purely metaphysical man. One of their greatest pleasures was to paraphrase antiquity, to live in a more or less close communion with the Greeks and Romans. You must then picture the writer as seated in his closet, surrounded by books; as respectful toward tradition, not taking a step without consulting his authorities; as wishing ordinarily only to produce variations on well-known subjects, always treating literature like a lady of fashion, who exacted all kinds of politeness, and placing, truly, the charm of the thing in refining these politenesses *ad infinitum*. In a word, the writer revels in pure letters, in the pleasure of some literary conceit, in discussions about the use of language, in elaborate painting of character, feeling, and passions, not probing them down to their real physiological truth, but setting them forth in tragic tirades and eloquent passages. There is an impassable gulf between the savant who experiments and the writer who describes. The latter never cuts company with philosophical and religious dogma; he is shut fast in the domain of the spirit, even when he possesses a revolutionary nature. Literature is really a world apart: the literary man cultivates a sort of garden where each flower has its own plot, tulips on one side and roses on the other. This garden is formal but pretty; with lots of rules and regulations, yet nevertheless is full of the peaceful pleasure of watching the long expected flowers bud forth in their season.

It was the *salons* which called forth the literary instinct and molded it. Books were dear and poorly circulated; the people did not read at all, and the middle class hardly at all; they were far removed from that great current of reading which to-day carries all society with it. It was an exception to come across an impassioned reader devouring all he could find on the booksellers' shelves. And the general mass of readers, what we call public opinion, the universal suffrage, as we might put it, that molds literature to-day, did not then exist; the *salons*, a few rare groups of chosen people, were the only ones to give a decisive judgment. These *salons* really governed letters. They were the ones who decided upon the language, the choice of subjects, and the best manner in which to treat them. They sorted out the words, adopting some, condemning others; they established the rules, laid down the fashions, and made men's reputations. From all this literature took a character such as I have endeavored to point out. It was a sort of witty conceit, an amiable pastime, a superior distraction indulged in by men of good company. Picture to yourself one of these *salons*, which made the law in literary matters. A woman gathered around her writers whose only thought was to please her; new works were read to a select few; there was a great deal of conversation, carried on with all the decorum and the politeness in the world. Genius, as we understand the word

to-day, with its irregular strength, would naturally be
very ill at ease in such quarters, but simple talent
blossomed forth in the sweet heat of a delightful hothouse.   Even in the first days of French culture, when
the *salons* were hardly born, and the great lords were
content to have in their train a poet, as they had a
chef, the very conditions under which letters existed
put them in the hands of a privileged class whom they
flattered and whose taste they had to accept.   This
gave them all kinds of amiable qualities: tact, moderation, pompous alternation, a showy method of construction, and brilliant language; and also all the
attractions that you find in the society of well-born
women, those subtle discriminations of heart and brain,
those keen discussions upon delicate subjects, lightly
touching upon all topics without ever stopping on
any one, those cozy conversations which resemble
musical airs, and in which you are content to listen
merely to the sad or gay melodies of the human
creature.   Such was the nature of the literary temperament of past ages.

Naturally the *salons* led up to the academies.   It
was here that the literary spirit blossomed forth into
beautiful rhetoric.   Freed from its worldly element,
with no more women to humor, it became grammatical
and wordy, it plunged into the question of tradition, of
rules and formulas.   You should hear Sainte-Beuve,
this liberal minded man, talking about the Academy
with the importance and anger of an honest official
who has gone to his office and is discontented with the
conduct and work of his colleagues during his absence.
A great many writers were fond of these ancient *séances*
where they disputed about the use of different words,

those talks where they wrangled in the names of the oracles of antiquity. They flung Greek and Latin quotations at one another's heads, and enjoyed the pleasure of a common pedantry, in the midst of an extraordinary complication of hates and jealousies, of petty battles and mean triumphs. During two centuries statesmen fallen from power, bilious poets mad with vanity, librarians, their heads stuffed with old books, went to the Academy for solace, enjoyed the illusion of glory, and sharply discussed their respective merits, without ever having the public with them.

If the true history of the Academy were written, with the letters in which the academicians have confessed the truth, you would have the most extraordinary comic poem about a group of men who had fallen into infantile pride, and into occupations astounding in their uselessness. Sainte-Beuve's writings are very valuable in this connection, for the reason that he gives us some excellent notes on the attitude of the writer in the last *salons* at the commencement of this century. You see the writer feeling very much honored at being received at the houses of the great. He gives them low bows, he is respectful, and shows that he knows his own place and recognizes their superiority. It is an acceptance of the social hierarchy at which he will smile, and skeptically analyze, as soon as his foot has touched the pavement of the street; but in the midst of it, among ladies and hobnobbing with the minister of to-day or to-morrow, he thinks he must bow as if he had still need of that protection, as if he worked only for this class, flattered by its politeness, captivated by the seductions of these aristocratic surroundings, in which letters appeared more noble. It is simply a remnant of court-flattery, a taste for the grace and delightful propriety of good society.   Immersed in such reading, Sainte-Beuve seems to forget that it is the presence of the entire nation behind him that gives him his power and his true celebrity.

In a word, in the past centuries, literature means the cultivation of letters, utterly divorced from any notion of scientific inquiry.   It is an idea of pure letters, taking the conception of a soul utterly separate from the body and superior to it as its primary philosophical basis, and then starting from this indisputable dogma to wrestle in books dealing solely with questions of grammar and rhetoric.   As a result the literary sense of the nation labors in *salons* and learned bodies toward the formation of the language, toward the creation of a well-balanced literature which expatiates in beautiful sentences on the character and emotions as they were laid down by the metaphysics of that age. Man and nature remain in an abstract condition ; writers do not feel that it is their mission to tell the truth about people and things, but to depict them according to the conventional method, tending always toward the type so as to obtain the greatest possible grandeur. Nowhere do they descend to the individual ; not even among the comic poets, who have written some masterpieces of general observation.   The study of separate facts, the anatomy of special cases, the collecting, classifying, and ticketing, of human data are still far off. It is simply a question of amusing an elegant society by writing for it works in which could be found its language, its politeness, its art of shading, its fine restrictions, all its life of half admissions and common civilities.

Certainly such a literary spirit has given birth to beautiful works. I state this, I do not pass judgment upon it. All our great national literature of the eighteenth century, and, above all, of the seventeenth, is the product of this relation between the writers and the chosen society for whom they wrote. The *salons* and the academies were the cultivated soil in which our classical *chefs-d'œuvre* were inevitably to take root. To them is due the beautiful arrangement and the solemn breadth of Racine's tragedy, the magnificent periods of Bossuet's orations, the logic and the genial good sense of Boileau. Our glory is still there, for the new centuries are barely begun ; and we must give the spirit which has arisen since the romantic insurrection time to gain strength and amplitude. My aim is not to deny the past ; I wish, on the contrary, to define it, to show that it is the past, and that French letters are entering upon a new period, which it is well to disentangle clearly, if you wish to evade useless regrets and march to the future with resolute steps.

This, then, is the old literary spirit. Let us now take up some historical documents.

II.

FOR a long time I have thought that it would be very interesting to examine the material and moral situation which writers occupied in the last centuries. What was their real rank and social position? What position did they hold with the nobility and the middle class? How did they live? with what money, and on what footing?

To make a complete reply to these several questions would be a considerable labor, a work of great research and compilation. It would be necessary to gather together all the data that are possible about writers, to penetrate into their inner life, know their fortune, examine their accounts, follow them in their daily cares; and it would be more necessary than anything else to study the condition of publishers at that epoch, to know what returns a book brought to its author, to judge if literary work was sufficient to feed a man. It is only thus that we can grasp the real causes of the literary spirit of this vanished society; for the soil explains the plant, and the existence of the parasite writer of the classical centuries is to be found especially in the question of money.

Naturally it is impossible for me to treat the subject to its full extent. I should need much more leisure than I have at my disposal. This can be nothing more than a very incomplete sketch, some notes which I have gathered together and which I give now, to

indicate the great and interesting work which there is
to do. I do not even try to put order into these notes;
I merely transcribe them in haphazard fashion, drawing
from each the several reflections which bear on my
subject.

To make the inquiry complete I ought to go back to
the early writers, but I will content myself with a writer
no further back than Malherbe. We read the following in Tallemant des Reaux, who, after explaining that
the king could not give the poet a sufficient pension,
says: " The king ordered M. de Bellegarde, then first
gentleman of the bedchamber, to take charge of Malherbe until he was able to put him on the roll of his
pensioners. M. de Bellegarde gave him a salary of
5000 crowns, with his board, and provided him with a
horse and lackey. Upon the death of Henry IV. the
queen, Marie de Medicis, gave Malherbe a pension of
5000 crowns, and from that time he was no longer
under M. de Bellegarde's care. M. Moraud, who was
at Caen, promised Malherbe and a nobleman, one of
his friends, who was also at Caen, to let each of
them have 400 francs, for what I do not know, and in
that did them a great favor. He even invited them to
dinner. Malherbe was not willing to go unless he sent
his coach for him. Finally the nobleman persuaded
him to go on horseback. After dinner their money
was paid to them."

Is not this a typical example? The pith of the
whole matter seems to me to be found in these few
lines. A writer is a luxury which a great lord allows
himself. When the king has not enough money, he
passes the writer over to a courtier, praying him to
feed him for a little while, as he would hand over an

expensive beast for safe keeping, whom he hoped to be able to afford the distraction of at a later date ; and in fact, if death hinders the king from gratifying his caprice, a queen steps in who takes charge of the poet. Writers were rare and priceless birds, whom the great nobles lent, gave, and transmitted thus to one another, to show their taste and to proclaim the amount of their fortune. But what struck me the most in Tallemant des Reaux is the pride which Malherbe maintains, notwithstanding this position of parasite which he holds; he wants M. Mourad's money, but he insists upon their sending a carriage for him in order to go and get it, and ends by being content with a horse. Is not this a charming commentary upon the ideas of the times? The present of a sum of money does not seem to wound his feelings, but he insists upon the greatest etiquette in the matter.

Tallemant is filled with the stories of pensions and the sums of money given to authors. He says, speaking of Racan : " He lived at the bidding of the soldiers of the Marshal of Effiat." Then, he says of Chapelain : " The Duc de Longueville took Chapelain away from M. de Noailles, who treated him brutally, and paid him a pension of 2000 francs. . . His ode to Cardinal Mazarin brought him a pension of 500 crowns. . . Later M. de Longueville raised his pension 100 francs." What do you think of M. de Noailles, who "treated him brutally" to such an extent that the Duc de Longueville profited by the circumstance to allow himself the luxury of Chapelain at a price which was very exorbitant for those days ? Valets change masters thus when their masters beat them unmercifully.

I will transcribe here a very well known document,

but a very interesting one, which is to be found in the
" Siècle de Louis XIV." by Voltaire.   It is an extract
of a list of pensions, discovered in Colbert's papers, and
made out more than likely by Chapelain.   These pensions were paid by the king : " To Sire Pierre Corneille,
first dramatic poet of the world, 2000 francs ; to Sire
Demaretz, the most fertile author and gifted with the
most beautiful imagination which was ever known, 1200
francs ; to Sire Molière, an excellent comic poet, 1000
francs ; to Sire Abbé Cotin, orator and French poet,
1200 francs ; to Sire Douvrier, savant and Doctor of
Letters, 3000 francs ; to Sire Ogier, consummate in theology and in *belles-lettres*, 2500 francs ; to Sire Racine,
French poet, 800 francs ; to Sire Chapelain, the greatest poet who ever lived and possessed of the soundest
judgment, 3000 francs."

If the title of "first dramatic poet of the world,"
awarded to Corneille, satisfies us still, we are a little
surprised at the present time to learn that Demaretz
was gifted with " the most beautiful imagination that
was ever known," and that Chapelain inscribed himself
as " the greatest poet who ever lived and possessed of
the soundest judgment."   But the interest is not alone
in that ; this list is a precious document, because it
shows the true meaning of the pensions which were
given to writers.   They were not only alms distributed
to the needy ; they were also pledges of satisfaction,
accorded by a master to his servants, who exerted
themselves to magnify his glory.   Later on I shall
touch upon the conditions under which the state to-day
comes to the help of letters.   Formerly these pensions
were given because of the precarious situation in which
the following of letters as a profession placed the

writers, but these pensions also brought with them a certain amount of honor, and this is so true that even authors who were rich humbly petitioned to become pensioners.

Tallemant des Reaux furnishes us with a very striking example on the subject, in speaking of Balzac: " This man, who was possessed of so many virtues, ventured on a cowardice to which he had no temptation; in writing to the Cardinal Mazarin he signs himself: ' The most humble, most obedient, and most obliged servant and pensioner of Your Eminence.' " Balzac was rich, and yet he asked for and obtained a pension of 500 crowns. This is the most striking example of parasitical literature I know of.

I quote Tristan's epitaph; he died in 1665, and belonged to Gaston of Orléans:

> Ébloui de l'éclat de la splendeur mondaine,
> Je me flattais toujours d'une espérance vaine,
> Faisant le chien couchant auprès d'un grand seigneur,
> Je me vis toujours pauvre, et tâchai de paraître ;
> Je vécus dans la peine, espérant le bonheur,
> Et mourus sur un coffre, en attendant mon maître.

Naturally all backs were not bowed in such submission. Men of talent stood firm and upright; but they were the exception, for, I repeat, the ideas of the period permitted this guardianship, this state of dependence in which the great kept the writers. The great men paid and the writers bowed. Later, in Voltaire's time, the manners were already changed. Thus, in Voltaire, we find the following lines on Mainard, a forgotten writer, born in 1582: " He was one of those authors who complained of the lack of fortune attached to talent. He failed to understand that the success of a good work was the only recompense worthy of an artist ; that if princes and ministers wished to honor themselves by recompensing this kind of merit, it was more honorable to await these honors than to ask for them ; and that if a good writer was ambitious for a fortune, he should make it himself." This is very far removed from Balzac's singular vanity when he signed himself as "pensioner"; yet Voltaire does not condemn pensions, he only says that a writer ought to learn to wait for them.

I will take a few more examples from Voltaire : "Descartes had an older brother, who was a counselor in the parliament of Brittany, who despised him greatly, and who said it was an indignity that the brother of a counselor should debase himself by being a mathematician." But here is a much more distinct judgment. He is speaking of Valincour : "He made a much greater fortune than he would have made had he been only a man of letters. Letters alone, apart from the laborious sagacity which makes them useful, will hardly ever be productive of anything but an unhappy and despised life."

In the life of La Fontaine is also to be found some excellent information. *L'Amateur d'Autographes,* a journal which has published some very curious letters, has given some very interesting ones of La Fontaine. In a letter dated "January 5, 1618," he thanks his uncle, M. Jannart, then deputy attorney-general of the king, for the great obligations to which he is under to him for the sum which he has put to his credit; "it is not the first time that you have given evidence of the good will which you bear me." In another letter to the Duc de Bouillon's steward (dated

September 1, 1666) he complains " that he has not had any salary for two years." La Fontaine might be regarded as the typical example of a very talented poet; his works were successful, and he lived with the great noblemen of the time, going from one to the other without feeling any very intense desire to earn his living by his own exertions.

It would be easy for me to continue to quote examples. Thus I find in *L'Amateur d'Autographes* the following documents : In the first place, here is a letter from Dacier to the Duc d'Orleans, who was then regent, in which he says: "For thirty-five years my wife has worked for the advancement of letters; and the approval with which V. A. R. deigned to honor her makes us feel her efforts have not been in vain. The late king gave her a pension of 500 francs; but she owed this pension to the great prince's pity, and not to his esteem for her." Another letter is addressed by Gilbert to Baculard d'Arnaud. I will quote these two phrases : " I am in need of a louis; I make bold enough to ask you for it. I do not doubt but that you are generous enough to lend it to me, if you can." Then this is what Mme. de Genlis wrote to Talleyrand under date of July 10, 1814: " My situation is frightful since the Duc d'Orleans' departure; I have neither pension, revenue, nor resources; I have lived by borrowing and by putting my things in pawn. If the king gives pensions to men of letters, it seems to me that I am more entitled to one than many others; no matter how modest it may be, it will be sufficient, even if it is but 1200 francs."

This picture of the general misery of writers of former times is very incomplete; but I can easily see what researches might be made, and I know what important data would be obtained. Then it would be necessary, on the other hand, to consider the resources which writers were able to obtain from their works, to expose in what way and for how much a work would sell. I frankly confess I have not pushed my investigations as far as that; the inquiry would be a difficult one, and would take a great deal of time. We do not know very much about the terms made between publishers and authors, nor the exact amounts which their works brought in to them at that time. To gain a thorough knowledge on the subject it might be well to read the memoirs and letters of that period carefully; here and there we might get glimpses of the truth. But one thing I do know, and that is that a book or a play brought in very little money to its author compared with the figures of to-day. There are no examples of men of genius being enriched by their works. Corneille's absolute poverty has been contested; but, in any case, he died in very straitened circumstances. Racine lived to the time of his death as a *bourgeois*. Molière barely earned his living, although he was an actor as well as a comic poet. Dramatic authors made hardly any money until Beaumarchais' time. As to novelists, poets, and historians, they were the publishers' prey. Baculard d'Arnaud, whom I mentioned further back, died poor, after having earned for his publishers more than a million francs.

This, then, was the true situation of writers in the seventeenth and eighteenth centuries, a situation which can easily be established by more positive proof still.

To sum up all that I have said : Literary labors could not feed the author, who thus became a rare bird, whom the king and the great lords were alone able to indulge in the luxury of. A contract was entered into between the protector and the *protégé ;* the protector clothed, fed, and lodged, or else he contented himself with pensioning the *protégé ;* who in return sang his praises, dedicated his works to him, in order to pass down to posterity his name and the recognition of his benefits. This entered into the rôle which the old *régime* assigned to the nobility; in exchange for its privileges its duty was to help those who were obedient to them, and letters were but one of their dependents, like the soil and the common people themselves. A whole pyramid of conventional distinctions ruled with absolute sovereignty, fostered by worldly respect. If the king or the nobles condescended to a familiarity. with a writer, it was but a passing condescension, for it never would have entered anyone's head to place King Louis XIV., for instance, and the actor Molière on a footing of perfect equality. Genius counted for nothing but part and parcel of the pomp belonging to the reign. And besides, as we have just seen, the pension granted to a writer was not only a help, which would assure him leisure in which to write fine works, but it was an honor much sought after, even by writers born with fortunes. It was a fine thing to belong to a powerful nobleman; it gave one a position in the world. All the intellectual life moved in the narrow circle of high society, in the *salons* and the academies. And as a result the literary world was, as I have defined it, devoted to leisure and elegant language, careful of all the proprieties ; a lovely, yet pompous plant, sunning itself in the ladies' smiles, but confined within narrow limits by academical disputes, and subsisting mainly upon rule and tradition ; above all, it had an instinctive hatred of science as of an enemy who would one day break all rules and introduce new formulas in triumph.

III.

LET us now examine the material condition of the writer, such as it is in our days. The Revolution has come, sweeping away all privileges; like a clap of thunder it has carried away the old distinctions and the old respect. In the new state of things the writer is among those citizens whose condition has been radically changed. Under Napoleon, Louis XVIII., and Charles X. things seemed once more about to resume their former aspect; but underneath these external appearances all things were being slowly transformed; the ways of living were no longer the same, and every day the new literary spirit was molded by the material conditions brought into letters by the young society. Every social movement brings with it an intellectual movement.

In the first place, the people have been educated, and thousands of readers created. The newspapers penetrate everywhere, the country people begin to buy books. In half a century books, which were formerly an *objet de luxe*, have become something within everybody's reach. Formerly they cost a great deal; to-day the most humble purses can purchase a small library. These are the decisive facts; as soon as people know how to read, and as soon as they can read cheaply, the publishers' business increases tenfold, and the writer finds a means of living by the work of his pen. For this reason he no longer seeks the protection of the great; parasiticism disappears from among us; an author is a workman like any other, and gains his livelihood by his work.

This is not all. Nobility has been pierced to the heart. It has abandoned its great train of retainers; it has lowered its head, little by little, under the universal leveling. It has sustained a slow but inevitable fall, which no longer permits it to have its poets and its historians, even though the latter should forever be reduced to the necessity of begging a bed and food. Manners have changed; who could imagine a palace in the Faubourg St. Germain indulging the luxury of a La Fontaine to-day? Thus not only can a writer earn his living by addressing his work to the public, but he would search in vain to-day for a *grand seigneur* who would pay him, by pensioning him, for dedicating that work to him.

Let us see now what influence money has in our literature. The newspapers, more than anything else, have opened out an immense field. To run a newspaper is an enormous business, and it gives the means of earning a living to a great number of people. Young writers, when they first start out, can in this way find immediate work which pays them well. Critics, celebrated novelists, without counting the regular newspaper men, some of whom occupy an important position, earn considerable sums in journalistic work. These high prices were not given from the very beginning; the returns were very small at first, but have grown larger little by little, and are growing still. Twenty years ago a writer who could earn 200 francs a month on a newspaper considered himself very fortunate; to-day the same man can easily earn 1000 francs and over.   Literature tends to become a very expensive merchandise, provided it is signed by a well-known name.   The newspapers cannot give an opening to all the beginners from the country, but they really support a great many young people, who have only themselves to blame if they do not cut loose some day in order to write good books.   Some people urge that even if the newspapers do come to the aid of these young writers, that, on the other hand, they weaken them, and render them incapable of great works.   This is a question which needs looking into.   Just now I simply mention the resources offered in our century to writers who wish to live by their pen.

It has become equally easy to publish a book, and upon a thoroughly fair basis.   It is childish nowadays to complain of the difficulty of approaching a publisher. They publish too much ; the number of volumes which appear each year in France amounts to thousands. When you look at the trash, the mediocre books which lumber up the shelves, one asks one's self what books the publishers could possibly have refused.   As to the contracts, they are actually drawn up in a very honest and reciprocal spirit.   It is not so very long ago that publishing was a regular game of chance.   A publisher bought the sole rights to a book for a certain sum during ten years; then he tried to get his money back, and to get back as much as possible by putting out the book to the best possible advantage.   As a result there was almost always a victim somewhere ; either the work obtained great success and the author cried out from the housetops that he had been robbed, or the work did not sell at all, and the publisher said that he was ruined by the lucubrations of a fool.   This explains the state of open warfare in which the publishers and authors lived. You should read Balzac's correspondence, you should hear the veterans in letters talk to-day, if you would get an idea of the quarrels and the proceedings which followed the productions of certain works. Now these ways are changed. If some publishers continue to follow the old method, the greatest number pay a certain fixed royalty; if this royalty is 50 centimes, an edition of one thousand copies will bring 500 francs to the author; and it will mean 500 francs as many times as the publishers put out a new edition. It can easily be seen that all recrimination becomes impossible under these circumstances; there is no longer any place for recrimination, as the author gains more or less according to the book's success, and the publisher is certain to pay no more to the author than a royalty proportionate to the sums which are coming to him. I must add, though, that the book, unless very much the fashion, will never enrich the author. It is considered a good sale when three or four thousand copies are sold; this would make 2000 francs if we compute the royalty at 50 centimes a copy, this being a big royalty—the usual royalty is generally 35 or 40 centimes. You can easily see if the work has taken one year to write, and even if it is so fortunate as at once to find a publisher, that 2000 francs is a very modest sum upon which to live in our days.

On the stage the gain is formidable, on the contrary. In the same way as with a book, you obtain a percentage on the receipts, only the receipts are enormous here, for the reason that a great number of people who would not pay three francs for a book will not hesitate to pay seven or eight for an orchestra chair;

hence it follows that a drama or a comedy brings much more than a novel. Thus, for example, suppose a play has a run of a hundred nights, which is the usual number to-day denoting success; the average receipts per night can be placed at 4000 francs, which brings into the box office 400,000 francs, and to the author a sum of 40,000 francs, if the royalties are ten per cent. of the profits. Now to earn the same sum by publishing a novel it would be necessary, putting the royalty at 50 centimes a copy, that 80,000 copies should be struck off, an output so extraordinary that I can only think of four or five examples during the last fifty years. And I am not speaking of its production throughout the rest of the country, of its reproduction in foreign countries, or of the revivals of the play. It is but a hackneyed truth to repeat that the stage brings in much more than the novel; a large number of men live by it, while you could easily count the number of authors who live upon the money their books bring them in.

I wish to spend a moment on this question of money as it presents itself to the young aspirant setting out for Paris. Let us suppose that a young man arrives almost without resources, or perhaps with a small sum of money which will keep him in bread for a little while. Want soon pushes him into journalism. This, at least, brings him in his bread, and he ends by devoting all his energies to this pursuit. If he is clever or simply persevering he will find a corner, will sell a few articles, will make a place for himself, which will bring him in 200 or 300 francs a month. He cannot very well starve on that. Some cry out against journalism; they accuse it of perverting literary youth, of warping talents. I have never been able to listen to these complaints without smiling. Journalism kills those who should be killed, that is all. It is certain that the money to be made in newspapers has taken many young men from their counting houses and their work-shops who might but for that be selling cloth or making candles all their lives; they were not born writers, they follow the trade of a journalist as they would follow any other; and that injures no one. But without taking into consideration that some men have the true newspaper instinct, a special ability for this kind of work, for this daily battle, let any point me out a born writer who has lost his talent by earning his bread on a newspaper during the difficult hours of the start. I am certain, on the contrary, that they gained, while thus engaged, more energy, more manliness, a more sorrowful, but much more penetrating, knowledge of the modern world. I have already expressed, else-where, this idea, and I shall perhaps develop it some day. In the meantime, let us go back to our beginner who earns money by working on the newspapers; without doubt the cold shoulders are numerous, the bread is hard to eat sometimes, without mentioning the fact that any hour you may lose the position. The struggle is entered upon, however; and if the beginner holds the reins well, if he is strong, he will write a book or a play outside of his daily work; he will manage to try his literary fortune. The book appears, the play is produced; it is a step forward. The battle continues, volumes succeed each other, play follows play, and all this without any very startling success. At last the writer succeeds in freeing himself from journalism. He is rich by his writings or from his stage work; he is his own master. Such is the story of nearly all the well-known writers of to-day. Some few, however, have been able to escape the bitter struggle of journalism, either because they had money in the beginning or because their earnings from the stage or their books satisfied their wants at once.

In the last fifty years large fortunes have been realized in letters. A few examples will be sufficient. Since the generation of 1830 the profits have been considerable. Eugène Sue, after the popular success of his " Mystères de Paris," sold his novels for a very high figure. George Sand, who in early life was in very straitened circumstances, and reduced to painting simple subjects on wood, ended by attaining, if not a fortune, at least a very comfortable income. But the one who made the most money was certainly Alexander Dumas, who made and ran through millions in his extraordinary existence of superhuman work and mad revels. Then we must not forget Victor Hugo, who married a poor girl and had a very bitter struggle until the success of " Feuilles d'Automne " and " Notre Dame de Paris " was the commencement of that triumphant life of honor and riches.

At the present time it is the dramatic writers especially who become wealthy. First, there is M. Alexander Dumas, *fils*, who is as prudent and sharp as his father was prodigal and intemperate. M. Victorien Sardou, starting from desperate poverty, is now living comfortably in his Château de Marly, on one of the most adorable hillsides of the Seine. I could multiply examples, but these are sufficient to show how to-day letters often bring fortunes to writers.

But I have not spoken of Balzac yet. We must

study the wonderful case of Balzac if we want to treat this question of money in literature to its fullest extent. Balzac was a true workman, who turned out books to clear his name from stain. Overwhelmed with debts, ruined by unlucky enterprises, he took up his pen again as the only tool he knew how to use, and which could save him. It was not only his daily bread that Balzac asked of his books; he demanded that they should make good the losses sustained by him in trade. The battle lasted a long time; Balzac did not gain a fortune, but he paid his debts, which was much better. How far removed we are from our friend La Fontaine, dreaming under the trees, seated in the evenings at the table of some great lord, paying for his dinner by a fable! Balzac put his own nature into his "César Birotteau." He struggled against bankruptcy with a superhuman will; he did not seek in letters glory alone, and he found dignity and honor.

It is curious to study the question of pensions to-day. The state, that impersonal being, has substituted itself for the king, who was supposed to help letters by means of the money in his pockets Then, further, pensions are no longer given as an honorary title, and as a guarantee of great admiration; they go to the needy, to the writers whose old age is unhappy; and oftentimes they are hidden under the gift of a sinecure to the pensioner, a fictitious employment which shields his dignity. In fact, pensions are given discreetly and secretly; they certainly denote no fall, but they indicate a certain condition of poverty which is best hidden. What happened to Lamartine when ruin came upon him perfectly characterizes the public's actual sentiments on the subject. To those who became indignant at the want of money in which France left the great poet, to those who endeavored to get up a great national subscription for him, it was replied that the country was not bound to pay the debts of all extravagant writers whose open hands had squandered millions. It was a very hard reply, but it was made in the spirit of our new society; it arose from that spirit of equality which says that every producer should be the artisan of his own fortune. France, as Lamartine's friends said, is rich enough to pay for its glory; but between a writer who has shown himself free and worthy by his works, and a writer who begs for help after he has lived in utter disregard of his talents and his debts, public opinion does not hesitate; she is kind to the former, severe to the latter. It is not to-day that Balzac—I speak of the Balzac of the seventeenth century—would soil his honor by touching a pension from the government. This is the great step which has been taken.

However, the pension is a very good thing in connection with scientific men and scholars. There are, in fact, researches and experiments which demand a great deal of time, and of which the final gain is almost nothing. The state intervenes, and it is perfectly right that it should; for remark, the question always puts itself in the same manner: either the writer makes his living, and cannot be supported without shame, or his work is not sufficient for his needs, and then he at least has an excuse for accepting assistance for his wants. It remains, however, an open question if the shoemakers and tailors, for example, might not have good cause for complaint; they too often end in misery, after thirty years of hard work, and yet do not think they have any right to say to the country: "I can no longer earn my bread; give me some!" Then there are also subsidies, orders, and honors, of which I wish to say a word. These honors cost the state nothing; it is an easy way in which to please people, and I only speak of them for the purpose of once more showing the spirit of equality. Formerly the cross never shone on a writer's breast, to-day there are some great dignitaries in letters. As to orders and subsidies, these are rarely to be found in letters, outside of the theater; and there, moreover, they are given as the testimony of approval to the whole performance, and not directly to the work of the writer. A great many people, young people principally, complain and accuse the government of not having done for letters what it has done for painting and sculpture. These are very dangerous protestations; the greatest honor which our literature enjoys is that of being independent. I repeat what I have already said elsewhere: "All that the government can do for us is to give us our absolute liberty." At this day the highest idea we can form of a writer is that of a man free from all pledges, bound to flatter no one, who owes his life, his talents, his glory, solely to his own efforts, and who is ready to place all these at his country's service without expectation of any return.

IV.

THIS, then, in our days, is the position money holds in literature. It will be easy now to characterize our feelings about literature, and to compare them with the spirit of the last centuries.

In the first place, there are no more *salons*. I know that ambitious women, the blue stockings of our democracy, pique themselves still upon receiving writers. But their *salons* are merely great meeting places into which the guests rush, mid a perfect babel of noise and hurry. There is no longer any gathering together of congenial souls, such as the women of other days called around them ; there is no longer any disinterested love of letters, no longer any holding of conversations as one does a concert. All you have is a conglomeration of desires, a great mass of people eager for power, and rushing to the houses of women whom they consider powerful in any way whatsoever. Politics is there, shrieking, devouring, reducing letters to the rôle of a bleating lamb, the lamb of the ideal, washed and decked out in blue ribbons. There is always the same insipidness; they play at feasting on literature, while in reality the human animal underneath crops up, desirous of enjoyment and his share of the good things of the world. It is thus an inevitable consequence that these *salons*, true centers of political agitation, throw themselves into a violent opposition against the literary movement of the period when it makes the pretension of marching at the head of revolutionary and progressive ideas; sweet verses are read there; they swoon at the names of Rome and Athens; they affect a passion for antiquity; they are lost in admiration after the manner of an undergoverness who has read her classics, as others have learned to play on the piano; and naturally they deny the living literature of the actual hour; they would gladly persecute it, without daring to do so. All this counts for nothing; we have here only a lot of gossiping women.

The disappearance of these *salons* is a very important matter, as it indicates the diffusion of taste, the growing enlargement of the public. From the moment that opinion is not the work of a few chosen groups or of certain *coteries*, each one pushing to the front its particular idol, it comes to be the great mass of readers who judge and award success. There is an evident tie between the rapidly increasing number of readers and the disappearance of the *salons;* the latter have sunk and disappeared, because they could no longer lord it over the former, who have become legion and refuse to obey. The few literary reunions which exist still, certain little groups, especially in the academic world, have been swamped and have lost all their power; frightened at the ever-increasing mass of books, they are obliged to take refuge in a past, forever dead. It is the dying agony of the old literary spirit, which Sainte-Beuve realized.

Add that the Academy has equally ceased to exist; I mean as a power and an influence in letters. The conferring of a *fauteuil* is still sharply contested, the same as that of a cross of honor, by the innate vanity we possess. But the Academy no longer makes our laws; it has even lost all authority over our language. The literary prizes which it distributes no longer carry any weight with the public; as they ordinarily go to the mediocrities, they have no meaning, they indicate and encourage no movement. The romantic movement was born in spite of the Academy, which later was forced to accept it; to-day the same thing is in a fair way to happen concerning the naturalistic evolution; so that the Academy appears like an obstacle placed in the path of our literature, which each new generation has to kick out of its way; after which the Academy gives in. Not only does it aid us in nothing, but it impedes us, and it is vain enough and weak enough to open its arms to those whom formerly it wished to devour. Such an institution can be of no account in the literary movement of a people; it has neither significance, nor action, nor result of any kind. Its only rôle, which certain persons still recognize, is the position of guardian of the language; and this rôle even has escaped it; M. Littré's dictionary, so learned and so great, is more consulted to-day than the Academy's dictionary; without taking into consideration that since 1830 the greatest writers have turned the latter topsy-turvy in an outburst of splendid independence; creating words and expressions, exhuming condemned terms, bringing new words into use, enriching the language in each new work so well that the Academy's dictionary bids fair to become a curious archæological monument. I repeat that its rôle is almost null in our literature; it remains at best simply a sort of halo.

Thus the great social movement, starting from the

eighteenth century, has had in ours its literary expression. New opportunities of earning his bread have been
opened to the writer, and at one bound the whole system of artificial distinctions has been demolished,
intelligence has become a badge of nobility, and work
a dignity. At the same time, by a logical consequence,
as the influence of the *salons* and the Academy has
disappeared, the coming of democracy in letters is
seen; in other words, the little *coteries* are lost in the
great public, a book is born in the crowd and for the
crowd. Finally science penetrates into literature, the
scientific inquiry extends even to the work of the
poets, and this above all other things characterizes the
actual evolution, this naturalistic evolution which is
sweeping us along.

Well, I say we must resolutely put ourselves face to
face with the situation, and accept it with courage.
Men lament, crying out that the literary spirit is dying
out; that is not true, it is being transformed. I hope
to have proved it. And do you wish to know what
has made us worthy and respected to-day? It is money.
People are foolish who cry out against money, which
is a considerable social force. Only the very young
writers will repeat the common cry about the degradation of letters, the sacrifice to the golden calf; they
are ignorant yet, they cannot understand the justice
and the honesty of money. Let them compare for one
moment the situation of a writer under Louis XIV.
and that of a writer of our own days. Where is the
full and complete assertion of personality? Where is
the true dignity? Where is the greatest amount of
work, the broadest and most respected existence?
Evidently on the side of the actual writer. And this

dignity, this respect, this breadth, this assertion of his personality and his thoughts, to what is it due? To money, without a doubt. It is money, it is the legitimate gain realized from our works, which has delivered us from all humiliating patronage; which has made of the old-time juggler, the ancient court fool, a free citizen, a man who looks up only to himself. With money to back him, he has dared to say everything; he has carried his habit of examination into all quarters; to the king, even to God, without fear of losing his bread. Money has emancipated the writer; money has created modern letters.

It makes me angry to read in the journals of young poets that a writer should simply aim at glory. Yes, that is understood, it is puerile to say it. But we must live. If you are not born with a fortune, what will you do? Will you regret the times when they cudgeled Voltaire, when Racine died of a sulk from Louis XIV., when literature was the hireling of a brutal and imbecile nobility? What! You push your want of gratitude toward our great epoch to the verge of not understanding it, accusing it of a mercenary spirit, when this means, above all, the right to work and to live! If you cannot live by your verses, by your first essays, do something else; enter politics and wait until the public comes to you. The state owes you nothing. It is not very praiseworthy to cry for a supported literature. Fight, eat potatoes or truffles, break stones in the daytime and write *chefs-d'œuvre* at night. Only understand this well: if you have talent, if you have force, you will reach glory and fortune. This is the law of life and of our age. Why childishly revile our age when it certainly will remain great among the greatest?

I know all that can be said if you look at the question from certain unfortunate sides, such as that a mercenary spirit arises from this new appetite for reading, from the ever-increasing number of newspapers. But in what way does this hurt true writers? They earn less, but what matter so long as they eat? Remark, besides, that if a Ponson du Terrail amasses a fortune, he works enormously, much more than do the sonnet makers who revile him. Doubtless, from a literary point of view, the merit is nil; but the great labor of the newspaper writer explains his gains, while, in addition, his work enriches the dailies. We do not treat directly with the public; there are between it and us, middle-men, publishers, business managers—a whole little world, who live by our works, who make millions by our work; we do not wish to share our profits, and yet we splutter out against money, under the pretext that money is ignoble! These are unwholesome ideas, empty and blameworthy declarations, to which it is high time to take objection. Those who speak thus are either very feeble beginners, who are suffering from not being able to live by the work of their pens, or writers who have never known want, and who treat literature as a mistress, whom they always recompense with costly suppers.

What I reiterate is that money brings forth great works. Imagine, then, in our democratic times a young man thrown on the streets of Paris without a cent in his pocket. I have shown you, a little while ago, this young man, living by newspaper work, faring rather badly than well, succeeding finally, by a determined effort, in writing books outside of his daily work. Ten years of his life pass by in this terrible struggle.

Then success comes to him ; he has not only earned glory, he has made his fortune; he has reached a haven, having saved his children from poverty, sometimes having succeeded in paying the debts left by his family. Henceforth he is free, he speaks his thoughts aloud. Is it not a splendid picture? Money here shows its greatness.

The question has always been very badly put. We should start from the point that all work is worthy of payment. In composing a book, naturally, the true writer does not seat himself at his table each morning with the idea of earning the largest possible sum; but the book finished, the publisher is there, who makes money with this merchandise which has been given to him to sell, and nothing is more natural than that the writer should accept the royalty fixed by his contract. I cannot understand this great burst of indignation against money. The business part is on one side, literature is on the other.

All great evolutions must have their bad side. Inevitably speculators spring up. I have spoken of the feuilletonists who throng the sidewalks in such crowds. According to my way of thinking they earn their money very legitimately, because they work hard, and some with a great deal of spirit; but it is certain that literature is not here in question. The beginners are wrong to cry out against the newspaper writers, for they do not in reality encroach on any literary path ; they have created a special public, who only read newspaper literature ; they address themselves to these new readers, who are illiterate and incapable of appreciating a beautiful work. In fact, I think we ought rather to thank them, for they polish up this uncultivated soil, these penny journals which penetrate to the backwoods. Besides, look at politics : there is no movement there without an excess; each step in a society is marked by struggles and deep upheaving. In the same way it was inevitable that the emancipation of the writer, that intelligence when it reached triumphant prosperity and had become an aristocrat, should bring with it regrettable facts. This is the bad side of things. Men traffic dishonestly with their pens, a mass of folly looks out at us from the front page of the newspaper, we are inundated with silly books. But what matters it; all this is part of that natural viciousness which shows forth in the hours of a social crisis. The progress which is accomplished on high, the efforts of great talent bringing forth from our daily battles a new beauty, life in its truth and its intensity—you should look only at these things.

A much graver consequence, and one which has always worried me, is the continuous effort to which the writer of to-day is condemned. We are no longer at the time when a sonnet, read in a *salon*, made a writer's reputation, and led him to the Academy. The works of Boileau, of La Bruyère, of La Fontaine, are contained in one or two volumes. To-day we must produce and continue producing. It is the work of a laborer who must earn his bread and cannot retire until he has made his fortune. Besides, if the writer stops, the public forgets him ; he is forced to pile volume upon volume, as a cabinetmaker adds table to table. Look at Balzac. That is terrible, for the question presents itself immediately : How will posterity treat a work of such magnitude as the " Comedie Humaine "? It seems incredible that it can retain it all, and yet what part can it reject? Remark that the books bequeathed by the centuries are all relatively short. Man's memory halts before a bulk. Besides, it hardly retains the books called classical; by classical I mean those which are imposed upon us in our youth, when our intelligence cannot defend itself. Then, again, I am always uneasy when I think of our feverish rate of production. If each writer has really only one book in him, we are doing a very dangerous thing for our own glory in repeating this book indefinitely under the lash of new necessities. This, to my way of thinking, is the only disturbing element in the actual condition of things. Then again, we must never judge the future by the past. Balzac will evidently stand in a different position from Boileau.

I now come to the scientific breeze which is sweeping more and more over our literature. The question of money is simply one result in the transformation which the literary spirit has undergone in our days, for the primary cause of this transformation comes from the application of scientific methods to letters, from the use of those tools which the writer has borrowed from the savant in order to take up again with him the analysis of nature and of man. The actual battle is waged on this soil: on one side the rhetoricians, the grammarians, the pure men of letters, who intend to continue tradition; on the other, the anatomist, the analysist, the experts in the sciences of observation and experiment, whose object is to depict anew the world and humanity, studying them in their natural mechanism, and extending their works so as to embrace the greatest amount of truth. These latter, by their triumph since the beginning of the century, have molded the new literary spirit. They are not a school, as I have said a hundred times; they are a social evolution, whose phases are easily stated. The abyss which separates Balzac from a writer of any kind in the seventeenth century immediately presents itself before our eyes. Let us admit that Racine formerly may have read "Phèdre," which is his most audacious tragedy, in a *salon;* the fine ladies listened to it, the academicians approved of it, all those present were delighted with the pompousness of the verses, with the correctness of the tirades, with the propriety of the sentiments and language. The work is a fine rhetorical and logical composition, made about abstract and metaphysical beings, by an author imbued with the philosophical opinions of his day. Now let us take "Cousine Bette" and attempt to read that aloud in a *salon* or in an academy. The reading would appear improper; the fine ladies would be scandalized; and this only happens because Balzac has written a book of experiment and observation on human beings, not as a logician or a maker of beautiful phrases, but as an analyzer, who is loboring at the scientific quest of his age. This comparison shows how large is the abyss. When Sainte-Beuve sent forth his despairing cry, "Oh, physiologists, I find you everywhere!" he sounded the knell of the old-time literary spirit, he felt that the reign of literary men of old times was over.

That is the situation. I sum it all up by saying that our epoch is a grand one, and that it is childish to lament before the century which is opening out to us. As it advances humanity leaves only ruins behind it; why always turn back and weep over the ground which we have left behind us, wasted and strewn with *débris?*

Doubtless the past centuries had their literary greatness, but it is a poor aim to try to keep us immovable
in this greatness, under the pretext that there could be
no other.   A literature is but the expression of a social
condition.   To-day our democratic society is beginning
to have its literary expression, and it is magnificent
and complete.   We must accept it without regret or
childish repinings ; we must recognize the power, the
justice, and the dignity of money; we must submit to
the new spirit which broadens the domain of letters by
means of science, which above all grammar and rhetoric, above all philosophy and religion, strives to attain
to the beauty of truth.

V.

AS a result of and as a conclusion to the pages which I have just written, I will finish by briefly touching upon what we call " the question of the young writers."

Our beginners make unreasonable demands, as is explicable and pardonable, for youth is by nature in haste to succeed. I know a great many boys of twenty who, upon the refusal of their second play by the directors of a theater, or at the return of their third article sent to the newspapers, hold forth on the decadence of letters, and demand in a loud voice to be protected. Our young littérateurs dream of something like this : A special publisher, empowered to edit and publish all the books which the writers present to him ; a theater which, thanks to a generous subsidy, will present all the plays which the beginner sends to the director. And in all this recriminations come in ; they remark that the government gives much more money to music than to literature ; they point out painters covered with crosses and orders, who live like pampered children, under the protection of the government. Let us for a moment look into the wishes of these young people.

The idea of a general encouragement makes me smile. There must always be some sort of selection ; a committee or delegation will be appointed to examine the manuscripts ; the young writers whose books are rejected will set up a cry of partiality on the part of the examiners, and will accuse the state of doing nothing for them and of trying to suppress them. Moreover, they would not be far wrong; subsidies in any case benefit mediocrities; a cross never goes to an unhampered and original talent. This system of encouragement has not been applied to books; in fact, there does not exist a publisher who receives one or two hundred thousand francs from the government as a set-off for agreeing to publish ten or fifteen volumes by young authors during the year. But in the theater the trial has been made a long time; the Odeon, for example, is open to dramatic beginners. And I would like these people who cry out for such encouragement to make a study of the talented authors whose pieces were first played at the Odeon. I am certain that they are relatively few, while the list of poor and already forgotten ones must be formidable. I quote this simply to come to this axiom: protection in literature only leads to mediocrity.

Sometimes young authors, and, above all, dramatic authors, have written to me as follows: " Do you not believe that there is a great deal of unknown talent?" Naturally, until talent has shown itself it cannot be known; but what I believe and what is true is this, that any great talent ends by showing itself and becoming known. This is the whole point. Genius does not need aid in being brought forth; it brings itself forth. Every year in the Salon, that bazaar of artistic fabrications, we see pictures by pupils, studies by scholars, perfectly insignificant in themselves, and which are there only for encouragement and by tolerance; but that does not matter; that does not count and can never count; it is only that the great wrong is committed of occupying a place in vain. Therefore, why should they make such a display of useless things in literature by the help of a subsidy? The state owes nothing to young writers; it is not sufficient to have written a few pages to find an excuse for posing as a martyr if no one prints them and no one plays them; a shoemaker who has made his first pair of shoes does not look to the government to find a market for them. It is the worker who should force his work on the public. And if he has not this power he is nobody; he remains unknown by his own fault, and justly.

The weak ones in literature deserve no pity. Why, being weak, have they the ambition to wish to be strong? Never was the cry, "Woe to the vanquished!" more applicable. Nobody obliges a young man to write; when once he has taken up his pen, he must accept the consequences of the battle; and so much the worse for him if he is overthrown by the first shock, and if a whole generation passes over his body. Lamentations in such a case are childish, and besides, they remedy nothing. The weak succumb in spite of protection; the strong reach their goal in spite of obstacles; and the whole moral of the affair is just there.

I know very well that if we keep to the particular, there are examples of writers of very great mediocrity of whom subsidies and protections have made fashionable authors. In what has France need of mediocre writers? If beginners are encouraged it is evidently in the hopes of finding a man of genius among them. Books and plays are not objects of regular consumption, as are hats and shoes, for example. Such consumption, if you like, has place, it is true, in our libraries and in our theaters. But this concerns only

inferior works, done away with immediately, destined
to satisfy our appetites for the time being.   I do not
wish to consider for a moment the greater or less
mediocrity with which we might be overwhelmed if
the state intervened to put these books on the market.
Why not at once open a class in the Museum of Arts
and Sciences?   Why not instruct young men how to
write books according to the most approved formula,
and then have them compose each summer the number
of novels and comedies which Paris will need as a pastime during the gloomy winter hours?   No, in all this
genius alone is the thing.   There is no excuse for
encouragements unless it be well understood they are
intended to facilitate the rise of men of superior genius
who are bewildered and lost in the crowd.

From this moment the question simplifies itself.
All you have to do is to let things take their course,
for no one can give another talent, and talent carries
with itself the necessary power for its own complete
development.   Look at these facts.   Take a group of
young writers, twenty, thirty, fifty of them, and follow
them through their life.   At the start all set out
together, on the same footing, with an equal faith, an
equal ambition.   Then very soon distances are established; some seem to run ahead, while others appear
to be glued to their places.   But judgment must not
be pronounced yet.   Finally the result is shown; the
commonplace ones, sustained, pushed ahead, praised,
still remain commonplace, notwithstanding their first
success; the weak ones have completely disappeared.
As to the strong, they have struggled for ten years, for
fifteen, perhaps, in the midst of hatred and envy, but
they triumph in the end, they rise and shine in the first

rank. It is the same old story. And it would be very unfortunate to try and spare the strong those hard years of novitiate, those first battles in which they have shed their first blood. So much the better if they suffer, if they despair, if they sorrow. The imbecility of the crowd and the rage of their rivals end by giving them genius.

Then, from my standpoint, this anxiety about young writers is misplaced. It is the way commonly that you delude the unfortunate hopes of the feeble. As I have already said, at no time have the doors of publishers and managers been more widely open; everything is played, everything is printed; and much better for those who are forced to wait, for they ripen. The worst of misfortunes for a beginner is to reach success too quickly. It must be understood that behind a solid reputation there is twenty years of effort and work. When a young man who has written half a dozen sonnets envies a well-known writer, he forgets that that writer may be deteriorating as the result of his fame.

For a long time it has been the fashion to appear interested in young writers. Lecturers burst into effusions; chroniclers petition the state to remember the beginners, and they end by thinking seriously of a model library. Well, all that is hollow. These people flattered the youths, and nothing more, with a more or less selfish object. Some were trying to make theatrical capital; others were improving their reputation as sympathetic men; still others wished to make believe that they enjoyed the admiration of the younger generation, and held the future within their grasp. I willingly admit that there are a number of naïve people simple enough to believe that the greatness of our literature lies in the solution of this pretended question of the young writers.   I, who like to tell brutal truth, and who put in my vote for freedom, I will simply say to the beginners in conclusion :

"Work; it all lies in that.   Count on no one but yourself.   Say to yourself that if you have talent your talent will open the most tightly closed doors, and that it will put you as high as you merit to go.   And, above all things, refuse benefits from the government; never ask protection from the state; you will leave your manhood behind you if you do.   The great law of life is to struggle.   Nobody owes you anything.   You will triumph necessarily if you are a power, and if you succumb do not complain, for your defeat is just.   Then respect money; do not fall into the childish fashion of crying out, with the poets, against it; money is our courage and our liberty.   We writers, who need to be free in order to say what we think, money makes us the intellectual leaders of the century—the only possible aristocracy.   Accept your epoch as one of the greatest in the history of humanity; firmly believe in the future, without stopping to look at the inevitable consequences, the invasion of journalism, the money-making spirit of the baser literature.   Lastly, do not mourn for the old literary spirit, as it was the expression of a society now dead.   Another spirit is springing out of the new society, a spirit which broadens daily in its search for and in its assertion of the truth.   Let the naturalistic movement pursue its own ways; geniuses will rise up and complete the work.   You who are starting on your career to-day, do not struggle against the social and literary evolution, for the geniuses of the twentieth century are among you."

THE NOVEL.

THE NOVEL.

THE REALITY.

THE greatest praise that could be formerly given to a novelist was to say that "he had imagination." To-day this praise would be looked upon almost as a criticism. This only goes to show that all the conditions of the novel have changed. Imagination is no longer the predominating quality of the novelist.

Alexander Dumas and Eugène Sue were gifted with imagination. In "Notre Dame de Paris" Victor Hugo imagined characters and a story of the most intense interest; in "Mauprat" George Sand knew how to impassion a whole generation by the imaginary loves of her heroes. But nobody has ever thought of granting imagination to Balzac and Stendhal. Their wonderful faculties of observation and analysis have been spoken of; they are great because they have depicted their epoch, and not because they invented stories. These are the men who lead this evolution; it is dating from their works that imagination no longer counts in the novel. Look at our great contemporaneous writers, Gustave Flaubert, Edmond and Jules de Goncourt, Alphonse Daudet: their talent does not come from what they have imagined, but from the manner in which they show forth nature in its intensity.

I insist upon this fall of the imagination, because in it I see the characteristic of the modern novel. While the novel was a recreation for the mind, an amusement, from which was asked only animation and vivacity, it is easily understood that the important thing was to show an abundance of invention before anything else. Even when the historical novel and the novel with a purpose appeared, even then it was still imagination which reigned omnipresent, either in calling up vanished times or in the form of arguments, which characters, formed according to the need of the author, expounded. With the naturalistic novel and the novel of observation and analysis, the conditions change at once. The novelist invents, indeed, still : he invents a plan, a drama; only it is a scrap of a drama, the first story he comes across and which daily life furnishes him with always. Then in the arrangement of the work this invention is only of very slight importance. The facts are there only as the logical results of the characters. The great thing is to set up living creatures, playing before the readers the human comedy in the most natural manner possible. All the efforts of the writer tend to hide the imaginary under the real.

One could write an interesting paper on the subject of how our great novelists of to-day work. They base nearly all their works on profuse notes. When they have studied with scrupulous care the ground over which they are to walk, when they have gotten information from all the possible sources, and when they hold in their hands the manifold data of which they have need, then only do they decide to sit down and write. The plan of the work is brought to them by the data themselves, because the facts always classify themselves logically, this one before that one. Inevitably the work takes shape; the story builds itself up from all the observations gathered together, from all the notes taken, one leading to the other, through the linking of the lives of the characters, and the climax is nothing more than a natural and inevitable consequence. You can easily see, in this work, how little part imagination has in it all. We are very far re-removed, for example, from George Sand, who, they say, put herself before a mass of white paper, and, starting out with the first idea, went on and on without stopping, composing in a steady stream, relying solely on her imagination, which brought her as many pages as she needed to complete a volume.

Suppose that one of our naturalistic novelists wishes to write a novel on theatrical life. He sets out with this general idea, without having as yet a single fact or a single character. His first care is to gather together in his notes all that he knows of this world which he wishes to depict. He has known such and such an actor, he has witnessed such and such a play. Here are data already, the best, for they have ripened within himself. Then he will set about the business, he will get the men who are the best informed on the subject talking, he will collect their expressions, their stories, and their portraits. That is not all; he then turns to written documents, reading up all that he thinks will be of the slightest service to him. Finally he visits the places, lives a few days in the theater, so as to gain a perfect knowledge of all its recesses; he passes some evenings in an actress' rooms, steeping himself as much as possible in the surrounding atmosphere. And, once his data are complete, his novel, as I have said, makes itself. The novelist needs but to distribute his facts logically. From what he has learned, the plot of his drama, the story of which he has need as a general frame for his facts, will shape itself. The interest no longer lies in the strangeness of the story; on the contrary, the more commonplace and general it is the more typical it becomes. Make your real characters move in real surroundings. To give your reader a scrap of human life, that is the whole purpose of the naturalistic novel.

Since imagination is no longer the ruling quality of the novelist, what, then, is to replace it? There must always be a ruling quality. To-day the ruling characteristic of the novelist is the sense of reality. And this is to what I am coming.

The sense of reality is to feel nature and to be able to picture her as she is. It seems at first that, as all the world have two eyes to see with, nothing ought to be more common than the sense of reality. However, nothing seems to be more rare. Painters know and realize this better than anyone else. Put certain painters face to face with nature and they will see her in the strangest manner in the world. Each will perceive her under a dominant color; one will dress her out in yellow, another in violet, and a third in green. As to shape, the same phenomena will be produced; some will round off objects, others will multiply the angles. Each eye has a particular way of seeing. Then, again, there are eyes which see nothing at all. There is doubtless some lesion, the nerve connecting them with the brain has become paralyzed in some way that science has not been able to determine as yet. One thing is certain, that it is no use for them to look at the life throbbing around, as they will never be able to reproduce a scene from it correctly.

As I do not wish to name any living novelist, it makes my demonstration a little difficult. Examples would make the point clearer. But each one can see that certain novelists remain provincial, even after a twenty years' residence in Paris. They excel in pictures of their own country, but as soon as they touch a Parisian scene, they make a nice mess of it, and never succeed in giving a correct impression of surroundings in which, however, they have lived for years. Here is one example of a decided lack of the sense of reality. Doubtless the impressions of childhood have been the most vivid; the eye has retained the pictures which it was first impressed with, then paralysis developed—it is no use for the eye to look at Paris; it sees it not, it will never see it.

The most frequent case, however, is that of complete paralysis. How many novelists think they see nature and only see her through so many distorted mediums. They persuade themselves that they have put everything in a picture, that the work is definite and complete. This is of a piece with the conviction with which they have piled error upon error in colors and forms. Their nature is a monstrosity that they have dwarfed or enlarged in trying carefully to finish off the painting. Notwithstanding their efforts, everything is touched up with false tints, everything is topsy-turvy. They might perhaps be able to write epic poems, but they will never be able to produce a true work, because the lesion of their eyes prevents it, and because, when you have not the sense of reality, you can never acquire it.

I know some charming story-tellers, some writers of adorable fantasies, poets in prose, whose works I admire very much. These do not attempt to write novels, and their books are exquisite apart from the truth. The sense of reality does not become absolutely necessary except when one attempts pictures of life. Then, with the ideas we have to-day, nothing can replace it, neither an impassioned style, nor a vigor of touch, nor the most meritorious attempts. You want to paint life; in the first place, see what it is, and then give it its exact reproduction. If the reproduction is unshapely, if the pictures are out of plumb, if the work runs to carica-ture, be it sublime or simply vulgar, it is a stillborn work doomed to rapid oblivion. It is not firmly founded on the truth—it has no reason to be.

This sense of reality seems to me very easy to detect in a writer. For myself, it is the touchstone which decides all my judgments. When I have read a novel I condemn it if the author appears to me to be want-ing in the sense of reality. Let the scene be laid in a ditch, or in the stars, below or above, it is equally indifferent to me. Truth has a sound about it which I think you can never mistake. The phrases, the lines, the pages, the entire book should ring with the truth. They will tell you that you need very delicate ears; you need a true ear, and nothing else. And the public itself, that cannot very well boast of a great delicacy of sense, clearly hears the works which ring with truth; it turns more and more toward these, while it soon becomes silent about the others, about the false works, which ring with error.

In the same way that they formerly said of a novel-ist, " He has imagination," I demand that they should say to-day, " He has a sense of reality." This will be grander and more just praise. The ability to see is less common even than creative power.

To make myself better understood I must return to Balzac and Stendhal. Both of them are our masters. But I must confess that I do not accept their works with the devotion of the faithful who believe without questioning. I find them truly great and superior only in the passages in which they have the sense of reality.

I know nothing more surprising in " Le Rouge et le Noir " than the analysis of the love of *Julien* and *Mme. de Rénal.* You must bear in mind the epoch in which the novel was written; it was the very height of romanticism, and heroes made love in the most disheveled lyricism. Yet here is a young man and woman who love each other just as we all do, foolishly, deeply, with the ups and downs of reality. It is a superior picture. I will give in exchange for these pages all those in which Stendhal complicates the character of *Julien,* sinking into those subtle analyses he is so fond of. To-day he is not really great, except in the seven or eight scenes in which he has dared to bring in the note of reality—life in all its truthfulness.

The same with Balzac. There is in him an aroused sluggard who nods now and then and sometimes creates curious figures, which certainly do not add to the novelist's greatness. I confess I have no admiration for the author of " Femme de Trente Ans," nor for the inventor of the type of *Vautrin* in the third part of " Les Illusions Perdues," and in the " Splendeur et Misère des Courtisanes." These are what I call Balzac's phantasmatography. I do not like his great people any better, which he has invented entirely out of his own brain and which make one laugh, if you except a few superb types called forth by his genius. In a word, Balzac's imagination, that ill-regulated imagination, which threw itself into every exaggeration, and which sought to create the world anew on the most extraordinary basis, it irritates me more than it attracts me. If the novelist had had but that, he would have to-day but a pathological interest and would be merely a curiosity, etc., in our literature.

But happily Balzac had, besides, the sense of reality, and the most developed sense of reality we have yet seen. His *chefs-d'œuvre* give proof of that : that marvelous "Cousine Bette," in which *Baron Hulot* is so colossal with truth ; "Eugénie Grandet," which contains the whole country at a certain date in our history. I ought also to mention "Père Goriot," "La Rabouilleuse," "Le Cousin Pons," and many other works which have been taken quivering and living from the entrails of our society. Here it is that you find Balzac's immortal glory. He founded the novel of to-day because he was the first to apply to it this sense of reality which gave him power to call forth a new world.

However, to see is not all : you must give it again. This is why, after the sense of reality, there is the personality of the writer. A great novelist should have the sense of reality and also personal expression.

PERSONAL EXPRESSION.

I KNOW some novelists who write very correctly, and who have finally obtained very great literary renown. They are very industrious, they approach all kinds of literature with the same facility. Phrases flow from their pens without any difficulty, and it is their practice to throw off five or six hundred lines every morning before breakfast. And, I repeat, their work is very good, there is nothing lame about the grammar, the movement is excellent, color appears at times in these pages which seem to say to the public, who are dumb with respect: "This is prettily written." In a word, these novelists have all the appearance of a genuine talent.

It is their misfortune to be without any individual expression, and that is enough to make them forever commonplace. It is no use for them to amass volume after volume, employing and abusing their incredible fecundity; they will never remove from their books the nauseous odor of stillborn works. The more they produce the more the pile becomes mildewed. Their correct grammar, their perfectly proper prose, their polished style may fool the public at large for a shorter or longer time; but all this will not suffice to keep their books alive, and will have no weight in the final judgment passed upon them by competent readers. They have no individual note, and so they are condemned. All the more that almost always they are lacking also in the sense of reality, which still further aggravates the case.

These novelists acquire the style which is in the air around them. They catch the phrases which are flying about them. Their phrases never emerge from their personality, and they write as if someone from behind was dictating to them; and it is for that reason, perhaps, that they only need to turn on the faucet to obtain their productions. I do not say that they plagiarize from this man, or that they steal whole pages from their companions; on the contrary, they are so fluent, so superficial that one cannot find any strong characteristic in their writing, not even that of some illustrious master. Only without copying they have, instead of a creative brain, an immense storehouse filled with well-known phrases, current expressions, a kind of mean of the common style. This storehouse is inexhaustible, shovelfuls may be taken out with which to cover paper. Here it comes and here it comes again. Always, always shovelfuls of cold and dull material which crowd the columns of the newspapers and the pages of books.

On the other hand, let us look at a novelist who has an individual note; for instance, M. Alphonse Daudet. I take this writer because he is one of those who live in their works. M. Alphonse Daudet is present at a spectacle, at a scene of any kind. As he possesses the sense of reality, he is struck with this scene, and he retains a very vivid impression of it. Years may roll by—the brain preserves the image; time but makes it sink in more deeply. It ends by becoming a possession; the writer must communicate it, must give back what he has seen and retained.

Then a phenomenon takes place, the creation of an original work.

At first it is a resurrection: M. Alphonse Daudet remembers what he has seen and he sees the characters again with their gestures, the horizons with their lines. He feels that he must give back all this. From that moment he acts his characters, he lives in their surroundings, he falls into a passion in which he confounds his own personality with the personality of the beings and even with the things which he wishes to depict. He ends by becoming one with his work in the sense that he becomes absorbed in it, and at the same time resees it for the sake of his story. In this intimate union the reality of the scene and the personality of the novelist are no longer distinct. Which are the absolutely true details and which are invented? This would be very difficult to say. What is certain, though, is that reality has been the starting point, the propelling force which has powerfully started the novelist; he has then continued the reality, he has extended the scene in the same way, giving it a special life and one which belongs to him, Alphonse Daudet, alone.

The whole machinery of originality is there in this personal expression of a real world which surrounds us. M. Alphonse Daudet's charm, this wonderful charm, which has won for him so high a place in our present literature, comes from the original flavor which he gives to the most insignificant phrase. He cannot relate a fact, present a character, without putting himself entirely into this fact or into this character, with the vivacity of his irony, the sweetness of his tenderness. You can tell one of his pages among a hundred others, because his pages have a life of their own. He is an enchanter,

one of those Southern story-tellers who act what they
relate, with gestures which create and a voice which
brings up. All becomes alive under their open hands,
everything takes a color, a smell, and a sound. They
cry and laugh with their heroes, they thee and thou
them, make them so real that you see them standing
before you so long as they speak.

How is it possible for such works not to move the
public? They are alive. Open them and you will
feel them palpitating in your hands. It is the real
world; and it is even more, it is the real world inhabited
by a writer of an originality both exquisite and intense.
He can choose a subject more or less happy, treat it
in a way more or less complete: the work will not be
less precious because it will be unique, because he
alone can give it that turn, that accent, that existence.
The book is him; that is sufficient. It will be classed
some day, but it is no less a book by itself, a real living
being. You are stirred up, you like or you do not like,
no one remains indifferent. You no longer question
about grammar or rhetoric, and you no longer have
merely a package of printed paper under your eyes; a
man is there, a man whose heart-beats and brain-work-
ings are heard at each word. You abandon yourself
to him, because he has become the master of the reader's emotions, because he has the strength of reality
and the all powerful note of individuality.

Do you now understand the radical powerlessness of
the novelists of whom I spoke a short time ago?
They never take possession of and hold their readers,
for they do not feel and they do not reproduce in an
original manner. You will vainly search in their works
for a new impression, explained in an original phrase.

When they employ certain modes of expression, when
they gather up here and there happy phrases, these
phrases, so full of life in another, with them have an
empty sound; there is not underneath a man who has
truly felt and who translates the same by a creative
effort; there is a manipulator of words, opening the
faucet of his production. And it is no use for them to
apply themselves, to wish to write well, thinking that
you can make a fine book as you do a fine pair of
boots, with more or less care; they will never bring
forth a living work. Nothing can replace the sense of
reality and the personal expression. When they do
not possess these gifts they might much better go out
and sell candles than meddle with writing novels.

I quoted M. Alphonse Daudet a while ago because
he offered me a most striking example. But I could
have named other novelists who are far from having
his talent. Personal expression does not necessarily
include a perfect form. You can write badly, incor-
rectly, like the devil, and yet, with it all, retain a true
originality of expression. According to my idea, the
worst style is, on the contrary, that correct style, flowing in an easy, soft manner, that deluge of commonplace, of known images, which calls forth from the
public this irritating judgment: "It is well written."
No, it is badly written as soon as it ceases to possess
a distinctive life, a flavor of originality, even at the
expense of correctness and propriety of language.

The greatest example of personal expression in our
literature is that of Saint-Simon. Here is a writer who
has written with his blood and his anger, and who has
left behind him pages of intensity and life that cannot
be forgotten. I was wrong even to call him a writer,

for he seemed not to care about writing; and he reached, with one stroke, the highest style in the creation of a language and in the living expression. Our most illustrious authors, they smell of rhetoric, of the preparation of the phrase; an odor of ink emanates from their pages. With him there is nothing of this; the phrase is but a palpitation of life; passion has dried the ink; the work is a human cry, the long monologue of a man who looks on high. This is very far from our romantic way of managing a work, in which we exhaust ourselves in every sort of artistic effort.

It was the same way with Stendhal. He pretended to say that in order to acquire tone he read several pages of the Civil Code every morning before commencing to work. This was, of course, a simple braggadocio thrown at the romantic school. Stendhal wished to say that style meant for him the clearest and most exact translation possible of the idea. He also had personal expression in a very high degree. His dryness, his short sentences, so incisive and penetrating, became in his hands a marvelous tool for analysis. You could not imagine him as a graceful writer. He had the style proper to his talent, a style so original in its incorrectness and its apparent thoughtlessness that it has remained typical of him. It was not the enormous stream of Saint-Simon, sweeping along wonders and ruins, magnificent in its violence; it was like a lake frozen on top, boiling, perhaps, in its depths, and which reflected with an inexorable truth all that was on its edges.

Balzac, like Stendhal, has been accused of writing badly. He has, however, in his " Contes Drôlatiques " given pages which are masterpieces of word-painting. I know nothing more prettily invented in the way of form, nor more finely executed. But they find fault with the heavy beginnings to his novels, his massive descriptions; above all, the bad taste in certain exaggerations in the painting of his characters. It is evident that he has an enormous foot, which is of too crushing a force sometimes. Then we must judge him in the colossal *ensemble* of his work. In this way you see a heroic struggler who has battled with everything, even with style, and who has come forth a hundred times victorious from the combat. Besides, without going into his unfortunate phrases, his style is always redolent of him. He kneads it, he remodels it, he remakes it entirely in each of his novels. He searches for a form unceasingly. You find this, in his life as a gigantic producer, even in his smallest paragraphs. He is there, the forge grumbles, and he slaps his arm in turn on his phrases until they bear his stamp. This stamp they will keep forever. Whatever may be his faults, his is a grand style.

I simply had the intention, by giving these few examples, to explain more explicitly what I meant by personal expression. A great novelist in our days is he who has a sense of reality, and who expresses nature with originality, making her live with his own life.

THE CRITICAL FORMULA APPLIED
TO THE NOVEL.

I LATELY read a biographical article, in which the novelist was very disdainfully treated by the critic. His novels were cast overboard; his literary essays were approved of, without perceiving that the faculties of the critic tend to-day to run into the faculties of the novelist. This is a question which seems to me to be worth looking into.

Everybody knows what criticism has attained to in our days. Without giving the complete history of the transformation which it has undergone since the last century—a history which would be most instructive, and which would recapitulate the general intellectual movements—it is sufficient for my purpose to quote the names of Sainte-Beuve and M. Taine to establish the distance there is between us and the judgments of La Harpe, and even the "Commentaries" of Voltaire.

Sainte-Beuve was one of the first to comprehend the necessity of explaining the work by the man. He replaced the writer in his surroundings, studied his family, his life, his tastes; in one word, he looked upon a written page as the product of all kinds of elements, which he must necessarily know in order to pronounce a complete, just, and definite judgment. From this point come the deep studies of human nature which he wrote with a flexibility capable of marvelous investigation, with a delicate perception of the thousand shades and complex contradictions of man. This was far, indeed, from the critics who judged after the manner of pedagogues, according to the rules of the school, making complete separation between the man and the writer, applying to all works the same common standard, and looking upon them simply from a grammarian's and a rhetorician's standpoint.

M. Taine came and made a science of criticism. He reduced to rules the method which Sainte-Beuve employed as a virtuoso. This gave a certain harshness to the new instrument employed by the critic; but this instrument acquired an indisputable power. There is no necessity for me to recall M. Taine's admirable works. Everyone knows his theory of surroundings and of historical incidents applied to the literary movement of nations. M. Taine is really the foremost critic we have, and it is to be regretted that he shuts himself up in history and philosophy, instead of taking an active part in the daily battle, instead of directing opinion as Sainte-Beuve did by judging the small and the great of our literature.

I simply wish to state fully and explicitly in what manner modern criticism proceeds. For example, M. Taine wishes to write the fine study which he has made on Balzac. He begins by gathering together all the documents conceivable, the books and articles which have been published about the novelist; he questions the people who have known him, those who can give him any certain information upon him; and yet this is not sufficient; he never rests until he has seen the places in which Balzac has lived, he visits the town in which he was born, the houses he has occupied, the districts he has traveled through. In this way every-thing is ransacked by the critic—the antecedents, the friends—until he possesses Balzac absolutely, in his most intimate recesses, as the anatomist possesses the body he has just dissected. Then he can read the work. The producer stands before him and explains the production.

Read this study by M. Taine. You will see the working of his method. The book is in the man ; Balzac, pursued by his creditors, piling up extraordinary projects, passing entire nights working to pay his debts, his brain always active, his end the " Comedie Humaine." I do not comment upon the system. I lay it bare, and I say there is real criticism with more or less bias. Hereafter the man will never be separated from his work ; the one will be studied to understand the other.

Our naturalistic novelists have no other methods. When M. Taine studies Balzac he does exactly what Balzac himself did when he studied, for example, the character of *Père Grandet*. The critic operates upon the writer in order to judge of his works, as the novel-ist operates upon a character to know his acts. On both sides there is the same attention to surroundings and circumstances. Recall to yourself Balzac determin-ing exactly the street and the house in which *Grandet* lived, analyzing the people who surrounded him, estab-lishing the thousand little facts which have decided the character and the habits of his miser. Is not that an absolute application of the theory of surroundings and circumstances ? I repeat again, the work is identical.

You will say that M. Taine is walking on real ground,

he accepts but proven facts which have really happened, while Balzac is free to invent, and certainly uses
this liberty. But you must always admit that Balzac
bases his novel on a primary truth. The surroundings
which he describes are exact and the characters which
he places in them have their feet on the ground.
Henceforth it is little matter the work which follows,
the moment that the method of construction employed
by the novelist is identical with that of the critic. The
novelist starts out from real surroundings and from
true human data; if afterward he develops in a certain
sense it is no more imagination according to the old
style of story-tellers; it is deduction after the manner
of savants. Further, I have not pretended to say that
the results were exactly the same in the study of a
writer and in that of a character; in the former case,
for a certainty, you touch reality the nearest, leaving,
however, a great deal to intuition. But I say again the
method is precisely the same.

Moreover, this is the double effect of the naturalistic
evolution of the century. In truth, if you dig deep
enough you will reach the same philosophical soil, the
positivist inquiry. In fact, to-day the critic and the
novelist no longer conclude. They are content to
expose. Behold what they have seen; behold how
such an author must produce such a work, and behold
how such a character must commit such an act. On
both sides they show the human machine at work,
nothing more. From comparing facts we end, it is
true, by formulating laws. But the slower we are about
formulating laws, the wiser we shall be, for M. Taine
himself, because he was a little hurried, was accused of
yielding to a system. We had best busy ourselves

collecting and classifying documents, above all, in the
novel. It is already a great work merely to search for
and to say what is. We must leave science to formulate the laws, as we can only trim out and arrange
the reports, we novelists and critics.

Therefore to sum up : The novelist and the critic
start to-day from the same point, the exact surroundings,
and the human data taken from nature, and they
employ the same method to reach a knowledge and an
explanation, on one side, of the work written by a man,
and, on the other, of the acts of a character, the written
work and the acts being looked upon as the products
of the human machine submitted to certain influences.
From this it becomes evident that the naturalistic
novelist is an excellent critic. It is but necessary to
carry into the study of any writer whatsoever, the tool
of observation and analysis of which he made use to
know the characters which he took from nature. It is
wrong to think that he becomes belittled as a novelist
when it is lightly said of him : " He is only a
critic."

All these errors come from the false idea which
people continue to hold about the novel. It is too bad,
in the first place, that we have not been able to change
this word *roman*, which no longer signifies anything
as applied to our naturalistic works. This word brings
with it the idea of a story, a fable, a flight of fancy
which clashes with the report which we are arranging.
For fifteen or twenty years we have felt the growing
impropriety of the term, and there was a time when we
were tempted to put on the book covers the word
étude. But that was too vague, the word " roman "
was kept in spite of everything, and to-day there

would be necessary a lucky hit in order to replace it. Besides, these changes should produce and impose themselves.

For my part, the name does not worry me if they are willing to admit that, though it is kept, the thing itself is completely modified. We find a hundred examples in the language of terms which formerly expressed ideas radically contrary to those which they express to-day. Our chivalrous, our adventurous, our romantic and idealistic novel has now become a true criticism of the manners, the passions, and the acts of the hero brought on to the stage, studied in his own person and under the influences which the surroundings and circumstances had upon him. As I have written, to the great scandal of my colleagues, imagination no longer plays the dominant rôle; it changes into deduction, intuition; it busies itself with the probable facts which could not directly be observed, and with the possible consequences of facts which we are trying to establish logically according to method. Such a novel as this is a true page of criticism, for in it the novelist places himself before the character whose passions he wishes to study in exactly the same attitude that the critic assumes toward the writer whose talent he wishes to exhibit.

Is it necessary for me to conclude? The affinity between the critic and the novelist arises essentially from this : that both employ, as I have already said, the naturalistic method of the age. If we turn to the historian we shall see him also performing the same labor in history and with the same tool. The same with the economist and with the politician. These facts are easily proven, and show the savant at the head of the movement leading human intelligence to-day. We are of more or less value as science has touched us more or less deeply. I leave the personality of the artist aside, I only indicate here the great intellectual stream, the breath which carries us all along with it toward the twentieth century, whatever may be our individual mode of expression.

DESCRIPTION.

IT would be very interesting to study the descriptions in our novels from the time of Mlle. de Scudéry until Flaubert. It would be the history of philosophy and science during the last two centuries; for under this literary question of description there is nothing but the return to nature, this great naturalistic current which has produced our beliefs and actual knowledge. We should see the novel of the seventeenth century, which, like the tragedy, sets in motion purely intellectual creations on a neutral, indeterminate, and conventional ground ; the characters are simple mechanisms of feelings and passions, who work outside of time and space, and in consequence the surroundings are of no importance and nature has no rôle to play in the work. Then in the novels of the eighteenth century we should see nature shooting forth but in philosophical dissertations or in the cut and dried manner of idyllic emotions. Finally, our century comes with the descriptive orgies of romanticism, this violent reaction of color, and the scientific employment of description : its precise rôle in the modern novel is not fully settled until the appearance of Balzac, Flaubert, the de Goncourts, and others. These, then, are the chief milestones of a study which I have not the leisure to undertake. It is sufficient for me to indicate it in order to give here some general notes on description.

In the first place, the word description is no longer

suitable. It is as bad to-day as the word *roman*, which has no longer any significance when applied to our naturalistic studies. To describe is no longer our end ; we simply desire to complete and determine. For example, the zoölogist who in speaking of a particular kind of an insect finds it necessary to study the plant upon which this insect lives, and from which it draws its being, even up to its form and its color, finds it necessary to make a description; but this description enters into the very analysis of the insect; there is in this the necessity of a savant and not the mere display of a painter. This amounts to saying that we no longer describe for the sake of describing, from a caprice and a pleasure of rhetoricians. We consider that man cannot be separated from his surroundings, that he is completed by his clothes, his house, his city, and his country; and hence we shall not note a single phenomenon of his brain or heart without looking for the causes or the consequence in his surroundings. There results from this what are called our eternal descriptions.

We have given to nature, to the spacious world, a place as large as that which we give to man. We do not admit that man alone exists and that he alone is of any importance, persuaded to the contrary that he is a simple result; and to have the human drama real and complete we must interrogate all that is. I know that this startles philosophers. This is why we place ourselves at the scientific point of view, at the point of observation and experiment, which gives us, at the present moment, the greatest certitude possible.

You cannot accustom yourself to these ideas, because they clash with our time-honored rhetoric. To want to introduce the scientific method into literature seems ignorant, vain, and barbarous. But it is not we who introduce this method ; it has introduced itself without help, and the movement would continue even if we wished to check it. We are but stating what has taken place in our modern letters. The character is no longer a psychological abstraction, as all the world can see. The character has become the product of the air and the soil, like a plant ; it is the scientific conception. From this moment the psychologist should become an observer and an experimentalist if he wishes to clearly explain the movements of the soul. We cease to remain among the literary graces of a description clothed in a fine style; we are busy studying the exact surroundings, stating the conditions of the exterior world, which correspond to the interior conditions of the characters.

Then I should define description: "An account of the environment which determines and completes man."

Now it is very certain that we rarely hold ourselves to this scientific rigor. All reaction is violent, and we shall react still against the abstract formula of the last centuries. Nature has entered into our works with so impetuous a bound that it has filled them, sometimes swamping the human element, submerging and carrying away characters in the midst of a downfall of rocks and great trees. This was inevitable. We must leave time to weigh the new formula and to arrive at its exact expression. Besides, in this riot of description, this overflow of nature, there is much to learn, much to say. There are precious data to be found here, which would be very valuable in a history of the naturalistic evolution.

I have already said that I did not care much for
Theophile Gautier's prodigious descriptive talent. I
find truly in him description for the sake of description, without a thought of any kind for humanity.
He is the direct descendant of the Abbé Delille.
In his books the surroundings never determine a living
being; he remains a painter; he has only words as a
painter has only his colors. This puts into his works
a sepulchral silence; there is nothing in them but
things; not a voice, not a human quiver arises from this
dead world. I cannot read a hundred pages of Gautier's in succession, because they do not stir me, they
do not take hold of me. When I have admired his
happy gift of language, the modes and ease of the
description, there is nothing for me to do but close the
book.

On the contrary, look at the de Goncourt brothers.
They do not any more always remain rigorously confined to the scientific study of surroundings, entirely
subordinated to the complete knowledge of the characters. They let themselves enjoy the pleasure of
describing, as artists who play with the language and
are happy to bend it to the thousand difficulties of
utterance. Only they always put their power of expression at the service of human beings. This consists no
longer of perfect phrases on a given subject, but of feelings felt before a spectacle. Man appears, mingles in
things, and animates them by the nervous vibration of
his emotion. All the de Goncourts' genius shows in
this so vivid translation of nature, in those carefully
noted quiverings, those whispered murmurings, those
thousand breathings rendered perceptible. With them
description seems to breathe. It overflows sometimes,

and their characters fluctuate in too enlarged a horizon ; but even if it presents itself alone it remains in its place as determining condition ; it is always noted in its connection with man and thus always retains a human interest.

Gustave Flaubert is the novelist who, up to the present time, has employed description with the greatest moderation. The surroundings occupy a discreet equilibrium with him ; they do not submerge the character, and nearly always content themselves with determining it. This is what gives " Mme. Bovary " and " L'Education Sentimentale " so much force. It can truthfully be said that Gustave Flaubert has reduced to strict necessity the long appraiser's enumerations with which Balzac lumbered up the beginning of his novels. He is temperate, which is a rare quality; he gives the salient trait, the main lines, the peculiarity which paints, and that is sufficient to make the picture a never to be forgotten one. I would counsel anyone to study Gustave Flaubert, for description or for the necessary painting of surroundings, each time that they complete or explain a character.

The rest of us, for the most part, have been less wise, less well balanced. The passion for nature has often carried us away, and we have given bad examples in our exuberance, and in our rapture over the open air. Nothing affects the brain of a poet so surely as a sun-stroke. He dreams of all kinds of folly, he writes books in which the springs commence to sing, the oaks to talk with each other, the rocks to sigh and palpitate like a woman overcome with the midday heat. And there are symphonies in the leaves, rôles given to the blades of grass, poems on light and on odors. If there is any excuse to be offered for such digressions it is because we have dreamed of broadening humanity, and that we have imbued even the stones in the roadways with it.

May I be permitted to speak of myself? What they reproach me with the most, even sympathetic spirits, are the five descriptions of Paris which keep returning and conclude the five parts of " Une Page d'Amour." They only see in this the caprice of an artist for a fatiguing repetition, as for a sort of conquered difficulty, in order thus to show his dexterity of hand. I may be mistaken, and I have certainly made a mistake, because no one seems to have understood me ; but, in truth, I had all sorts of good intentions when I became infatuated with these five pictures, all of the same scene viewed at different hours and seasons. This is the history of it. In the poverty of my youth I lived in a garret in the faubourgs, from which the whole of Paris can be seen. This great, motionless, and indifferent Paris, which was framed by my window, seemed to me the mute witness, the tragic confidant of my joys and my sorrows. I have been hungry, and I have wept before her ; and before her I have loved, I have experienced my greatest happiness. Well, then, since my twentieth year I have dreamed of writing a novel, of which Paris, with her ocean of roofs, should be a character something like an ancient chorus. I needed an intimate drama, three or four people in a little room, then the immense city on the horizon, always present, gazing at the frightful torture of these miserable creatures with her eyes of stone. It is this old idea which I have tried to realize in " Une Page d'Amour." That is all.

But I do not defend these five descriptions. The

idea was bad, since it has found no one to understand and defend it. Perhaps I put them in the work in a form too stiff and too symmetrical. I quote the fact only to show that, in what they call our rage for description, we never succumb to the need for mere description alone; but mingled with it there is always a harmonizing or human purpose. The entire creation belongs to us; we make it enter into our works; we dream of depicting the whole of heaven's wide vault. To wish to shut us up in a descriptive mania is to unjustly lessen our ambition, not allowing us to get beyond the more or less correct outlining of the conditions.

I will finish by a declaration : in a novel, in a study of humanity, I blame all description which is not according to the definition given further back, an account of the environment which determines and completes man. I have sinned enough myself to have the right to recognize this truth.

THREE DÉBUTS.

I.

LEON HENNIQUE.

A BEGINNER'S book is like virgin soil. Before cutting the pages you have the sense of the unknown. Who knows—perhaps there is the first cry of a great genius in this book? A veiled lady passes by. The heart beats. You follow her. *Mon Dieu,* if she is the one for whom one waits! I know that women and books often bring disenchantments; the woman is ugly, the book puts you to sleep. What matters it—you have had the charm of hope.

I have just felt this rare pleasure in reading " La Dévouée " of M. Leon Hennique. You go from discovery to discovery. You are astonished by a new accent. You say naïvely: " What! this boy has already as much talent as this? " And this is great praise, notwithstanding the joking tone of the exclamation. When I receive the last novel of a writer whose good qualities are already known to me, I only have the pleasure of once more remarking these qualities. But here is an unknown ground, of which my spirit takes possession.

Here is the plot in a few words. A certain *Jeoffrin,* sprung from the *liaison* of a scholar. and a girl, has grown up in the household of a day laborer. He

has wished to be a clockmaker. Then, after having
amassed a fortune, he is attacked with the inventor's
fever; he gives himself up, heart and soul, to the problem of directing and steering balloons. This *Jeoffrin*
is a modern hero, as M. Hennique calls him with terrible truth. I mean to say that he fights his way into
society unscrupulously, indeed in a rascally fashion,
attaining his ends after the manner of an able man
whom nothing could stop.

Then the pith of the drama follows. *Jeoffrin* has two
daughters, *Michelle* and *Pauline*, to whom an uncle has
left one hundred thousand francs, fifty thousand to
each. It happens that the father finds himself at the
end of his resources; his inventions have swallowed a
fortune, and he lives in a condition of impotent rage,
seeing his hands tied just at the moment when he
thought he had discovered a way to steer balloons.
If he only had money it would mean success and triumph. He first tried to borrow *Michelle's* fifty thousand
francs. But she refused; this money is all that remains
of the former wealth of the family. Then crime begins
to grow in *Jeoffrin's* brain as naturally as a plant which
is one day to bloom. He begins by poisoning his
daughter *Pauline*, which he arranges in such a way that
Michelle is accused. She is arrested, tried, found guilty,
and guillotined. *Jeoffrin* has got rid of the two children
who stood in his way, and he has inherited the hundred
thousand francs. Now he has the power to construct
his balloon. The story stops here. It is simple and
frightful.

I will say that this subject troubled me greatly, and,
besides this trouble, there was a sort of irritation against
the novelist. Why should he write so black a drama?

Life is more commonplace, events run along with more simplicity. Then, even while accepting the drama, *Jeoffrin* worried me. He disarranged my preconceived ideas about inventors, whom I considered, I do not know for what reason, as mild and inoffensive cranks. This one killed his daughters too quietly. I thought he might have got the hundred thousand francs by some less radical means. A great many other objections arose in my mind. Briefly, the subject was displeasing to me; I could not force myself to accept *Jeoffrin.*

When I had reached this point I re-read certain passages, and from the bottom of my judgment a voice, feeble at first, cried out to me: "Why not?" It was the first crack! This devil of a *Jeoffrin* possessed me; I argued about him with myself every minute of the day. He grew, he stood out clearer and clearer, he took a more and more solid outline. Yes, why not? Why should not this man have killed his two daughters in his passion for a fixed idea, which changed his whole being? I could mention a hundred facts of the same kind. *Jeoffrin* was admirably drawn; the novelist's analysis showed him to us as he should be; murder was but a natural development in him. I ended by thinking that if he had not committed murder this rogue's character would have been incomplete.

Such were the impressions through which I passed before becoming convinced that *Jeoffrin* was a very original and very bold creation, set up by a vigorous hand and studied subsequently by a science already great. Remark that through it all he remains a brave man. He has nothing in him of the ideal traitor of a melodrama. He poisons as the father of a family who

desires to do the thing properly. He is an actor playing the rôle of a hypocrite in a superior manner. He
loved his balloons better than his daughters, and he sacrifices his daughters. This seems fair to him. All
human madness lies below this; one hears it rumbling
under the usual good nature of this crime. And this
is just what constitutes *Jeoffrin's* depth. Is he a man
of genius? Perhaps. Is he a fool? He may be. He
is the human abyss, that is all we know. The assassin
in his nature is but the acute condition of his intelligence. You feel a shiver creep over you; you will
never forget this terrible man, who is a deranged
colossus.

I have laid great stress on *Jeoffrin* because he is the
entire book. But beside him there are some secondary
characters drawn with a stroke. I would mention the
police commissioner *Barbelet*, the *Misses Thèry*, and
the more delicately drawn silhouettes of young *Guy de
Lassalle* and *Poupelard*, the Bohemian. M. Hennique
seems to me to possess that gift of creation which
makes a character live, which places him in his true
atmosphere, gives him a natural gesture and the proper
voice. A phrase is sufficient to create. Only you
must have the sense of reality, and I know writers of
great merit as stylists who will exhaust themselves for
months on the perfection of a phrase without ever succeeding in breathing life into it.

The novelist is content to unroll before us pictures
taken from everyday life. This is what he has seen;
he has noted the details, he reconstructs the whole.
Let the reader in his turn feel and reflect. The naturalistic method is there in its entirety. A work is no
longer but an intense calling forth of humanity and

nature. The author strives to put a corner of creation in a work. People read it later as though they themselves moved in the surroundings described and among the characters analyzed.

Thus the first chapter of the "Dévouée" is simply the recital of a promenade *Michelle* and her godfather *Barbelet* take across the fields which surround Moulineaux. Their conversation is broken here and there by descriptions of this corner of the Parisian suburbs. Little by little the twilight falls, the sun sets over Paris. There is here certainly something of the virtuoso. The writer who, in spite of his youth, is already master of his style, delights in these conquered difficulties. But who will dare absolutely condemn this extended beginning, this conversation which sets forth the facts, these descriptions which open the dark history with a puff of fresh air? Must not the surroundings be firmly established? *Jeoffrin* would become an impossibility if Paris, behind him, did not smoke in the evening mists.

The second chapter describes a dinner at *Jeoffrin's* house, in which M. Hennique has gathered together all his secondary characters. Nothing could be more full of movement. But I cannot analyze each chapter thus. I will content myself by indicating those points which struck me most vividly, and especially the superb picture of *Pauline's* death and burial. The effect is startling. There is no inflated style, however. Only small details, true observations, a relentless reality, which little by little takes you by the throat and reaches the most violent emotion. It was so intense that you felt this must be true.

In my opinion the most astonishing part of the

book is *Jeoffrin's* day on the morrow of *Michelle's* execution. *Jeoffrin* has fled to Montmartre, to a hotel
there. Knowing nothing he enters a saloon and calls
for a beefsteak, and then it is that he casts his eyes
over a newspaper and finds that his daughter had been
guillotined that morning. This makes his heart jump.
" His balloon seemed vibrating in the blue sky, floating
without encumbrance, rising and descending according
to his fancy, flying to the left, then to the right, like
a trained eagle obeying his gestures. Then he ate his
beefsteak and called for some cauliflower. At last he
was free ! "

Then commenced a whole day of happy loafing.
Jeoffrin quietly trod the boulevards in the bright sunshine. He seated himself before a table in the Café
Rich, parched with thirst. He drank, but he was
always thirsty. His limbs became heavy. He rose,
he entered another *café*. In a few moments he entered
into conversation with a neighbor. I will give a few
lines here :

" The clammy mouth, feeling the necessity of repos-
ing confidence in the waistcoat of someone, after mut-
tering to itself for an instant, said :

" ' They guillotined my daughter this morning.'

" And as the great, red-faced man sniggered in an
incredulous manner, he added :

" ' Upon my honor ! ' "

However, he dines that evening at Brebant's. Then he
goes to the Folies Bergère. The intoxication became
greater. He could not quench his thirst. He felt no
remorse ; only he had a hell in his throat. The day
had been warm ; a violent storm burst forth. He, with
the obstinacy of a drunkard, must go to Moulineaux,

to see again the model of his balloon, a plaything which he has in his cabinet. And this journey under the rain and in the mud should be read. He slipped, he fell, he picked himself up. The thunder rumbled overhead, but he had the obstinacy of a beast. At last he arrives. " In the same corner as formerly the model of the balloon swayed to and fro, with a singular motion, under its covering; it seemed to be alive. Jeoffrin uncovered it. It lifted itself up a little——"

Here I stop. I hope I have given an idea of the " Dévouée." I think it a very remarkable beginning. M. Hennique must work. He has the sense of reality, he carries the gift of creation, he possesses, besides, a style already very supple and solid. When he shall, by work, have disengaged somewhat more distinctly his personal note he will certainly be one of the most vigorous workers in the present task.

II.

J. K. HUYSMANS.

NOTHING interests me so much as the young generation of novelists who are growing up around us at present. It is this generation who will be the future. Will it decide in our favor, walking in the broad path of naturalism opened by Balzac, pushing always further the inquiry opened upon man and nature? I am indeed happy when I see the analytical and experimental spirit taking firmer possession of our young writers and bringing out from the ranks new fighters, who come to battle beside the elders the good fight for truth.

I wish the writers of novels and absurd melodramas on the people would conceive the idea of reading " Les Sœurs Vatard " of M. J. K. Huysmans. They would then see the people as they are. Without doubt they would cry out against its obscenity, they would affect disgusted airs, they would talk of taking pincers to turn the pages with. But with it all it is a little amusing comedy upon hyprocrisy. It is the regular thing for the dabblers in letters to insult the writers. I should be even very much chagrined if they did not insult M. Huysmans. But I will not worry. I know they will insult him.

Nothing could be more simple than this book. It is not even a complicated plot, for a complicated plot necessitates a drama. There are two sisters, *Céline* and *Desirée*, two sewing girls, who live with a dropsical mother and a lazy, philosophical father. *Céline* leads a fast life. *Desirée*, who is keeping herself for a husband, enters into an honorable love affair with a young workman, whom she leaves in the end; then she marries another, and that is all—this is the book. This bareness of plot is characteristic. Our contemporaneous novel becomes more simple every day from its hatred of complicated and false plots. One page of human life and you have enough to excite interest, to stir up deep and 'lasting emotions. The slightest human fact takes stronger possession of you than any other of no matter what imaginary combination. We shall end by giving simple studies without adventures or climax, the analysis of a year of existence, the story of a passion, the biography of a character, notes taken from life and logically classified.

Behold the power of human data. M. Huysmans has cast aside all arrangements of scenes. No straining of the imagination, but scenes in the workman's world, Parisian sights bound together by the most ordinary story in the world. Well, the work is full of intense life; it clutches you and impassions you; it raises the most vexing questions; it has the heat of battle and victory. Whence comes this flame that darts from it, then? From the truth of the pictures and the personality of the style, and nothing else. Modern art is here exemplified.

In the first place, let us look at the surroundings. These surroundings, these sewing girls' workshops, which M. Huysmans paints with a frightful intensity, have a terrible odor. Doubtless many people would say they were exaggerated. Dare to enter a sewing

woman's workroom. Question, inquire, and you will
see that M. Huysmans has still remained outside of the
truth, because it is impossible to print certain things.
All this workingman's atmosphere, this corner of misery
and ignorance, of tranquil degradation and naturally
tainted air, has been treated in the " Sœurs Vatard "
with a scrupulous exactitude and rare firmness of touch.

Then come the characters. They are marvelous portraits in resemblance and in tone. You may be certain
that they were taken from nature.

Here is *Père Vatard*, who has only two mortifica-
tions—his wife's disease and the conduct of his
daughter *Céline*. Her first fault filled him with emotion. I quote: " He had a moment of sadness, but he
consoled himself quickly. Desirée was old enough to
care for him, and to take her mother's place; and as to
Céline, the best thing for him to do was to close his
eyes on her conduct. He had acted a father's part,
moreover; he had reproached her, in court of assizes
terms, for the impropriety of her manners; but she had
become angry, had thrown the house into a topsy-turvy
condition, threatening to overturn everything if she
were annoyed again. Vatard then adopted an air of
great indulgence; besides, his daughter's terrible gabble
amused him in the evening." This is complete. This
is the father of our faubourgs, such as most commonly
the promiscuous mingling that springs from poverty
and the degradation of his surroundings, make him.
We do not wish to understand that the moral sense is
merely relative, and distorts and changes itself according to its conditions. What is an abomination in the
middle class is but a sad necessity with the people.

And this *Céline*, is she strongly encamped in her

reality? She is but one of a thousand. It is not the question of an exception, but of a majority. Go and see for yourself instead of protesting.

Desirée is of a rarer type. But she exists, and she will console pure souls a little. Not that at bottom she follows any conception of virtue, for she really only follows her instinct. She is an apathetic girl, who is not drawn toward man, and whom her sister's example restrains. She dreams of marriage. Nothing could be more admirable than her idyl with *Auguste*, an idyl of the outdoor boulevard life, of dining in a saloon, strolling in the vague night of the long avenues, of good-by kisses given behind the walls of some unfinished building. No impurity of any kind. He did not wish to marry, but he is captivated, and they held long conversations on the future, filled with touching nonsense, the eternal duet which the idealists have put in the clouds and the naturalists place on the sidewalks. This homeless love is just so much the more the tender that it is lived, and that you jostle it on each boulevard of our faubourgs.

I reach the climax, one of the most deeply touching passages that I have read for a long time. Little by little the two lovers have become cold. *Desirée*, detained by her mother's illness, has missed several rendezvous, and when she meets *Auguste* again they are both embarrassed. The young man already thinks of marrying elsewhere. The young girl, now that her father has given his consent to her marriage, listens to her sister, who speaks of another man. And it is *Céline* who brings matters to a climax in provoking an explanation and a last adieu. The scene takes place at the doors of a *café* on the corner of the Quay de la

Tournelle and the Boulevard Saint Germain. I know nothing so piercing, stirring the human heart as it does to its depths. All our loves, all our joys dreamed of and lost, all our hopes ceaselessly killed and ceaselessly being born again, are they not there in these two simple creatures, who are leaving each other after having loved, who are going far away from one another to live a life apart which they had sworn to live together? They talk for the last time sweetly, softly, they give each other details on their respective marriages, they thee and thou each other again, and all at once memories are awakened; they recall what they did on such and such a day, at such and such an hour; tears spring to their eyes; perhaps they would have come together again had not *Céline* hastened to separate them. It is ended; they are now two strangers.

I would like to quote this episode entirely to make my readers feel the thrill which passed through me as I read it. What misery and infirmity are ours! How everything falls from our fingers and is broken! These two young creatures disclose the depth of our frailty and our nothingness.

The only criticism which I shall make on M. Huysmans is an abuse of rare words which at moments takes away from his best analyses their living air. These words cover the first part of the book especially. I also prefer the second part, which is more simple and more human. M. Huysmans has a style that is marvelous in its color and in throwing objects into relief. He inserts into beings and things an admirable intensity of life. This is really his principal quality. I hope they will not style him a photographer, although his pictures are very exact. The people who

have made the innocent discovery that naturalism is
nothing more than photography will understand this
time, perhaps, that, though priding ourselves upon
absolute reality, we mean to breathe life into our productions. Thence comes the personal style which is
the life of our books. If we refuse to admit imagination in the sense of invention added on to truth, we put
all our creative force into giving truth its proper life,
and the labor is not an easy one, as there are few
novelists who have this gift of life.

There are some marvelous descriptions in " Les Sœurs
Vatard ": the Rue de Sevres, the Rue de la Gaieté, all the
Quartier de Montrouge, so thoroughly characteristic, the
sewing girls' working-room, a frolic in a railway station,
in which locomotives were being run in and out, a ginger-
bread fair. The frame is as truthful as the characters.

Evidently they will try to pretend that M. Huysmans insults the people. I know that political school
which speculates in lies; these men who flatter the
workmen in order to gain their votes, who live upon
sores which they do not wish touched. We have
already told the truth about the higher class; now we
will tell the truth about the people in order that they
may be frightened, pitied, and helped to rise. It is a
work for courageous men. Yes, such is the truth; a
great portion of the people are like this. And all know
it well. They lie from motives of policy, that is all.
But our contempt is higher than their hypocrisy.

I wish to see M. Huysmans dragged through the
gutters of criticism, denounced to the police by his
colleagues, to hear the whole troop of the envious and
impotent ones howling at his heels. Then he will
commence to feel his strength.

III.

PAUL ALEXIS.

"LA FIN DE LUCIE PELLEGRIN" is dedicated to me, and I will not conceal that the author, M. Paul Alexis, is one of my old friends, a fellow of great talent, and whom I think a great deal of. It is ten years now since he reached Paris in one of those freaks of literary enthusiasm which leave families desolate. He came from that Provence in which I grew up; he had the great hopes and the fine indolence of the Latin temperament, whose sleep is full of dreams of battles and triumphs. In the first days Paris seems to belong to these young men, and many fall asleep. They have left their windows open, but success has not come in to them. I did not worry about M. Paul Alexis; I knew his hour would come, because he was that kind of man. And this is his first book; he has made us wait a little while for it, but it has a flavor that indicates the analyst and painter in his blood. He has gained his footing; he needs but to walk straight ahead.

Volumes of short stories are not very much in vogue at present. The taste of to-day is not for short stories, which are so delicate and of an art so polished, sometimes. It is the same in the theater: each débutant wishes to present a piece of five acts for his first, knowing that the public like long plays. If M. Paul Alexis had spent on a novel the talent which he has put in

these four stories which compose his volume, his success
would have been very great. This is why I wish to
emphasize these stories in order that they may be read
and that their high merit may be felt.

The first, the one whose name has given the title to
the collection, is certainly the best, from the point of
view of its style and artistic arrangement. It is a
series of little etchings, short chapters, depicting the
agony of a young girl dying for want of a kindness,
in the midst of the imbecile gossip of four women who
have been drawn to her bedside by the curiosity which
a deathbed excites in some minds. Nothing can be
more simple than the subject and nothing stronger than
the vigorous and clear observation. One end of our
Parisian pavements is to be found here analyzed and
reproduced in an astonishing manner. The wine merchant's little room in which the action passes ; the conversation of the four women, with their ever increasing
curiosity ; then the scene by *Lucy's* bedside, this apart-
ment stripped of all furniture by the creditors, while the
poor unfortunate coughs on her hard bed, the dying
woman drinking a glass of absinthe and dreaming of
her last hour—this whole tableau is depicted so truly,
so powerfully, as to make the picture an indelible and
definite one of a corner of Paris.

This is an example of the great force of the truth.
It is eternal. The data brought forward are incontest-
able ; fashion has no power against them. Add that an
artist is back of the observer giving to the observed
facts the fire of his nature, the arrangement of his
taste. It is not an idealization, a distortion ; it is a
composition logically classifying the facts and giving
them value. The imagination, as I have often said, is

no longer an irregular invention launching out into a fantastical folly, but a remembrance of witnessed truths and the connection of ideas between them. For example, the imagination in " La Fin de Lucie Pellegrin " is shown in the dog, who comes into the action and gives birth to her pups on the bed while her mistress is dying on the ground. All the little story is full of a careful art under an apparent simplicity.

The story which follows," L' Infortune de M. Fraque," is like the plan outlined and completed in certain parts of a great observational novel. M. Paul Alexis, who was brought up in a country town in Aix, has recalled the remembrances of his childhood and has given us a very curious study of the little town of Noirfond. Nothing could be prettier or more original than the subject, a true history, bearing traces of hardly any arrangement in its details. The trouble is a great fight between *M. Fraque* and his wife, *Zoë de Grandval*, a terrible fight, in which the latter, after having incensed her husband by a series of questionable maneuvers, finally beats him completely by throwing herself heart and soul into religion, and leaving all her fortune to a young priest with which to build chapels. *M. Fraque*, to protect himself, has no other resource than to throw himself into the raising of pigs and to exaggerate a growing deafness. Later, when his wife devotes herself to the *Abbé de la Molle*, *M. Fraque* turns to the Protestant pastor *Menn :* a delightful religious battle, which ends the story.

We no longer have the perfect little pen pictures of " La Fin de Lucie Pellegrin" here. You feel that the author has got his breath. There are paragraphs of very penetrating analysis laying bare the country.

The only fault in it is, as I say, that the subject has not
been fully developed throughout; there is the material
for a novel in it, but certain scenes need greater space.
But it is in this incomplete work that you can foresee
the fine qualities of the novelist, the breath, the amplitude, and the ability to produce vast subjects and the
power to realize them. He belongs to the strong
family of Balzac. He will certainly attack the great
questions of social analysis, and he will not dally in
the exquisite pictures, in the jewels of rhetoric that all
beginners end by turning out to-day. It is by strong
studies of nature and man that our young writers will
rise.

With "Les Femmes du Père Lefèvre" we come back
to what I shall call the fantasy founded on truth. But
the subject is so pretty that this little story is, perhaps,
the happiest of the book. It is a simple fact, hardly
an anecdote. The students in a small town are dreaming
of giving a ball the Thursday of Mi-Carême, but come
to a full stop for entire want of ladies, and are then
saved by an old officer, who promises to obtain some
ladies from Marseilles, and finally lands in the city
thirteen frights, whose presence upsets the inhabitants.
This is all the plot there is; it is nothing, and yet it is
decidedly comic in its charming irony, in the correctness of its observation and its rendering. No exaggeration to force a laugh, only a jest which enlivens one
discreetly. The comical side of it is in its truth, in the
impatience and anxiety of the young men from lack
of girls, going to each train vainly expecting *Père
Lefèvre*, who does not come; then the arrival of these
ladies, in the midst of cries of enthusiasm from the
young men; the lazy curiosity of the *bourgeoïses*

stationed in front of the Café des Quatre-Billiards; the complete topsy-turvy condition of the city, where the train of women's dresses after the ball was heard and felt for months.

I have used the words " fantasy founded on truth." We have, in the actual naturalistic current, poems based on the truth, which mark the epoch. These are no longer airy constructions of sylphs and fairies, imaginations floating in an immaterial world ; they are true facts and real creatures, but presented in a form of melancholy or railing animation arranged so as to obtain the greatest possible effect, and in such a manner that observation and analysis never depart from nature. You might even say that the generation of novelists who to-day follow in the footsteps of Balzac and Victor Hugo are also poets of the truth. And I mention " Les Femmes du Père Lefèvre" as one of those charming fantasies founded strictly on realities, illuminated by the flame of observation and analysis.

The last story, " Le Journal de M. Mure," leads us back to a severe analysis. The plot is again of the simplest nature, for the point is here a psychological and physiological study. *M. Mure,* a magistrate of a little city, watches *Hélène,* the daughter of *Captain Derval,* grow to womanhood. Little by little he becomes completely infatuated with this young girl; he never has the courage to declare himself, and his whole life passes in a longing for this woman whom he sees possessed by others. First he marries her to a silly substitute, *M. Moreau ;* then he has the misery of knowing of her flight with a *M. de Vaudrieilles,* with whom she lives in Paris ; then she falls lower, even to the gutter; finally he reconciles her to her husband, and dies in the joy of her return and her triumph, surrounded by the society of the little town which she had so dreadfully scandalized in her younger days. This poor *M. Mure* is but a continual miscarriage his whole life long. He is a study of paternity in love. He makes others happy without ever gaining any satisfaction himself; and in this fact lies the great originality of the work—an analysis of infinite delicacy: the pleasure of working for *Hélène's* felicity, saddened by the jealousy of knowing she belonged to another; all sorts of half avowals, abnegations, and regrets; an exquisite prudery troubled by a persistent desire, even in his old age; then a final resignation with solitary contentment. There is in all this a very personal creation.

This last story is a shortened novel like " L'Infortune de M. Fraque." Only it is barer and of a much broader conception, according to my way of thinking. At this time the evolution which is taking place in the novel seems to point more especially to this simplicity of daily life, to the study of human miscarriage so magnificently analyzed by Gustave Flaubert in his " Education Sentimentale." It is the inevitable reaction against the passionate exaggerations of romanticism. You throw yourself into the everyday routine of existence, you show the emptiness and the sadness of all things, so as to protest against the hollow deifications and the false sentiments of the romantic works. This is excellent, for it is by this means that we shall return to a simple and true art, to human sentiments, and to a logical language. I speak now of method, of the good and bad paths, always taking into consideration the question of temperament.

This, then, is M. Paul Alexis' book. They will classify it as follows : It is the work of a young naturalist, one of those dreadful naturalists who respect nothing and who copy one another. The current criticism, in its hatred and carelessness of justice and truth, repeats these ready-made judgments, which are radically false. The truth is that those young novelists, whom they think to crush under the epithet of common naturalists, are precisely of the most opposite temperament you could possibly imagine ; not one has the same personality, not one looks at humanity from the same angle, and yet they are called the fervent disciples of the same religion, with this fine *un*intelligence which distinguishes our sorry criticism of the present time. One day I will certainly make a study of these novelists, to point out their dissimilarity. For a long time it has enraged me to see the perfect mess of judgments which have been passed upon them. But just now there is but the question of the author of " La Fin de Lucie Pellegrin."

M. Alexis is, beyond everything else, sensitive. With him analysis is preceded by sensation. He needs to see in order to know, to be touched in order to paint. His book is entirely composed of reminiscences. He relates the stories which have happened around him, hardly modifying them. Evidently he must work from nature ; he dissects only people he has known and associated with. I do not think he will ever conceive any great figures, types drawn from his own brain ; but he will employ with a true power of penetration the data which life will furnish him with.

Add that he is an artist. I mean by that a man of style and symmetry. In the " Journal de M. Mure," the last story of the series, the broadest in conception and composition, the arrangement shows a highly evolved art, under the apparent confusion of these short or long notes thrown on the paper at all hours and all times. As I have said, it is no longer a composition, it is a classification. But the temperament of the writer asserts itself not less in a vivid perception of the facts and the putting forth of thoughtful observations.

M. Paul Alexis must write a novel, for he is lost in a short story, and he has in him the making of great works. The crudities and cruelties of analysis in his first book will perhaps provoke a great many people, but I am certain that all will recognize the solid back of an originality which already makes itself felt with great force.

HUMAN DOCUMENTS.

IN the essay which I devoted to M. Huysmans'
remarkable novel, "Les Sœurs Vatard," I wrote
this phrase : "We shall end by giving simple studies,
without adventures or climax ; the analysis of a year
of an existence, the story of a passion, the biography
of a character, notes taken from life and logically
classified." I do not doubt but that this phrase will
scandalize a great many of my colleagues. Some will
be angry, some will make fun of it ; all will accuse me
of denying imagination, of killing invention, of urging
as a rule that novels should be ordinary and vulgar.

What always puzzles me is the manner in which my
words are read. For more than ten years I have been
repeating the same things, and I must really express
myself very badly, for the readers are very rare who
will read " white " when I write " white." Ninety-nine
people out of a hundred persist in reading " black."
I will not utter hard words about stupidity and unfairness. We will admit that their sight is impaired.

For example, do they not say foolish enough things
about this poor naturalism ? If I were to gather
together all that has been published on this question,
I should raise a monument to human imbecility.
Listen to what everybody is saying : " Ah, yes, those
naturalists, those men with dirty hands, who want to
have all the novels written in slang, and who choose
deliberately the most disgusting subjects among the

lower classes and in bad districts." But not at all; you lie! You make naturalism, in a miserable fashion, a question of rhetoric, while I have always striven to make it a question of method. I have called naturalism the great analytical and experimental movement, which started in the eighteenth century and which is growing grandly in ours. It is stupid to pretend that I restrict the horizon, that I insist upon finding our literature in the faubourgs, that I have reduced it to obscene language, while, on the contrary, I maintain the literary domain is extending more and more and mingling with the scientific domain.

"L'Assommoir," always "L'Assommoir"! They are trying to make some kind of absurd Gospel of this book. Oh! I wrote ten novels before that one, and I will write ten more. I have taken the whole of society for my subject; I have already placed my characters in twenty different worlds, even in that of dreams. Do not say that I have the idiotic pretension of only depicting life in the gutter. Have eyes; see clearly. That does not even need intelligence; it is sufficient to ascertain the facts. And, above all, do not accuse me of inventing a literary religion, because that is not true, because I am simply a critic studying his epoch, going back to the last century to search for its sources in Balzac's novels, and then tracing it down to our own days, to find out what the movement that the author of the "Comedie Humaine" has determined in our literature consists of. This is my task. Naturalism does not belong to me, it belongs to the century. It acts in society, in the sciences, in letters and in art, and in politics. It is the power of our age.

Have I made myself understood this time? Will

they still shut naturalism within the four walls of the sink of the Ambiguous? In truth, it is irritating.

I allow myself to get angry, and that is wrong. Let me come back to imagination in the novel. The idea that the novel tends toward becoming simply a monograph, a page of existence, the recital of one single fact, has seemed monstrous and revolutionary. In truth, our story-tellers, with the complications of their soporific stories, must have befogged their brains. Without going back to "La Nouvelle Heloise," to "Werther," to "René," which are but the analyses of a psychological fact, I will cite M. de Goncourt, in "Manette Salomon" and "Mme. Gervaisais," two novels published ten years ago, which owe their interest to no plot, and are of value only as the study of a place or a character.

M. Edmond de Goncourt is about to publish a new work, "Les Frères Zemganno." It is the story of two circus júmpers. But, fearing that I may be suspected of analyzing the book from my point of view, I prefer to take the account of it from a charming article which M. Alphonse Daudet has just published.

"The subject," he says, "is very simple: a life devoted to art and love. The elder becomes father and master to the younger. Life goes on, new tricks astonish Paris; then comes fortune, almost glory. Then one day the spite of an equestrienne causes the younger one to miss the trick and throws him in the sawdust, both legs broken, and the elder, not without regret and bitterness, renounces his art, swearing to the invalid to lighten his sickly repinings, that not with another, nor alone, would he ever perform again. No other *dénouement.* Reality has very nearly as much."

This is an excellent *résumé*. I said no more for the "Sœurs Vatard" of M. Huysmans. I admit, to-day, that I was thinking of M. de Goncourt's works as I wrote my phrase on the tendencies which the novelists appeared to have toward simplifying more and more the plot and suppressing theatrical effect and climax, giving to their readers only their notes on life, without binding them by any arrangement whatsoever. Personally, I will add that I am in favor of more complete studies, embracing a larger amount of human data, without inferring that they can, in my opinion, exhaust a subject. I was trying, then, only to state a fact. And by reason of this strange phenomenon in their vision of which I have already spoken, this is what they read in my article : that I wished to suppress imagination and make vulgarity the rule in novels.

You must understand what I mean by the words imagination and vulgarity. Certainly I reject imagination if you mean by that the inventions of the newspaper story-tellers, although such writers be endowed with the genius of their kind, and even if they are called Alexander Dumas and Eugene Sue. Nothing is more monotonous, in short, than their adventures. They have one or two dozen combinations which reappear continually. It is a mechanical theater, of which they turn the crank in the side, and the same characters reappear periodically, under other names and in other costumes. I will not speak of the nothingness of all this. At the bottom of all their long speeches there is only emptiness. They are read as you play with a musical box, to pass away an hour.

Imagination, the faculty of imagining, is not wholly in that. There it has only its coarsest application.

To invent a story out of the whole cloth and push it to the last limits of probability, to interest by the most incredible complications, nothing can be easier, nothing more within the reach of all the world. On the contrary, take facts, facts that you have seen around you, classify them according to a logical order, fill up the gaps by intuition, obtain the marvelous result of giving life to human data, a life fitting and complete, adapted to certain surroundings, and you will have exercised in a superior manner your faculties of imagination. Well! our naturalistic novel is properly the product of the classification of the notes and of the intuition which completes them. Look at Balzac's "Femme de Trente Ans" and "Eugenie Grandet"; any novelist whatever could have put his name to "La Femme de Trente Ans," while it would have taken a naturalistic novelist to write "Eugenie Grandet." The reason is that the first of these novels was invented, while the other was seen and divined.

I come to this reproach of commonplaceness. There is first a question of appreciation here. It is difficult to specifiy what is commonplace. You will say that what you see every day is commonplace. And what if, seeing it every day, it had never been looked at, and what if you can draw superb and unknown truths from it! This is the story of the great scientific movement of the eighteenth century. Nobody thought of analyzing air, because air was commonplace; Gay-Lussac analyzed it and founded modern chemistry. We are then accused of being commonplace because we take up the study of truth from the beginning, from nature and from man. But then there immediately comes up the question of form. *Bon Dieu!* tell me how many people have accused M. Huysmans of being common-place? Why, he is rather an exaggerated poet, a colorist of the Holland school, who has let himself slip into a general debauch of violent tones. This is what I reproach him with. If he is commonplace as a writer, then we must accuse the novelists of the *Revue des Deux Mondes* of reveling in orgies of style. No, no! the contemporaneous naturalistic novel is not commonplace, it is not enough so, and I myself have complained of it; but they did not understand me, as usual. The idea that I could be a purist, has made many laugh.

I wish, however, that they would cease to ascribe to me opinions which are not mine. I do not set up the commonplace; as a rule I do not reject imagination, above all, deduction, which is its most elevated and strongest form. It is like the horror for poetry which they credit me with. Have I ever written two lines which were silly enough to call for the suppression of poets? When and where have they surprised me in the act of clouding the sky of fantasy, of denying in man the necessity to lie, to idealize, to fly from reality? I accept man in his entirety, only I explain him by science. I have said twenty times that it made me angry to be deceived, and nothing more.

If you are a writer of dramatic fantasies, a poet, write me some fairy tales, and I shall take great pleasure in reading them. But if in a drama or a comedy you pretend to give me men, and your men are things of straw, you make me angry. The same way in a novel; write poems freely if you experience a need to idealize; Do not give me grotesque and impossible stories if you wish me to believe that all this has happened in this way. Give me no illegitimate and hypocritical works, that is all; no inacceptable mixture; no monsters, half real and half fabulous; no pretense of arguments, based upon lies, which reach a moral and patriotic conclusion. You are either an observer who gathers together human data or you are a poet who tells me your dreams, and I only ask from you genius in order to testify my admiration. I add that the present evolution operates evidently in favor of the observer, of the naturalistic novelist, and I explain this by social and scientific reasons. But I accept the whole, I rejoice in the whole, because I love life after the manner of a savant who observes it from day to day.

Thus, for example, M. Edmond de Goncourt, in " Les Frères Zemganno," was taken with the original whim of deserting the immediate reality in order to enter the domain of dreams. After the technical novel of " La Fille Elisa " he wished to show that he could flee from and get away from the observation. His new book belongs to poetical psychology, if I may be permitted to use this term. Well, nothing could be better; I approve of this attempt. It will be curious to learn how one of the authors of " Germinie Lacerteux " thinks and writes under the garb of poetical prose. The honest, respectable citizens whom " La Fille Elisa frightened will see that, when we wish to, we can make women weep and young girls dream. Did not the unworthy author of " L'Assommoir " write the second part of " La Faute de l'Abbè Mouret," a Garden of Eden idyl, a species of parable about ideal loves in pastures which never were?

Fourteen years ago, in 1865,* I was the only critic who

* This essay was originally published in 1879.

dared to call "Germinie Lacerteux" a *chef-d'œuvre.* To-day I announce the coming appearance of "Les Frères Zemganno" as the great literary event of the season. But I do not wish them to make use of the last work to attack the first. I will go further. Let one read "Les Frères Zemganno" and "Les Sœurs Vatard": there is between these two productions only this difference: one is the work of a master, the other that of a beginner. I like them because they both start out from the same literary method: one through a dream, the other through reality, and both are filled with life.

"LES FRÈRES ZEMGANNO."

THE PREFACE.

I WILL first touch upon the preface which the author has written for his book. This preface, which has all the importance of a manifesto, is excellent. Only as it appeared to me a little succinct I wish to be permitted to comment upon it here. I desire, while developing the ideas of this preface, to prevent the public from giving a meaning to the opinions expressed by M. Goncourt which never entered into his thought.

The thesis maintained by the author is that the decisive triumph of the naturalistic formula will be complete when it shall have been applied to the study of the higher classes of society. He says as follows: "We can publish 'Assommoirs' and books like 'Germinie Lacerteux,' and by them agitate, stir up, and excite one part of the public. Yes, but to my thinking the success of these books are only brilliant skirmishes by the advance guard, and the great battle which will determine the victory of realism and naturalism, and of analysis according to nature in literature, will not be fought on the ground that the authors of these two novels have chosen. The day in which the cruel analyses which my friend M. Zola and perhaps myself have brought to bear upon the picture of life in our lower classes shall be taken up by a writer of talent, and employed in the reproduction of fashionable men and women, placed amid surroundings of education and

distinction—on that day only classicism and its following will be killed."

This could not be better put. I have expressed
these ideas a hundred times. I am worn out repeating
that naturalism is a formula, and not any mode of
expression; that it does not consist of any form of
language, but in the scientific method applied to
surroundings and characters. From this it becomes
evident that naturalism does not confine itself to a
choice of subjects; in the same manner that the savant
applies his magnifying glass as much to the rose as to
the nettle, the naturalistic novelist has for his field of
observation the whole of society, from the *salon* to the
hovel. Fools alone make naturalism the literature of
the slums. M. Edmond de Goncourt expresses in an
excellent manner this very fine thought, that for a
certain prejudiced public, frivolous, unintelligent, if you
wish, the naturalistic formula will never be accepted
until this public shall perceive by examples that it is a
question of a formula, of a general method which is as
applicable as well to duchesses as to *grisettes*.

For the rest, M. de Goncourt completes and
explains his idea by adding that naturalism " has not
in fact only the mission of describing what is low, what
is repugnant, what is disgusting; it has come into this
world to define in artistic expression that which is
elevated, pretty, and noble, and, still more, to give to
the world a picture of the doings and appearances of
refined men and women and their rich and sumptuous
surroundings; but it will do this in a cons'stent,
vigorous, unconventional, and unimaginative study of
beauty, a study such as the new school has just made
these few years back of ugliness."

All this is perfectly clear. People affect to see but
our brutalities, they pretend to be convinced that we
shut ourselves up in the horrible ; all this is a maneuver
on the part of our enemies, made in very bad faith.
We wish to depict the whole world, we mean to submit
to our analysis beauty as well as ugliness. I will add
that M. de Goncourt might have been a little less modest
for us. Why should he leave it to be imagined we
have only depicted ugliness? Why does he not show
us carrying out the same work under all conditions, in
all classes of society at the same time? Our adversaries
alone play us this villainous trick of only speaking of our
" Germinie Lacerteux" and our "Assommoirs," keeping silent about our other works. We must protest, we
must show the general whole of our efforts. I will not
speak of myself ; I will not recall the fact that I have
undertaken to show in a series of novels the picture of
a whole epoch ; I will not draw attention to the fact
that " L'Assommoir " will remain a single note in the
midst of twenty other volumes—I will content myself
with mentioning " La Curée," in which I have already
tried to picture a little corner of what is " pretty " and
what is " refreshing." But I shall insist upon doing
M. de Goncourt justice ; I wish to show him writing
" Renée Mauperin " after " Germinie Lacerteux,"
touching the higher classes after the people, and writing
a *chef-d'œuvre* after a *chef-d'œuvre.*

What an exquisite and deep study " Renée Mauperin "
is! We are no longer in the midst of the roughness
and savageness of the lowest class. We have gone up
into the middle class, and the conditions become terribly complicated. I know very well that this is not yet
the aristocracy, but it is, at any rate, " an environment

of education and distinction." At this time the classes
are so intermingled, the pure aristocracy hold so small
a place in the social machinery, that the study of it is
not very interesting. M. de Goncourt, when he asks
for the aspects and profiles of refined people and costly
things, evidently speaks of the Parisian world, so elegant, so modern, and so variegated. He has already
presented one side of this Parisian world in the publication of " Renée Mauperin," fourteen years ago. In
that book will be found all that his great modesty asks
from those writers of talent who are to come after him.
Why, then, should he wish to remain the author of
" La Fille Elisa" and " Germinie Lacerteux," when
he has written " Renée Mauperin " and " Manette
Salomon," that other *chef-d'œuvre* of rare and vigorous
charm ?

It is true that M. de Goncourt has left one point in
obscurity, which it is necessary clearly to establish. He
demands " a well carried out study, rigorous, non-conven-
tional, and non-imaginative, of beauty " ; and further on
he adds that human data alone make good books—
" books which set mankind, as it truly is, standing
squarely on its legs "—an opinion which I have
defended for years past. There is the tool, the naturalistic formula, that we can apply to all conditions
and to all characters. Then the worst of it is that we
at once reach the human beast under the black broad-
cloth coat as well as under the blouse. Let us look
at "Germinie Lacerteux." The analysis is cruel there, for
it uncovers terrible sores. But carry the same analysis
into a higher class, into educated and distinguished
surroundings ; if you tell everything, if you probe
below the skin, if you expose man and woman in their

nakedness, your analysis will be as cruel there as with the lower classes, for it will only mean a change of scene and many more hypocrisies. When M. de Goncourt shall desire to depict a Parisian drawing room and to tell the truth, he will certainly have some pretty descriptions to make of beautiful toilets, flowers, politenesses, refinements, with an infinite variety of shadings. Only if he undresses his characters, if he passes from the *salon* to the bedchamber, if he enters into the intimacy, into the private and hidden life of every day, he must dissect monstrosities so much more unpardonable from the fact that they have grown and been cultivated in a richer soil.

And besides, is not " Renée Mauperin " a proof of what I have just said? Is not the refined wickedness of that book much more disgusting than the instinctive and desperate dissoluteness of *Germinie Lacerteux,* this poor sick girl who was dying for want of love? Yet M. de Goncourt has surfeited us with delicate tints in " Renée Mauperin. " The surroundings are luxurious; they smell good. The characters are respectable; they do not talk slang, and they are careful of all the proprieties.

It is necessary to state this plainly. Our analysis will always be cruel, because our analysis goes to the bottom of the human body. High and low we throw ourselves at the beast. Certainly there are veils more or less numerous, but when we have described them one after another, and when we have lifted up the last one, we see behind it more dirt than flowers. This is why our books are so black, so severe. We do not seek for what is repugnant—we find it; and if we try to hide it we must lie about it, or at least leave it incomplete. The day that M. de Goncourt conceives the notion of writing a novel on the fashionable world, wherein all will be pretty, or where there will be no bad odors, that day he will have to content himself with painting light Parisian pictures, sketches made on the surface, observations taken in the vestibule. If he goes down into the psychological and physiological study of characters, if he goes below the laces and jewels, well! he will write a novel which will poison the minds of delicate readers, and which they will look upon as frightful lies, for nothing seems less truthful than truth as soon as you search for it in the more elevated classes.

Another remark of M. de Goncourt's struck me very forcibly. He explains that a man of the people is easier to study and to paint than a gentleman. This is very true. A man of the people can be read immediately, while the well-educated gentleman hides his true nature under the thick mask of education. Then you can paint the man of the people in stronger outline. This makes the work amusing; vigorous silhouettes are obtained, violent contrasts in black and white. But I do not admit that there is more merit in leaving behind you a *chef-d'œuvre* on the people than a *chef-d'œuvre* on the aristocracy. The work is not judged by its subject, but by the talent of the writer. As to knowing, if the model poses better or offers more resources, that is a secondary question; it is only necessary that the model should be reproduced with genius. M. de Goncourt speaks of the difficulty that is experienced in grasping in all its truth the distinctive attributes of a Parisian man or woman, but it is as great a difficulty to grasp those of the peasant. I know some very careful studies on Paris life, while you can hardly find even a few true notes on country life. Everything lies in the manner of studying ; that is the truth.

At last I am come to the principal sentence in the preface. M. de Goncourt explains why he has written it, saying : " This preface aims to say to the young writers that the success of realism lies there [in depicting the higher classes] and only there, and no longer in the *canaille littéraire,* as it is exhausted in our day, by their forerunners." I agree with him precisely, only I ask the right to comment upon the phrase as I understand it.

Evidently M. de Goncourt could not have meant that the study of the people was already an exhausted subject because he has written " Germinie Lacerteux." That would be conceited and false. The field of observation cannot be exhausted by a single crop when it is as vast a field as that of the people. What ! we have been given a " freedom of the city " as regards the people in the literary domain, and back of us, all at once, there is nothing more to say about it. We may have made mistakes, but in any case we have not seen everything.

Besides, M. de Goncourt speaks of the *canaille littéraire.* I do not understand this expression, and for my part I do not accept it. In my opinion " Germinie Lacerteux " is not of the order of *canaille littéraire ;* it is a superb study of living, throbbing humanity. I would rather think, then, that by this expression of *canaille littéraire* M. de Goncourt intends to designate a certain mode of expression in which crude words are the invariable rule. On this understanding I agree with him. I beg of our young writers to break away from all special modes of expression. The naturalistic formula is independent of the writer's style, as that is independent of any choice of subject. It is, as I have said before, but the scientific method applied to letters.

I take up M. de Goncourt's conclusion again, and I say to our young novelists that the success of the formula lies not in imitating the process of their literary forerunners, but in the application of the scientific method to all subjects. I must add that there are no exhausted subjects; that the literary methods alone are exhausted. M. de Goncourt rightly desires no pupils. But let him be reassured : he will have none ; I mean by this that simple imitators die quickly, while the newcomers who bring a temperament of their own with them will soon break away from any fatal traditions. We must not definitely settle writers by their beginnings ; it is better to aid them in asserting their originality, which the crowd does not see, but which is often very real. We need no more masters, we want no more schools. What keeps us together is a common method of observation and experiment.

I go even further. I entreat our young novelists to get up a reaction against us. Let them leave us to draggle along in " artistic writing," according to M. de Goncourt's happy expression, and endeavor on their part to acquire a more solid, simple, and human style. All our sentimentalisms, all our excessive refinements of form, are not worth one good word in its proper place. This is how I feel and this is what I desire, if I could have it. But I am afraid I have mingled too much in the romantic mixture; I was born too soon. If I sometimes am angry with romanticism it is because I hate it for the false literary education which it has given me. I am tainted with it, and it enrages me.

I come back to M. de Goncourt, and I find in " Les Frères Zemganno " a last proof of the necessity of lying when you want to console yourself and others. He says that his new novel is an attempt " at a poetic reality " ; and he adds : " This year I found myself in one of those hours of life when one feels his increasing years; I felt ill and cowardly in the face of the sharp and agonizing labor of my other books, in a condition of soul when the truth, too true, was distasteful to me —and I have used this time some imagination, and have written a dream intermingled with a remembrance." This is just what I could have written of myself in regard to " La Faute de l'Abbé Mouret." Everyone has these cowardly hours in his life as a writer. I hope that M. de Goucourt will write the fashionable novel which he has announced. He will not decide the victory of naturalism by it, however, for this victory he has already won, and he was one of the first in any estimate. But he is mistaken if he thinks he will gain any sympathizers while carrying his knife into the more complicated organisms and into a more knowing corruption. They will only accuse him of insulting the aristocracy, as they have already accused us of insulting the people, even though he merely employ imagination in constructing a dream.

As for me, I only wish for one more triumph for naturalism, the reaction against our literary methods. When we have put our phrases, which compromise the scientific formula, to one side, when we shall have applied that formula to the study of all conditions and all characters, without the tra-la-la of our romantic frills, we shall write true, solid, and durable works.

THE BOOK.

In the first place, this is the plot:

Two brothers, *Gianni* and *Nello*, grew up among a troupe of circus people, of which their father, an Italian named *Bescapé*, was the director, and which scoured the villages and smaller cities of France. Their mother, a Bohemian, died first, to the great sorrow of her place and people. The father died not long afterward. Then the two brothers, fired with ambition, sold their rolling stock and went to England, where they passed several years, and where they found employment as gymnasts in several circuses. They finally returned to make their début at a circus in Paris, which had been their secret desire for some time. *Gianni* had for a long time been trying to invent some trick which would make them famous. He finds it at last, and they are starting to perform it in public for the first time, when an equestrienne, who had been repulsed by *Nello*, wreaked her vengeance on him by causing him to have a frightful fall, in which both his legs were broken in such a manner as to incapacitate him from ever performing again. *Gianni*, seeing *Nello* suffer intensely from a strange jealousy every time he touched a trapeze, finally renounces his art of his own free will. This is the *dénouement*.

Latterly, when I have stated that the novel of the present day tended to simplify the action more and more, and to confine itself to one fact, instead of the complicated inventions of our story-tellers, I was mocked at, and they even reviled me, as happened when they threw reflections on my character by saying of me that if I wished to suppress invention in the novel it was because I showed a lack of invention in my own works. In the first place, I am not foolish enough to wish to suppress anything ; I am but a critic, whose only work is to arrange the actual statement. Then, I only speak with proofs. For example, here is " Les Frères Zemganno," which affords me a very characteristic proof.

You can see M. de Goncourt this time has not confined himself to a strictly exact analysis. As he says himself, he has used imagination in constructing a story out of a dream, mingled with a remembrance. Since the public demand imagination, here it is. Only just see what imagination can become in the hands of a naturalistic novelist when he takes the notion not to press too near the reality.

Evidently M. de Goncourt did not exercise this imagination as regards the facts. It is impossible to build up a more simple drama. There is but one unexpected change, the equestrienne's vengeance, in substituting a cask of wood for the cask of cloth, which *Nello* was to carry, thus bringing about his fall. And again, this incident holds but a very small place in the story. You feel that the author had need of it, but that he disdained it. He passes over it quickly, and he prolongs the climax; he stops at the situation he has obtained as soon as *Nello* is wounded. Thus when M. de Goncourt speaks of imagination he does not mean by it what the critic does, the imagination of Alexander Dumas and Eugene Sue ; he means a particular poetical arrangement, an individual fancy, made in the face of the truth, but based all the same on the truth.

Nothing could be more typical, I repeat, than "Les Frères Zemganno" from this point of view. All the facts which are presented to us are facts strictly taken from reality. The author does not invent a plot; the most everyday history is sufficient to put his heroes forward; the secondary characters hardly mingle in the action at all; it is a matter of analysis that he desires, and not the symmetrical and opposed elements of a drama. Only when he has this matter for analysis before him, when he possesses the needed amount of human data, he gives the rein to his imagination, he builds upon these data the poem which pleases him. In a word, the work of the imagination is, in this case, not in the events nor in the characters, but in the way the analysis is turned into another path and the incidents and characters are made to symbolize a certain truth.

Thus it is evident that *Gianni* and *Nello* do nothing that circus athletes could not do. They are constructed according to exact data. But they are idealized; they represent a symbol. In their ordinary condition things would not happen with such refined sensations. We have here very delicate minds in very coarse bodies. M. de Goncourt has lifted these clowns out of the material atmosphere of violent exercises, to place them in one of exquisite nervous sensibility. Notice that I do not deny the reality of this story; roughs might have these adventures and feel these sensations, only roughs would feel them in a different way—more confusedly. In a word, in reading " Les Frères Zemganno " you immediately understand that the work does not ring with the exact truth; it rings with truth transformed by the imagination of the author.

What I have said of the two principal characters I could say of the less important ones. I could also say it of the surroundings. These people and these things have reality as their basis, but they are a little touched up later on: they enter into what M. de Goncourt has so happily called " a poetic reality." You must then, I repeat once more, make a great difference between the imagination of the story-tellers, who turned the facts topsy-turvy, and the imagination of the naturalistic novelists, who set out from facts. This is poetic reality, that is to say, reality taken and poetically treated subsequently.

Certainly we do not condemn such imagination as this. It is an inevitable escape, a flight from the bitterness of truth, a caprice of the writer, whom the truths torment which have fallen from him. Naturalism does not restrict the horizon, as they so falsely say. It is nature and man in their universality, with their known and their unknown. The day they escape from the scientific formula they but play truant among the truths as yet undemonstrated.

Besides, the question of method dominates everything. When M. de Goncourt, when the other naturalistic writers add their fantasy to the truth, they still keep the analytical method, they prolong their observation beyond what is. It becomes a poem, but it still remains a logical work. They admit, besides, that their feet no longer rest on the earth ; they do not pretend to give out their work as a truth. On the contrary, they warn the public of the exact moment when they enter upon the dream, which is, to say the least, an act of good faith.

Now, to come back to " Les Frères Zemganno," it

would be very easy to tell how this book was conceived
by M. de Goncourt. He felt the need, at one moment
of his life, of symbolizing the powerful tie which united
his brother and himself at every hour of the day in an
intimacy and joint work. Recoiling from an autobiog-
raphy, looking simply for a frame for his memories, he
said to himself that two gymnasts, two brothers, who
risked their lives together, who had become united
together as much through the body as through the
mind, would actualize in a powerful and original manner
the two beings, blended into a single whole, whose sentiments he wished to analyze. But, on the other side,
from an easily explained feeling of delicacy, he recoiled
before the brutal surroundings of a circus, before certain uglinesses and certain monstrosities belonging to
the characters whom he had chosen. " Les Frères
Zemganno " is, therefore, the result of a conception
materialized and then idealized.

The result is a very touching book, startling in its
strangeness. As I have said, you soon feel that you
are not in a real world; but, under the caprice of a
symbol, there is in it a throbbing humanity. I will
point out the bits of analysis which struck me most.
The childhood of the two brothers, their tenderness
growing with their years, their mutual absorption; then,
later, their two bodies, which became but one body in
the dangers which they faced, this perfect union of the
two gymnasts entering more and more the one into the
other, living their life in common; and then, when *Nello*
can no longer perform, his anger at the thought that his
brother would perform without him; his jealousy, like
a woman's, happy in knowing the beloved being would
never love elsewhere, and demanding in his unreason-

ableness that the Zemganno Brothers should both die from the moment that one was dead to the circus. These are the pages which give to the work an intense life, a life lived, outside of the reality of characters and surroundings. Human data are so touching here that they are felt even under the poetic veil which is thrown over them.

In his pure descriptions M. de Goncourt has retained his exact and fine touch. There is, in this connection, at the commencement of the book, a marvelous description : a landscape at the hour of twilight, with a little city in the distance whose lights twinkle on the horizon. I will also cite the description of the circus the night *Nello* broke his legs; the silence of the audience after the fall has a superb effect. And what beautiful episodes—that of the death of the gypsy mother in the traveling wagon which served them for a home; the different exhibitions on the road; the evening that *Nello*, convalescent, wished to see the circus again, and is seated in the Champs-Élysées on a rainy night, before him the brightly illuminated windows; then he goes away silently without wanting to enter.

Such is the book. It brings a new note into M. de Goncourt's work, and it will remain by its originality and its emotion. The author has written simpler and completer books, but he has put into this one all his tears, all his tenderness, and that often is sufficient to render a work immortal.

MORALITY.

ONE of my good friends had a novel in course of publication in a newspaper. The editor in chief had him summoned one evening and spoke to him with great indignation of a paragraph which was to appear in the paper the next day; I do not know exactly what it was the editor found fault with—the lovers were not behaving well, there was a kiss which was thought to be too tender. My friend, blushing at the idea of having shocked the sensibilities of the whole editorial staff, consented to suppress the paragraph. The next day what was the astonishment of this young man to read on the third page of this same newspaper, in the same edition from which they had made him expurge his paragraph, the story given at length and in all its details of a most atrocious criminal affair, such as the most romantic imagination alone could have been capable of conceiving. No horror was spared, neither the details of the horrible crime nor the abominable circumstances accompanying it.

Well, I must say I cannot understand it. The question stands thus : How is it that the newspapers are so bashful on their ground floor, and so improper on their third page ? I do not enter upon the literary discussion concerning imagination and reality; I merely examine one fact ; I say that there is an absolute lack of logic in speaking of the dignity of a newspaper and the respect due to families. If after exercising police supervision with the novel they publish without hesitation all the infamies of the courts, why exact in one place a *couleur de rose* lie and then accept all the ferocities of existence in another?

For a long time I have wanted to make a certain study and I have begun keeping a scrapbook toward this end. My idea is very simple: I cut out of the news-papers with the largest circulation, those which pride themselves on being read by mothers and young girls, the most frightful episodes, the details of crimes and lawsuits which put most cynically in all its nakedness the filth of man; then I propose some day, when I have a pretty little pile of these experiences, to publish the collection, contenting myself with printing after each extract the name and the date of the newspaper. When this work shall be completed we shall see with what a dignified air the editors will speak to their subscribers at the least trace of boldness in analysis shown by the naturalistic novelist.

And you may believe that my collection will be a rich one. I already have the story of an old woman who was thrown into the water and taken out three times by her murderer for his pleasure; I have that of the other old woman killed by two young men after a frightful orgie; I have that of Menesclou with her chemise spotted with blood; without taking into consideration all kinds of occurrences: the minute details of the cutting up of murdered bodies, young girls kidnapped, adul-teries. Without doubt the newspapers neither make vices nor crimes; they content themselves with relating them, but in such clear terms, or with paraphrases which but aggravate the obscenity to such a point, that they do well truly to dispute with us the liberty of saying everything.

I know very well what the editors will reply. They are for the most part splendid fellows, loving a broad joke, and cutting capers like other simple mortals. Only they do not jest with their subscribers. In their heart of hearts they do not care a fig for the dignity of their journals; what they desire is that the subscriber should be satisfied; and they would give him arsenic if only he asked for it. Admit if you wish that the inconsistency comes from the public; the public which tolerates the bloody sewer of the courts, asks in novels for little birds and daisies to console itself with. It is a convention; that which is scandalous in one place becomes inoffensive in another. And if you have the misfortune to lack the proper credentials you are a scamp, the whole press drags you in the gutter. Liberal public!

At this moment a divorce suit is stirring up Paris. I do not intend to judge the people concerned therein, and I do not even care what the courts' decision may be. What interests me is simply these stories told by the newspapers, those which they print, the soiled linen which is shaken out with so much ease and complacency.

Apropos of this let me hazard an observation: you know very well that the judges dare go much further than we can, the novelists. They enter into truly scandalous details; the liberty of their questions is such sometimes, and they go so deep into the obscene, that they are obliged to order the doors closed. I know well that their mission is to know all, in order to judge. Well, our mission is also to know all, in order to judge. Between

judges and writers there is only one difference, and that
is that sometimes the writers leave works of genius.

Thus, my friends, we must confess our impotence.
We shall never put forth truth with this degree of
cruelty. The newspapers, which become indignant at
our works, and which publish in all their details these
obscene pictures, no doubt think that we are turning into *berquinades.* Consider the nature and the
details of the great scandal the newspapers are reveal-
ing so plainly at this very moment, and which is dragging through the mud the names of living people, who
are known to all of us, and you will realize how mean,
small, and youthful, timid and colorless, our stories are—
bread and milk for children in pinafores. I am ashamed
of this simple water.

Is it not my great friend Edmond de Goncourt who
advises you, you young writers, to study the world of
fashion, to carry observation and analysis up into the
higher classes in order to write good novels, which will
give forth a clean, sweet smell? The advice is excellent,
but where is this world? It is unquestionably not
among the officials and the millionaires of the lawsuit
now going on. Is it a question of the fashionable world
with open doors or with closed doors? If we are curious,
if we should peep through the chinks, I doubt not that
we should see in these higher classes, what we saw with
the lower people, for the human beast is the same
everywhere—it is only the clothing that differs. Such
is the opinion that I have expressed at other times, and
now the echoes of the Palais de Justice furnish me
with reasons for continuing in this same way of thinking.

We others, common folk, of ordinary appearance and
little fortune, we only know of this high society by the

scandalous divorce suits which burst upon us every winter. I do not speak of the *salons* to which we may go ; you are exposed to the eyes of the public in these *salons*, you behave there at least fairly well. I speak of the dining room, the boudoir, the alcove. From each lawsuit we learn some nice bits of information. Monsieur swears like a car-driver, calls his daughter an outrageous name, and his lady companion a worse one ; madame meets gentlemen in churches ; the father-in-law is a fool and the mother-in-law insupportable. They slap each other as the result of hard words ; they pull each other's hair before the domestics. *Grand Dieu!* are we in a wretched hole of La Chapelle? Not at all ; we are in the best society in the world, a world frequented by princes.

What do the public imagine ? When we put an oath in the mouth of a well brought up man ; when we note an obscene conversation, whispered just a few steps away from some ladies in a drawing room ; when we find the lackey and the prostitute under the black coat and the velvet robe—will they still tell us that we lie ? will they shrug their shoulders, affirming that we do not know the fashionable world? will they accuse us of defaming it and soiling it for our own pleasure? The fashionable world! Behold it as it is when a great passion shakes it, when a terrible drama throws it outside of its politeness and its conventionalities.

Obscenity is at the bottom of it all. Sometimes a lawsuit appears and breaks the surface, like an abscess. Everybody is astonished. They seem to think the fact exceptional, because most people recoil before a scandal ; but how many people have quietly separated after scenes of violence, how many brutalities and obscenities are concealed ? A lawsuit is simply an experimental novel, which unrolls itself before the public. Two temperaments are brought forward, and the experiment takes place, under the influence of exterior circumstances. This is the truth ; a true drama brings sharply out into broad daylight the true mechanism of life.

CRITICISM.

CRITICISM.

POLEMICS.

I.—M. CHARLES BIGOT.

MY attention was called lately to an essay entitled
"The Naturalistic Cult," which the *Revue des
Deux Mondes* has asked M. Charles Bigot to write. I
was filled with curiosity to know what M. Charles
Bigot, that lettered and conscientious critic, could possibly say on naturalism in that grave temple, *La Revue
des Deux Mondes*. I started to read it with all the
attention I possessed. Here are the impressions of
my reading, just as they came to me:

First, he is guilty of a deception. The critic starts
out by making those little jests which have been
current in the small newspapers for the last three years.
It is certainly a good thing to laugh, but it is necessary
to laugh appropriately and on your own account. Consequently I was slightly irritated on finding that the
critic took up again those old accusations, styling me
a Messiah, a Pope, the head of a school, crushing me
because I have not brought a new religion in my
pocket, crying out that naturalism is as old as the
world, and subsequently becoming angry with it while
calling it an incongruous novelty. I confess that I am
a little weary of replying to all this sort of thing. It

was no use for me to say once more that I was simply
a recorder drawing up the report of the course of the
intellectual current; no use to cry aloud that there was
no school and that I was not a leader; that I had a
horror of all revelation and of all pontificate; the
pleasantries continue none the less, the confusion
remains complete, the light is not thrown on my position nor on my true rôle. It seems as if a password
were given; each one makes over his neighbor's article
without trying to understand, without having even the
fairness to quote me as the basis of his reasoning. Let
that pass when it is only a question of the petty newspapers. But here comes *La Revue des Deux Mondes*,
which with all solemnity opens its mouth and lets fall
the same empty judgments, with utter uselessness and
insignificance.

How can I make M. Charles Bigot understand that
he has written a dull article, in which he says nothing
at all? This is, however, the strict truth. He starts
out from a radically false standpoint, he gives me an
attitude which I have not, he makes me say what I
have never said, and does not tell rightly what I have
repeated twenty times. Then how can one suppose
that he does good work? He can only paw the ground,
raising merely a lot of dust I have called naturalism
the return to nature, the scientific movement of the century; I have shown the experimental method brought
to bear upon and applied to all the manifestations of
human intelligence; 'I have tried to explain the evident
evolution which is being produced in our literature by
establishing the proposition that the former subject of
study, the metaphysical man, is being replaced by the
physiological man. Is all this so difficult of compre-

hension ? And why speak of a new religion, when we have just broken away from all religions ?

My irritation grows greater, then, at each page. Picture yourself talking to a deaf person, and that you cannot draw from him one word which fits in with what you are saying. You talk to him of the fine weather, and he replies to you that he feels very well. You ask him for news, and he is disconsolate because the grapes will not ripen well this year. This is exactly my situation with regard to M. Charles Bigot. Not one of his phrases responds to mine. He has made a little naturalism for his own use, or rather he bestrides naturalism for the sake of a joking criticism, and once started he rides off alone. Positively, monsieur, in this fashion we shall never come together.

However, pages succeed pages, I actually feared to come to the end of the essay without finding anything. It threatened to be absolute emptiness. But not at all. I at last fell upon a very serious passage. M. Charles Bigot, who has just devoted ten pages, and God knows what very full pages they are, to flitting around the question without entering upon it, to jesting, to battling with windmills, confusing everything and judging at random his own imaginations—M. Charles Bigot all at once steps on the ground itself of the discussion, comes to the decisive point. And remark that he does not seem to perceive that he has reached it, for he goes and slurs over the point, he who is so lavish in his favors at the beginning. It is seemingly by chance that he stops there for the space of a paragraph. A little more and he would have passed by the subject completely, and we should only have had a pretty dance about nothing.

I will quote it, which is more than he has done for me.
After granting that the naturalists have at least the
originality " of mixing up in their painting of monsters
physiology with psychology, or rather of suppressing
psychology to the advantage of physiology," he cries
out: " This is not the moment to examine into this
great philosophical question of mind and matter, nor
that of freedom and human responsibility, formidable
problems which were not made to be solved in a few
lines." But yes, monsieur, on the contrary, it is the
moment. I pray you wait a moment. I am perfectly
willing that you should not place us on philosophical
ground, which has no solidity, but place us on scientific
ground. And then, if you like, do not move us, for
here we possess certainty.

Further on I read again: " . . . I shall reply that
physiology ought to be left to physiologists; beware
of literary physiology as much as of amateur music."
Nothing prevents me from crying out in my turn: " I
shall reply that psychology should be left to the psy-
chologists ; let us beware of literary psychology as much
as of amateur music." I will not recommence here my
essay " Le Roman Experimental " (" The Experimental
Novel "), to which I refer M. Bigot. This time will he
understand that I am not a Messiah, that I am content
to search for what, according to my way of thinking,
will be the decisive influence of scientific methods on
our literary analysis of man and nature. I do not ask
him to think as I do. I beg him simply not to distort
my thought. Let him attack it if he will, but let him
understand it first.

Nothing is so astonishing in our age of inquiry as to
hear a man of such intelligence as M. Bigot give utter-

ance to the following lines: " What does it matter to me as a spectator whether *Phèdre* is or is not suffering from an hysterical illness? That is the business of the doctor who has her health under his care. What occupies me is to know what is to be the effect of her furious love, what ravages this love will work in her conscience, and if the innocent *Hippolyte* will perish. . . . The artist is not a savant who seeks out causes, the task he sets himself is to paint effects, to have an emotion sweet or terrible burst forth from his work." Then, monsieur, let us keep to the novels of Ponson du Terrail. If the domain of literature is only in the effects, if you forbid the search for causes you cancel with one stroke of the pen all human analysis: story-tellers must suffice us.

This is precisely what we wish to do : recommence our study of *Phèdre.* You are in the midst of our ambitions, or rather of our duties. We find that since the metaphysical ground is yielding place to the scientific, the theological and classical literature should yield to the naturalistic literature. Notice that this transformation has taken place of itself, and all I do is to state the fact. This is not a personal fantasy of the head of a school, it is a fact laid down by a critic. *Phèdre* is ill: well, let us see what her illness is, demonstrate it, let us master it, if it is possible ; that is of more value than for you to amuse yourself by merely enjoying the spectacle of this illness, which is not right, monsieur.

I pass over M. Charles Bigot's patriotic couplet condemning true pictures, intending us to understand that M. de Bismarck is watching us. I have already said elsewhere that our defeats were due to our disdain of scientific principles. Let us love truth and we shall conquer.

In the same way I make no comment on the singular tactics employed by M. Charles Bigot to annihilate naturalism. He speaks of " La Dévouée " by M. Leon Hennique and "Les Sœurs Vatard " by M. Huysmans without giving, for the matter of that, the title of these novels, without mentioning the names of the authors, as if the majesty of *La Revue des Deux Mondes* was unwilling freely to occupy itself with two young novelists at their first appearance ; and he starts out from that place to accuse the school, always the school! of not having yet made itself master of the world. Yes, he would like us to treat the whole of humanity in two volumes. *Bon Dieu!* what unreasonableness! You wait!

And now I come to this question : How is it possible that M. Charles Bigot, assuredly a man of great merit, could write for a review of such importance as *La Revue des Deux Mondes* an essay so confused and insignificant, when this review ordered an article on naturalism? This seems to me a very curious case.

M. Bigot is capable of better things than this essay. He was a good scholar at the Normal School ; he even, I think, has taught at Mines. His is a very cultivated mind, knowing a great number of things, writing remarkable political articles, putting more than the ordinary amount of good sense and conscience into his literary studies. But as soon as he touches upon this question of naturalism he becomes scared, he loses his footing, he does not even give himself the trouble to seriously study the question in the original documents, so much is he under the current prejudices, so much has he allowed himself to be carried away by the need to cleave the monster in two.

In the first place, without knowing it, M. Bigot accedes to certain philosophical beliefs. It is no use to affect a flippant air, he knows very well that these are conceptions of men and nature which are in question. I do not say that M. Bigot is a hardened idealist. I shall incline, on the contrary, to think of him as floating in an eclecticism made up of odds and ends. His ideas smell of the school—he who sees schools everywhere. Add the literary disposition. Science is an enemy to him. This idea of a literature governed by science surprises and disconcerts him. It would mean to remake his education entirely anew. You should see his indignation and astonishment at finding that you can admire the ligament of a muscle, the play of an organ, the mechanism of a body.

But this is not all. M. Charles Bigot lacks strong opinions, and this is a more serious thing in criticism than you might suppose. Look at M. Sarcey. Certainly his judgments are often rough. He passes more than once squarely to the side of truth, but he has none the less acquired an authority, and that often legitimately, because he shows his real feeling entirely, such as it is. On the contrary, M. Charles Bigot wishes to use tact in dealing with all subjects; he seeks the perfect equilibrium between yesterday and to-morrow. I must personally thank him for the efforts which he has made to drag me out of the fray in his massacre of the naturalistic novelists. Only, with this desire for the strict justice of a school-teacher, with this ambition to distribute the prizes to the most meritorious, he will end by no longer keeping count of the great evolutions and by losing interest in the general movement of minds. I will venture to say that it would be better sometimes to risk an exaggeration and take a position, to carry your personal action into the labors of the century and do the work of a man. No true convictions, no action!

This is no doubt the reason why the essay published in *La Revue des Deux Mondes* is a dilution of all the essays without reflection and weight which have appeared elsewhere. I am waiting for an adversary who will consent to meet me on my own ground and to fight me with my own weapons.

II.

M. ARMAND SILVESTRE.

IN the last *Revue Dramatique*, in an article written by one of my colleagues, M. Armand Silvestre, a poet of great talent, and who rows with us in the critical galley, I came upon a theory on the unworthiness of the novel and the excellence of poetry which I wish to reply to. This theory is that a poem alone is immortal, while a novel can look, at the very most, for only fifty years of success. And M. Silvestre adds: " I cite here a purely experimental fact, and one for which M. Émile Zola could surely not reproach me."

Certainly, yes ; I base all science on facts. Only the facts must be clearly established and clearly explained. Let us see the facts.

In the first place, I shall reproach M. Armand Silvestre for a phrase which has no doubt fallen from him unwittingly. He says, in comparing Balzac and Flaubert to Victor Hugo and Théophile Gautier : " There will always be an abyss between the artists who work for their epoch and those who attempt immortality." The idea of Balzac and Flaubert being accused of not caring a fig for immortality, of working for only their own generation ! I do not advise M. Silvestre to maintain that opinion about Flaubert, who spent ten years in writing one novel, and who had the high and great ambition of engraving each word as though on marble.

I also think his affirmation as to the approaching and complete disappearance of Balzac's work a little risky.

Truly the poets are wrong when they deny us the desire for immortality. That is a noble fever which consumes all writers of talent, whether they write in prose or in poetry. It is an outrage to say to us: "You do not write in rhyme, therefore you are but reporters." Ah, *bon Dieu !* what courage should we have for our work if the most humble among us did not soothe ourselves with the pleasant dream of living through the ages? Our whole strength lies in that. Perhaps we mislead ourselves, but it is glorious to be mistaken in this way, and the worst unhappiness which can overtake us is the thought after writing a page: " Here is a page which will die before I do."

Thus we all work for immortality. The impulse is universal and superb, and it is this impulse which makes the grandeur of letters. It remains to be seen if inevitably, by a law of nature, the novel is condemned to disappear at the end of half a century, while the poem by a special grace will be from its essence immortal.

M. Armand Silvestre pretends to base his opinion on facts. Evidently he is thinking of antiquity, of Homer for the Greeks and of Virgil for the Latins, without mentioning authors of tragedy. The names of great prose writers could be mentioned, especially in Rome. But if we do admit that epic poetry is the highest form of expression with the two ancient languages which are taught to us in our colleges, we must bear in mind that there are for this, historical conditions to be taken into account. A literature is but one form of logic.

All pagan philosophy tended to poetry, to the culti-

vation of one form of expression, to accept as absolute
one definite kind of beauty. For my part, I deny that
there is one absolute form in the matter of beauty ; this
is so true, and the rules of each nation and each age
differ so much, that the numerous attempts which we
have made toward epic poems ended in monstrosities.
We were obliged to fall back upon dramatic and lyric
poetry, which, in the ancient rhetorics occupied a secondary place.

Moreover, our pride as writers must admit one thing,
and that is that our immortality often comes to us
from secondary causes. Thus classical education for
the last three centuries has done more for the glory of
Homer and Virgil than has even their genius. How is
it possible for us to escape feeling admiration for these
poets, when they have been dinned into us from our
very childhood? You might well say that there are
truly no immortal books but those which have become
classical. I should like to know where Boileau would
stand to-day, for example, if our professors did not
hammer his writings into our brains. And by the side
of Boileau how many forgotten poets there are, known
only to literary men, and who are superior to him.
They are not between the hands of schoolboys, and
that condemns them. There is a species of ready-made
admiration, which one generation transmits to the following generation like articles of faith. This is, perhaps, the only practical immortality, while waiting for
a new deluge to carry our works on its waves like
straws—our poor human works, of which we are so
proud, and which do not count in the great evolution
of worlds.

Evidently verses have a better chance of living a

long time, if you look upon immortality as a simple result of the memory exercises in our schools. Verses are learned with more facility; there is a music to them which fixes the words in our memories. Then poems are generally short, and it must be remarked that the generations prefer short works, which they read and retain without effort. Homer has but two works—the Iliad and the Odyssey; and the Odyssey is, in a certain measure, discarded, because it does not enter directly into classical education. All Virgil's works are contained in a thin volume. These are things which ought to make us modern writers tremble when we think of our incredible fecundity. Look at Voltaire; already two or three masterpieces alone survive. And Victor Hugo. M. Armand Silvestre, who places him on the pinnacle, does he think that he will live, with his thousands of verses? For my part, I am certain that posterity will glean out from this pile of rhymes fifty pieces at most, a volume which will remain the *chef-d'œuvre* of French lyrical poetry.

This is the only superiority, then, which I am willing to admit that the poem holds over the novel: it is shorter, and it is retained with greater ease; this is what gives it preference in our schools as an exercise for the pupil's memory. Every other idea, above all, the idea of any absolute form, is an æsthetic jest. Written works are the expressions of a certain society —nothing more. Greece in the heroic age wrote epic poems, France of the nineteenth century writes novels. These are natural incidents of production which are one as good as the other. There is not one particular beauty, and this beauty does not consist in the arrangement of words in a certain order; there are but human phenomena coming in their time and possessing the beauty of their time. In a word, life alone is beautiful.

But, putting the dead languages to one side, in our own French literature let us see the facts to which M. Armand Silvestre refers. Who are our poets? Ronsard, Malherbe, Corneille, Racine, Molière, Lafontaine, and then the lyrical group of our own century, Musset, Hugo, Lamartine, Gautier, and still others. Who are our prose writers? Rabelais, Montaigne, Montesquieu, Pascal, Bossuet, Saint-Simon, Voltaire, Rousseau, Diderot, Balzac, Flaubert, Edmond and Jules de Goncourt, and still others. Well, I think this is pretty evenly balanced; and I myself consider that the prose platform is the stronger. M. Armand Silvestre may say to me, perhaps, that these men named by me have not written novels. If he makes this objection, it will only be because we do not understand this word "novel" in the same sense; as, indeed, I suspect is the case. As for me, I look upon " Pantagruel," "Les Essais," "Les Lettres Persanes," "Les Provincials" as novels, or, I should rather say, as human studies.

Has not " Pantagruel" lived for more than fifty years? Can M. Armand Silvestre quote me a poet of that epoch who to-day, after more than three centuries, eclipses the glory of Rabelais? There is Ronsard, but can Ronsard, notwithstanding the exhumation which the romanticists in 1830 attempted with his works, do more than tread on the heels of Rabelais? "Pantagruel," after having been the Bible of the sixteenth century, has remained an indestructible monument in our literature. The language has become antiquated, but it keeps its place nevertheless. Thus poetry-verse is not indispensable to immortality.

I could still continue these comparisons. The reader will easily make them for himself. I think that M. Armand Silvestre's mistake lies entirely in the restricted meaning which he has given to the word novel. He, no doubt, sees in the novel what Mlle. Scudéry and Le Sage saw, a simple amusement for the mind; and yet " Gil Blas " holds its own pretty well after 150 years. Since the eighteenth century the novel with us has broken loose from the narrow frame which inclosed it; it has become historical and critical; I could easily prove that it has become poetical. With Balzac it has absorbed all forms of expression; I have said this before, and I repeat it here. Whoever does not see and comprehend this great literary evolution, that a social evolution has caused, is, in one second, thrown outside of his epoch.

M. Armand Silvestre quotes Charles de Bernard, and states that he is no longer read. I can easily understand that; Charles de Bernard was only a poor copy of Balzac, and possessed not one original quality. But does he not go a little too far when he writes, after having named Balzac and Flaubert, " I should consider it altogether an impertinence to place their glory anywhere near that of Victor Hugo and Lamartine, Alfred de Musset and Théophile Gautier." This impertinence I permit myself the pleasure of committing. Balzac has been dead for more than a quarter of a century, and his glory does but grow; to-day he is a colossus— he is at the summit. We shall see what will be thought of Victor Hugo twenty-five years after his death.

Please to notice I have the same contempt for success that M. Armand Silvestre expresses. He says rightly that the infatuation of a generation proves nothing. This has been shown in the case of Chateaubriand and Lamartine; it will yet be seen in the case of Victor Hugo. A book attains to its fiftieth edition; this only means that it is in the fashion. But why does M. Armand Silvestre say that novels alone have " the exclusive privilege of repeated editions and a brilliant success"? And what of Béranger, one of his colleagues in poetry? and Delille, and Lebrun, and Casimir Delavigne? I think, on the contrary, that the bad poets are specially lucky in stealing undeserved successes; they are decorated, they are elected to the Academy, and they are embalmed even while alive. It only needs a sonnet to infatuate a public. The least bit of verse assures a name for its author, while it is sometimes necessary to write ten volumes of prose before you succeed in making people take you seriously.

Now, to conclude, I will say this : that immortality comes to genius. It matters little what form is adopted. The form is secondary; it is that which is fabricated, and ranks second to the fabricator. M. Armand Silvestre chases us out of posterity, we novelists, who believe in life and deny the absolute. I will be broader minded than he is, I will open the centuries to the poets. Let us go up together; that will be more brotherly, for our efforts are the same. I do not admit that he accuses me of knowingly writing on sand when I am very willing to believe that he rhymes on bronze.

"LE RÉALISME."

I HAVE had the good fortune to come across the file of a journal called *Le Réalisme*, which Edmond Duranty published in collaboration with a few friends during the first years of the Empire. I have looked over this file, and in it I found such curious notes that I could not resist the desire which came over me to devote a few pages to this subject. In my opinion *Le Réalisme* is a date, a very important and significant document in our literary history.

Observe that the newspaper had only six numbers. It appeared on the 15th of each month, in the form of a quarto, of sixteen pages of two columns each. The first number bears the date of November 15, 1856, and the last that of April–May, 1857. Evidently the funds were exhausted, there was the delay of a month, and that was its deathblow. The journal boasted of only three regular editors: M. Edmond Duranty, proprietor and editor-in-chief; M. Jules Assézat, later editor of *Les Débats*, and to whom we owe the publication of a fine edition of Diderot, but who has been dead now for several years; lastly, M. Henri Thulié, to-day a distinguished doctor and the author of several very remarkable works, and who has been latterly president of the Municipal Council of Paris.

You cannot imagine with what vigor these young men flung themselves into the fight. They were then twenty or twenty-five years old; they slept with boots and spurs on, whip in hand, and lived in a devil of a noise. I have the six numbers of the *Réalisme* on my desk before me, and there comes forth from these yellowed pages a smell of battle which intoxicates me. I have been all through this myself; I know these passionate convictions of the twentieth year, these fine errors and these fine injustices. You do not know much yet, you are searching still, and your desire is to get a cleared space to demolish everything in order to reconstruct it all again without being frightened at the immensity of the labor, thinking in all good faith that you are about to give birth to a world. These are splendid years, and happy are those who have known them. Later, when we have become wise, we mourn these vast desires.

But making a noise is nothing; the most astounding thing is that these young men brought on a revolution and formulated a complete body of doctrines. Certainly realism is a theory as old as the world ; only it is rejuvenated at each new literary period. Admitting that they invented nothing, that they only continued the movement of the eighteenth century—they had nevertheless the astonishing foresight to raise the flag of realism before the dying agony of romanticism had commenced ; before anyone had yet foreseen the great naturalistic movement, which was about to take place in our literature after Balzac and Stendhal had set the example. They were critical forerunners, they announced with a great deal of noise the new period, and they were so audacious that there was against the little paper an unprecedented outburst. The whole literary press made fun of them, hurled thunderbolts at them. Nobody seemed to understand them.

They themselves, I must confess, did not seem to be well settled in their doctrine. M. Duranty in several places explains that he is yielding to an instinctive impulse in establishing his paper. He is imbued with a feeling of the future; he has thrown himself headlong on this side in order to follow the light. As he put it in the last number: "In the first number the beast Realism could be seen crawling on his belly like those animals born of chaos; later, little by little, their figures became clearer, and finally the wolf, with bristling hairs, walks in the roadway, showing his teeth to the frightened passers-by." This was said in good faith; these young men felt that ideas would come to them in the struggle, that they would become hardened, and that they would in the end succeed in finding the victorious formula. But it was too soon, without doubt. I will tell directly why this first effort was bound to miscarry, in my opinion.

A doctrine does not grow by itself. Men are necessary to stir up people's minds. Our three enthusiasts set out in this fight in M. Courbet and M. Champfleury's footsteps. They were the paving stones which they threw at triumphant romanticism. They took the examples which they had at hand without even distinguishing between the talents, so different, of their two patrons. Moreover, *Le Réalisme* simply contains a study on M. Champfleury, and there are even restrictions in that; as to M. Courbet, he rules still less, he receives commendation only here and there. M. Duranty and his friends widened the question, going back to original principles; spoke of renovating all the arts. A very good story has been told me: It seems Courbet and M. Champfleury were very much frightened at the zeal these young men displayed in immolating all the powerful ones in literature on the altar of realism ; fearing to be compromised, they publicly cut themselves loose from their terrible defenders.

In the main this furious attack was directed against romanticism. We must remember that this was in 1856, and that Victor Hugo reigned in his far-away exile. Just there is the audacity of the innovators, the foreknowledge of the movement which was to increase in speed later. Naturally their theories remained rather cloudy. The articles are a little heavy, a little confused. I am far from accepting all their ideas. They seem like minds, still searching, who struggle to reach a just and precise formula. I am going to indicate by two quotations the points which seem to me absolutely clear.

In the first place it is no school : "This terrible word realism is the opposite of the word school. To say the realistic school is to talk nonsense ; realism signifies the frank and complete expression of individualities ; what it attacks is precisely conventionality, imitation, every kind of school."

Here is the new formula :

"Realism aims at the exact, complete, and sincere reproduction of the social surroundings of the time in which we live, because studies in such a direction are justified by reason, the needs of the understanding, and the public interest, and because they are exempt from all lies and all trickery. . . This reproduction, then, ought to be as simple as possible, so as to be understood by everybody."

I stop here, because we have put our fingers on the principles of the realists of 1856. Remember that they are sunk in the midst of romanticism, and they are going forcibly to accomplish a work of reaction. Then, as to the character of the movement they wished to cause, it is to do just contrary to what the romanticists did. They exalted sincerity, simplicity, and natural-ness; they meant to take their subjects from the *bour-geoisie*, from the common people. And as it was a question of exaggerating to make themselves heard, they restricted the literary field to a singular extent. This was one of their greatest faults. No one will listen to them, because their revolution is too radical, and because a literature cannot shut itself up in the nar-row world in which they seemed anxious to put it.

Yes, without doubt, a literature is more complex than that. We must admit the depicting of all classes. I see no place in which they counsel the application of the naturalistic method to all characters, prince or shep-herd, highborn ladies or dairywomen. You will say this is understood. Not at all; the realism of 1856 was exclusively *bourgeois*. It did not go out of a certain limited circle either in its theories or in its works. It did not possess the breadth which compels recognition.

Another fault which they committed, and which was to be very much regretted, was their violent attack on our entire literature. I have never seen a parallel slaughter. Balzac, even, is not spared; they discussed him, and told him just what they thought of him, and all the time they expressed much admiration for him. I do not speak of Victor Hugo, against whom they launched a thunderbolt. It was essential to strike romanticism on the head. The most unfortunate note is a short criticism on "Mme. Bovary," which had just appeared, so unjust in its tone that it is a matter of profound astonishment to-day. How was it that the realists of 1856 did not understand the decisive argument which Gustave Flaubert brought to bear upon their cause? They were condemned to disappear the next day, while "Mme. Bovary" was to continue their labor victoriously by the all-powerfulness of its style.

To deny poetry, to deny all contemporaneous productions—this savors of the glorious boldness of innovators. But in this case it is necessary to fill up the void which has been made. But M. Champfleury's shoulders were not large enough to fill it up. His talent was very individual, very fresh, and of charming flavor; only he lacked the amplitude, the masterly production which decides literary battles. The soldiers were conquered, because the general refused to march and would not lead them to victory. I put Courbet to one side; I content myself with literature. Courbet is a schoolmaster.

Besides, facts have decided the quarrel. The battle was but a skirmish. But outside of this defeat of the individuals engaged in the affair remains the programme of these three young men, who started up one fine morning with their hands full of truths. They speak first and with a superb haughtiness. Nothing frightens them, they attack every question. Duranty takes charge of the question of doctrine, and furnishes six severe articles in each number; Henri Thulié publishes a great revolutionary essay on the novel; Jules Assézat, the calmest of the three, makes a charge at full speed against the theater of that time. Novel, theater, painting, sculpture—they reform them all! And when the journal was about to go under, M. Duranty, in his

last article, indicated the subjects which had been
mapped out, an endless list of essays of which I will
quote a few: "A Discussion on Literary Prefaces which
have appeared since 1800"; "The Affiliations of the
French Intellect in its Affectation, from the Hotel Ram-
bouillet to Our Own Days"; "A Little History of
Literary Variations;" "A Work on the Comic, the
Tragic, the Fantastic, and the Honest"; etc., etc.

Read these lines which M. Duranty wrote when
addressing those who should continue his work:

"I would advise them to be severe and haughty.
For one year everyone will ask with anger and raillery,
'Who are these young people who have never done
anything and yet who wish to regenerate the world?'
At the end of eighteen months they will have become
men of letters. A writer's value can never be stated
at his beginning. They commence by trying to
scratch him with their nails, with their beak, with
iron, with a diamond, and all the hard and sharp instruments used by a critic; and when they find, after
many vain endeavors, that he is not friable and that he
resists, everyone doffs his hat to him and begs him to
be seated."

Then read this passage: "However, the newspaper
will have lived for six months, without funds, battling
against everything, and I consider that a sufficient
defense. Everything has been agitated. Young men
under thirty years of age, with the gayety born of
want of foresight, have disowned us with all the wit
that any Frenchman whatever can marshal for a
defense or an attack of a position. Others, older and
more experienced, have recognized the cloud which
announces the tempest, and the tidal wave which is

destined to drown them, and they have filled the reviews and the newspapers with their angry lamentations. The more resistance realism meets with, the more inevitably it will conquer. Where there is to-day but one man there will be one hundred when the drum shall be beaten."

These lines are prophetic. They have impressed me deeply. To-day romanticism is dying, naturalism is triumphant. On all sides the new generation is rising. The formula is enlarging; it keeps pace with the century. It is no longer a war of school against school, a quarrel of phrases more or less well constructed : it is rather the movement of the intelligence of the day.

THE "PARISIAN CHRONICLES" OF SAINTE-BEUVE.

IT is known that these chronicles are notes which Sainte-Beuve sent in the most secret manner to *La Revue Suisse*. M. Jules Troubat, in an excellent preface, has explained all the mechanism of these transmissions.

Now that we have attained to the distance necessary to judge the great critic, he appears to us to be possessed above all else with a supple intelligence, curious about all things, but relishing more particularly what was delicate and complicated in things. He himself maintains a happy equilibrium, having a horror of extremes, and irritated by the outbursts of very violent temperaments. To-day all of us who love life are often charmed by Sainte-Beuve's acuteness when we come across certain of his pages in which he has set forth with quiet bravery the experimental method which we are using to-day. Then, on the other hand, we are disconcerted and sorry on finding a Sainte-Beuve who does not carry out his opinions to their natural end, who parades the tastes and the opinions of a *bourgeois*, frightened by the logical conclusions of what he had exposed the day before. Evidently the writer does not tell all that the man thinks; and besides, there was in him something feminine which delighted in hidden implications and vaguenesses.

Nothing proves this better than the " Parisian Chronicles." At Paris he was choked by every kind of relation, and he dreamed of being free somewhere in order to say what he really thought. He therefore sent these notes to the *Revue Suisse*, notes which the editor of this review made into articles forming a regular series. This was not very brave, in my way of thinking. But it would be wrong for us to see in these masked judgments any betrayal of trust. It all depends upon the opinion which Sainte-Beuve held of the rôle which a critic should play. He looked upon it as a public charge. He assumed somewhat the position of a magistrate in discharge of official duties. From this arises his idea that the truth might be brutal and in bad taste. He seemed to think that he had charge of souls; all sorts of other than literary considerations entered into his judgments; you never had the exact truth from him, but a truth set up to meet the wants of the moment; and if you wanted to know just what he thought you must read between the lines, and be well acquainted with the subject which he was treating, know it as well as he did, and re-establish your facts from that by means of discreet deductions. It was a very amusing task, but a horribly complicated one.

Really we ought first to examine this question : the true purpose of criticism, and how attained. I believe, in fact, that an absolute frankness is healthier than all this crafty politeness. If it is necessary to kill a man you might as well cut his head off at once as assassinate him with pin pricks. I know very well that under this brutal system of saying everything, worldly relations are no longer possible; besides, it has a scientific rigor which frightens men of letters. But the work seems to me more honest and more moral. Moreover, on Sainte-Beuve's part it was not only prudence, it was the way he was made.

To return to the "Parisian Chronicles": the revelations which they make are not very terrible. I do not know whether the editor has stricken out the things which seemed too harsh to him, but it surprises me that Sainte-Beuve thought it necessary to disguise his authorship in order to express such opinions. Here is found again his desertion of the romantic camp, his criticisms of Hugo, whom he flattered the day before. Then the instinctive horror which he felt for Balzac; but these are all attitudes with which we were familiar. It must be that truth frightened Sainte-Beuve very much to make him think it necessary to go to Switzerland when he had such simple things to say.

What has impressed me is this, that the day after the production of "Les Burgraves" Sainte-Beuve expressed about the stage almost the same ideas which I defend, and which still seem revolutionary to-day. Here I will give a few quotations.

This is what Sainte-Beuve says of "Les Burgraves," which he has not even seen played yet: "It seems indeed that it is fine, but above all solemn, writes Janin; in good French, tiresome. You listen to it, but without feeling any pleasure." This same Janin, who has praised it through necessity in *Les Débats*, said out loud in the crowded foyer of the theater, so that anyone who wanted to could hear him: "If I were Minister of the Interior I would decorate the one who hissed it first." This really showed some courage. And later on he writes these lines, full of delightful wickedness: "'Les Burgraves' has not really succeeded; the piece is not a success, notwithstanding the reports. The first

three times the house was filled with friends ; the fourth
or fifth time the public hissed so much toward the end
that they found it necessary to lower the curtain.
Since that time the representations are always more or
less stormy. The newspapers favorable to Hugo . . .
say that this fact is unexplainable, and that there is I
know not what cabal against it. Nothing is easier to
explain. They hiss ; Hugo does not like this word, and
says before the actors : ' They disturb my play.' The
actors, who are a little malicious, have said since that
day ' disturb ' instead of ' hiss.' It is to be hoped
that ' Judith ' (or any other play) will succeed, and
that it will not be ' disturbed.' This word is a curious
one, coming from the school of proper words."

Upon the whole, Sainte-Beuve greets " Lucrèce," by
Ponsard, as a protestation against the romantic school.
It manifestly won his sympathy, even though he does
not hail it as a *chef-d'œuvre*. However, I suppose he
was not deceived about the absolute value of the work ;
he regarded it simply as a good howitzer in the war he
was waging.

But here is the passage which has impressed me
most : " Decidedly the school is drawing near its end [the
romantic school] ; we must ' bore for another ' ; the
public will not awaken except for an unforeseen novelty.
I hope that this revolution will come from the theater,
and from the midst of our anarchy ; there will burst
forth from that direction a literary 18th Brumaire. The
theater, the ground most affected by modern art, is also
the one which, with us, has produced the least, and has
belied all our hopes. For what admirable yet unfruit-
ful preparations have we not made for more than
twenty years. Translations of foreign plays, analytical

and critical studies, essays, and specimens of written
dramas: ' Barricades,' ' États de Blois,' ' Clara Gazul,'
' Soirées de Neuilly,' dramas by M. de Rêmusat,
modern prefaces, ' Cromwell ' — and then what?
' Hernani '! then nothing—a heavy fall ! Dumas has
squandered his powers ; De Vigny has never exerted
himself ; Hugo has overloaded himself. It is in the
theater that so much remains to be done, and here
finally, before a *blasé* public, which they will awaken—
the great ideas stirring in the air for the last fifty years
will be given expression."

Remember that this was written in 1843, thirty-six
years ago. Now I do not say anything different to-day.
However, it has come to pass in a way that Sainte-
Beuve never foresaw. The awakening, which he expected by means of the stage, has taken place through
the novel. It is Balzac—this Balzac whose power he
never understood—who has accomplished the literary
18th Brumaire of which he spoke. To-day the situation
on the stage is almost the same ; we look, as usual, for
a stroke of genius to drag us out of our anarchy ; only
it has become evident that the theater will never emerge
from its mess but by following the naturalistic novel
on its path. Sainte-Beuve exhibits the situation, but
he foresees nothing. The facts, as we see them now,
show where the strength of the century lies—in Balzac
and his followers, who, I think, will next conquer the
stage by the employment of their methods.

At the end of the volume Sainte-Beuve laments the
dramatic miscarriage of his age. He does not clearly
see why all has crumbled, but he states the fact of the
disaster. According to him, we can still hope even after
" Hernani." " At the commencement of 1830," he says,

" ' Hernani ' came, bringing a change, and was like the awakening of a new hope; it was strange, it was partly historic, it was more than human, and decidedly supernatural; but, more than that, it had sparkle, poetry, novelty, and audacity." However, this hope was soon disappointed by what followed " Hernani "; the plays which the romantic school produced afterward provoked him, and he burst forth with this cry : " History falsified, an absence of study in the subjects, something monstrous and furious in the sentiments and the passions—this is what has burst forth and overflowed us ; we believed we were clearing the way and opening a passage to a chivalric and audacious army, but withal civilized, and it has turned out to be an invasion by a horde of barbarians."

Sainte-Beuve remains bewildered. He no longer knows in what direction things are going, he no longer dares to prophesy at all. The labor of the century escapes him entirely. He does not even seem to understand that if romanticism goes to pieces so quickly, it is because it brings with it the immediate causes of dissolution. He does not understand either that the outburst of 1830 was a simple cry for deliverance, that the true man of the century is Balzac, that romanticism, in a word, is the initial and troubled period of naturalism. From this come his perplexities on the dramatic side of the epoch. He talks about this thing with the intelligence of an amateur ; he has not thrown a single ray of light on the literary evolution which has been accomplished in the novel and which will be accomplished on the stage.

Besides, in my opinion, a critic who has not understood Balzac may be a very delicate analyzer and may possess a very flexible intelligence, but he is not, most assuredly, one of those superior intellects who have a perfect understanding of their age. I am well aware that there was in this case a natural antipathy, but, while loving neither the man nor his work, the point was to divine the decisive influence which Balzac was to have over the second half of the century.

Listen to the way in which he speaks of Balzac, apropos of the success which Eugène Sue had just attained with his " Mystères de Paris : " " What is best in his coming [the coming of Eugène Sue] is that he sweeps the ground clear and simplifies it. Balzac and Frédéric Soulié are put to one side. Balzac, ruined, and more than ruined, has gone to Saint Petersburg, giving out in the newspapers that he has only gone for his health and that he has decided to write nothing on Russia." Can we stand this to-day? " Les Mystères de Paris " sweeping away Balzac's works ! Eugène Sue and Frédéric Soulié put for one instant on a par with the author of " La Comédie Humaine "! These are some of the foolish criticisms that a short-sighted critic alone could make. When a man can see no more clearly into the work and the strength of a writer than this, doubts arise as to the soundness of his critical faculty in general, and he loses at once all the rights which he may have had to lay down definite judgments.

I will give one more quotation : " Balzac's novel ' Modeste Mignon ' is dedicated to ' a foreigner, daughter of an enslaved land, an angel in her love, a demon in her imagination,' etc. Has anyone ever read such gibberish ? Why does not ridicule scourge such writers, and through what concession does a newspaper which respects itself open its columns to them ? This novel of Balzac's was announced several days ago, in *Les Débats*, by a letter from the author the most ambiguous, the most affected and ridiculous that anyone could read, all this to get up some curiosity in the public mind. They who insert such fiddle-faddle despise it, doubtless, but they think they must serve to the public what they ask for."

All Sainte-Beuve's method of working is shown here. He stops at the romantic style of a dedication, and he does not penetrate to Balzac's true strength, that naturalistic method which is about to appear. He utters the judgment of an exasperated rhetorician ; he does not rise to the rôle of the analyzer, who with thorough self-mastery sets forth clearly the strength of a writer. Passion blinded him. The exuberant temperament of Balzac took away his sense of justice. In the last years of his life he still showed himself stupefied at the decisive influence of Stendhal and Balzac on the French novel. He died without caring to understand. This is for me a fact which settles the caliber of Sainte-Beuve. He was like one of those nobles of the old *régime*, who, after having adopted the ideas of the Revolution, refused to go to the end, profoundly worried and not understanding it. He applied the scientific method to criticism, only the old-fashioned man in him revolted when he saw this method carried into the novel with a revolutionary violence. Thence come these contradictions in a. critic who wished to master everything, and who, after having thrown light on a thousand minor points, refused to understand through what new gaps the broad daylight was to come.

HECTOR BERLIOZ.

I HAVE just read a book which has profoundly touched me—" The Unpublished Correspondence of Hector Berlioz." I do not intend to speak of music —I should be incompetent. I wish merely to exhibit a particular point of view, to study in Berlioz only the man of genius, for so long a time misunderstood, exasperated by the fierce daily struggle, hooted at and hissed at in France, while they applauded him in foreign lands, triumphing at last only in his death, after having borne for six years the agony of the final failure of " Les Troyeans."

Further than this my work will be very simple, as I shall confine myself to quotations. Here are the true facts :

In an excellent biographical notice with which M. Daniel Bernard has introduced " La Correspondence " I find, in the first place, some precious information. You must call to mind the stories which were current about Berlioz during his life. They made him out to be a fool and a knave, an artist whose immeasurable pride could tolerate no rival. The newspapers of the time painted him thus: " This unappreciated musician despises profoundly what is commonly called the public, but in compensation he has only a moderate amount of esteem for the artists who are his contemporaries. If you mention Meyerbeer—' Hum ! hum ! he has some talent, I do not deny it, but he sacrifices it to the demands of fashion.' And M. Auber? 'Composer of quadrilles and songs.' Bellini? Donizetti? 'Italians! Italians! Light musicians, much too light.'"

And this is not all. As M. Daniel Bernard tells us, they credited Berlioz with the most ridiculous criticisms. A man of struggles, having to battle in order to assert his ideas, he had fortified himself behind his regular short article in the *Journal des Débats*, in which he bombarded his numerous adversaries, who treated him with the current stupidity. It was no use to say white; they made him out to have said black. This is a strange, astonishing phenomenon, which is always taking place. The thing written, which everyone can read, ought to be a fact, it would seem. Well, it is not at all. Berlioz, writing about Mozart's "Idoménée": "What a miracle of beauty! What music! How pure! What an odor of antiquity!" And they read: "Mozart has no talent; nobody has any talent; I alone invented music." Explain this phenomenon if you can; it takes place every time that an artist sure of his own power addresses the limited mind of the average fool.

"Once for all," says M. Daniel Bernard, "let us establish the fact that Berlioz never made any pretension to the rôle which certain composers have claimed since. He did not boast of being the 'only' one of his kind, and did not believe that before he came music was an unknown, shadowy, uncultivated science; far from despising the ancients he bows before them, reverently worshiping the gods of symphony. He only claimed (what it seems to us he justified) that he was continuing and enlarging the old musical traditions, and improving them, thanks to modern resources."

Moreover, he had ardent likings. He defended Liszt with an extraordinary passion. If he made a continual massacre of comic operas, he was seized with a veritable rush of devotion toward the works which he loved. He was a believer in himself, with a tinge of fanaticism in his ideas, violently irritated by the injustice of his contemporaries. I borrow a few more lines from M. Daniel Bernard, which recapitulate very clearly Berlioz's troubled life :

" There existed excellent reasons why Berlioz should be attacked, discussed, and calumniated by his competitors, who, having talent, could not forgive him for having genius, and by those, much more numerous, who, possessing neither talent nor genius, rushed to the assault of no matter what genuine reputation, without hope of benefiting themselves in any way, and only for the mere pleasure of destruction. Crowned with laurels in foreign lands, Berlioz was irritated on finding in the leaves of these triumphant crowns Parisian mosquitoes which stung him. He was more preoccupied with the hatred which he encountered in his own country than the triumphant ovations which awaited him beyond its borders—in London, in Saint Petersburg, in Vienna, in Weimar, and Lowenberg."

One last quotation of M. Daniel Bernard, a phrase which struck me as being very well put : " Certain critics thought they had destroyed him once and for all, or they imagined that they so thought ; for, in truth, they were not very sure of it."

But it is time to let Berlioz speak for himself. I will take paragraphs from here and there, in which he gives expression to all his bitterness against Paris and France. It is an ever open wound ; it is a continual revolt ,against stupidity, mingled with a deep sorrow, at finding himself chased from his own country.

The 14th of January, 1848, he writes from London to M. Auguste Morel: "As to France, I no longer think of her. . . The reason is this: after comparing together the impressions which my music has produced on all the audiences of Europe who have listened to it, I am forced to conclude that it is the Parisian audiences who understand it the least. Is it not strange that at the concerts of the Conservatoire they play the works of all those who have any name whatsoever except mine? Is it not offensive for me to see the Opera having always recourse to those musical bunglers, and its directors always armed against me with prejudices which I should blush to combat if I tried to force their hand? Does not the press become every day more base? Do you ever see anything now (with rare exceptions) but intrigue, base transactions, and idiocy? . . . And do you suppose that I am the dupe of a crowd of people, with forced smiles on their faces, who conceal their nails and their teeth only because they know I have claws and means of defense? To see everywhere only imbecility, indifference, ingratitude, or terror—that is my lot in Paris."

The 15th of March, 1848, he writes from London to M. Joseph d'Ortigue: "I can no longer think of a musical career anywhere except in England or Russia. It is a long time ago now since I gave up France as hopeless; the last revolution makes my decision more firm and more indispensable. I had to struggle under the old government against hatred disseminated by newspaper critics, against the absurdity of those who govern our theaters, and the indifference of the public;

I should now have in addition the great crowd of grand composers which the Republic has just hatched, with their music—popular, philanthropic, national, and economic. France, from a musical point of view, is but a country of idiots and rogues; one must be devilishly patriotic not to recognize this."

The 21st of January, 1852, he wrote from Paris to M. Alexis Levoff: "Nothing further is possible in Paris; and I think that next month I shall return to England, where the desire to love music is, at least, real and persistent. Here every place is taken; men of little ability eat up everything among them, and one witnesses the fights and repasts of these dogs with as much anger as disgust. The judgments of the press and the public are so absurd and so frivolous that no other nation can approach them."

The 9th of January, 1856, he writes from Paris to M. Auguste Morel: "On every side all you can see are tricks, meannesses, fooleries, knaveries, nonsense, roguery, knaves, fools, mean men, and tricksters. I remove myself more and more apart from this empoisoned world of poisoners."

The 21st of February, 1861, he wrote from Paris to his son Louis Berlioz: "The professors of notes [musical notes] have provoked me at last; you have seen in my article of the 19th to what lengths they have gone, and what a knock on the head they obliged me to give them. Read this to Morel, who was insulted by them some years ago. . . I have never had so many windmills to battle with as this year. I am surrounded by all kinds of fools. There are times when I am choked with anger."

I could multiply these quotations, in which we see

this poor, great man exasperated in the struggle against the attacks which are made against his genius. Anger carries him out of himself; epithets run out one after another; he is continually under arms to repulse the attacks; and you perceive an incurable sadness in his bosom, the cut of the knife that the frivolity of his dear and detested Paris has planted full in his heart, and from which he will die. In his sadness consolation comes to him only from foreigners. When he smiles it is at his triumphs in some distant place, in Berlin or in London.

"I received a letter yesterday, from an unknown gentleman, on my share of ' Les Troyeans.' He told me that the Parisians were accustomed to a music more indulgent than mine. This expression has delighted me." (Letter to Mme. Ernst, Paris, December 14, 1864.)

"Here is another bulletin from the great army of bulletins. . . The second representation of ' Beatrice ' at Weimar was all they had told me it would be; I was called before the curtain after the first and second acts. I will spare you all the charming flatteries addressed to me by the artists and the grand duke." (Letter written to M. and Mme. Massart, Lowenberg, April 19, 1863.)

"I write you three lines so that you may know that I obtained a wonderful success last evening. Called before the curtain I cannot tell you how many times, hailed both [*sic*] as composer and leader of the orchestra. This morning I read in *The Times, The Morning Post, The Morning Herald, The Advertiser*, and still others, dithyrambics such as have never been written about me before. I have just written to M. Bertin, so that our friend Raymond, of the *Journal des Debats*, can make a *pot-pourri* of all these articles, so that they will at least know the thing as it is." (Letter to M. Joseph d'Ortigue, London, 24th of March, 1852.)

And such was his life to his last hour: hooted at in France, applauded by foreigners. I will terminate my quotations by a page of cruel irony. It had been announced that Berlioz was about to set out for Germany, where he had been appointed chapel master. It was then the 22d of January, 1834; he wrote the following letter to M. Brandus :

" The fact is that I am about to quit France some day for several years, but the orchestra the direction of which has been given to me is not in Germany. And since everything is known in this devil of a Paris, I wish to tell you now the place of my future residence. I am appointed director-general of the private concerts of Queen Ora, at Madagascar. The orchestra of her Majesty Ora, is composed of Malayan artists, who are very distinguished in their own country, and a few Malgaches of great talent. They do not like white people, it is true, and I should have a great deal to suffer in this strange country, in the first days, if so many people in Europe had not taken pains to blacken me. I hope thus to reach my new surroundings bronzed against their viciousness. In the meantime, be kind enough to say to your readers that I shall continue to dwell in Paris as much as possible, to go to the theaters as little as possible, but to go there nevertheless, and to fulfill my duties as critic as before, nay, even more carefully. I wish as a conclusion to give myself up to it to my heart's content, all the more that there are no newspapers at Madagascar."

Now what moral can be drawn from all this? Since Berlioz's death we know what his triumph has been. To-day we bow reverently before his tomb, and proclaim him the glory of our modern school. This great man whom they vilified, whom they dragged in the gutter during his life, is applauded in his coffin. All the lies circulated about him, all the odious and ridiculous stories, all the silly attacks, all the efforts of hatred and envy to soil him have disappeared like dust swept away by the wind ; and he remains standing alone in his glory. It is London, it is St. Petersburg, it is Berlin, alas! which were right in opposition to Paris. But do you think that this example will cure the crowd of its frivolity, and fools of their spite, when brought face to face with individual talent? Ah, no! To-morrow an original musician may be born, and he will find exactly the same hisses, the same calumnies, and will have to commence exactly the same battle should he desire the same victory. Stupidity and unfairness are eternal.

CHAUDES–AIGUES AND BALZAC.

I HAVE made a find. I have discovered a volume entitled " The Modern Writers of France." It was published by Gasselin in 1841, and its author was a critic named Chaudes-Aigues, who has been dead some twenty-five or thirty years, I believe, and who to-day is completely forgotten. I remember to have read in the *Revue de Paris* an article in which Asselineau speaks of this Chaudes-Aigues as a talented man of letters, endowed with a delicate and sagacious mind. At any rate, without being in the first rank, Chaudes-Aigues occupied an honorable place in the literature of the age. One may say that he represented the average opinion; that he occupied then such a place as many of our critics who are attentively listened to do to-day. Besides, the proof that his essays were valuable is that he found a publisher willing to gather them up into a book.

Now, in turning the leaves of this volume, I have come across a criticism on Balzac which nowadays is the height of absurdity. It is complete, and it sums up the absurdity of an epoch. Here we witness this everlasting rage of commonplace natures and this eternal negation that the blind throw at powerful personalities. But what makes it funny is that we are already posterity, and we are seized with laughter when we put Balzac face to face with Chaude-Aigues, this giant of the modern novel, beside this ridiculous nonentity, who tries to bespatter him with mud and only succeeds in bespattering himself. What a fine spectacle, and what a lesson! Snarl, insult, lie, be fools, denounce, make yourselves spies and jailers, drag their works into the mud, and see the result. Those whom you defame have grown and shine in the light of your grandchildren's admiration, while your odious and imbecile judgments, when they are found again, make the remembrance of you an object of shame and a laughing-stock.

I wish to resurrect Chaudes-Aigues. It will be a good example to hold up before our barkers of to-day. It is necessary to make a certain school of criticism smell its own filth. You will see that nothing is changed. The accusations are always of the same nature, and talent does not fare any worse.

I will therefore content myself with certain quotations. It will be sufficient to have some samples under our eyes. In the first place, Chaudes-Aigues sings a triumphant pæan, filling ten pages, because Balzac has taken the liberty of making certain changes in the classification of his works. We know that the great novelist conceived only as an afterthought the idea of connecting his novels by a common tie, under the comprehensive title of " La Comédie Humaine," and even then he hesitated a little, and modified the order of the different parts several times. There was evidently nothing in all that that lessened the novelist's talent ; we do not busy ourselves with these things to-day ; but Chaudes-Aigues is exultant ; he imagines that he has confounded Balzac in waging this war of details against him ; and when he has proved that certain works are not in their proper place he exults, he

boasts of having put "La Comêdie Humaine" in the
dust. Poor man! He says in conclusion: "Once we
have brought to the meditations of M. de Balzac's
most enthusiastic admirers this new inventory of his
works, we shall listen with indifferent ears to M. de
Balzac's unbounded boasts of the architectural marvels
of which he dreams. Who could think, however, without smiles of this future cathedral of M. de Balzac?"
Certainly we smile to-day, but we smile at M. Chaudes-
Aigues.

What put Chaudes-Aigues beside himself was more
especially Balzac's attitude. Listen to him: "Each
time that M. de Balzac rolls into the public square
one of the stones of his edifice, it is to the sound of a
trumpet, and with a blatant preface in which he takes
a particular care to announce that if the temple is not
yet finished it is only on account of the immensity
of the design." Naturally Balzac would be accused of
being a charlatan; that was in the order of things.
He had his ideas to defend. He fought boldly in the
midst of heated adversaries; and this was pure char-
latanism! Besides, his masterpieces were so outrageous as to create a great noise, and his publishers
committed the crime of wishing to sell them. Chaudes-
Aigues, in addition, shrugs his shoulders over "La
Comêdie Humaine." He is filled with pity for it. "It
is now five or six years since M. de Balzac," he says,
"conceived a singular way of escaping from the sovereign jurisdiction of the critics; he declared haughtily,
with an imperturbable *sang-froid*, that his novels
could not finally be judged, nor, indeed, at all, at present,
because his novels were not distinct works, separate one
from the other, rivals, so to speak, each one starting from

an individual inspiration, and reaching conclusions essentially diverse ; but rather were they fragments of a gigantic monument, indispensable stones of a colossal palace in which he desired to lodge his country. Moderately irritated by this injunction on the part of the writer, so as to protect from attack his own incompetency, the critic contents himself with shrugging his shoulders in indulgent pity." See this man of genius, whose ambition it is to build a monument, and who prays the critic to give him time ! Such pretenses, can they be tolerated ? Folly has no patience.

But this is only the beginning. Chaudes-Aigues, with a fillip, overthrows "La Comédie Humaine." Balzac is accused of lying and of inability ; he has no general plan ; he only wishes to impose upon the critic, and he exhausts his powers in meaningless efforts. Then he goes on to prove that his novels, taken separately, offer neither originality, nor interest, nor talent—nothing, nothing at all, absolute emptiness.

In the first place, Balzac invented nothing. In all his works there are but two types, a man of genius misunderstood and struggling, a woman of heart devoted to all kinds of sacrifices. " *Louis Lambert* and *Mme. de Vienmesnil,*" said Chaudes-Aigues, "to continue a very just comparison, are the first proofs of the only two portraits which he has drawn. Unhappily for M. de Balzac, the invention of these two portraits cannot be ascribed to him ; he has only the merit of being a skillful reproducer, in this case. Like the engraver reproducing the painter's idea on wood or steel, or like the pupil guiding the timid pencil over the traces left by the master's brush, he has copied pictures created by other brains than his own." And further on:

" M. de Balzac has not been very careful in hiding his
larcenies when, instead of principal characters, it is a
question of secondary ones and of details. In order to
attack him only on a ground which shall be favorable
to him, we will quote, in support of our assertions, his
two most popular works—'Eugénie Grandet' and 'Le
Lys dans la Vallée : the first one in which *L'Avare* and
Melmoth, a little affected and contracted, it is true,
are constantly before the author, each in turn; the
second which, in the general dispositions and scenic
effects, is made up of the shreds and patches of 'Le
Volupté'! Molière! Mathurin! Hoffman! Sainte-
Beuve! We must be just. M. de Balzac goes about
it in earnest, and it is not to the poor that he betakes
himself." Balzac pillaging from Sainte-Beuve—that is
the last straw, as we say to-day. Besides, the accusation of plagiarizing is equally in the order of things.
Chaudes-Aigues would not be complete if he did not
treat Balzac as a robber. The Chaudes-Aigueses of
to-day continue the tradition.

Now let us pass to his criticism of Balzac's style.
You are going to see how radically ignorant Balzac is
of the proper use of language. "M. de Balzac is a perfect stranger to the most common notions of syntax;
there is not in the art of writing any elementary principle of which he seems to have even a vague idea.
According to his pleasure he makes passive verbs
active, and *vice versa ;* or else he ranges in the category
of irregular or absolute verbs those which are properly
neuter. Nearly every word is forced, under his pen,
into impossible connections. With an audacity and an
assurance truly fabulous he establishes between nouns
of which he knows neither the precise significance nor

real origin, and adjectives of whose proper force he is entirely ignorant, alliances which run counter at one and the same time to tradition, vocabulary, and taste. As to pronouns, relative and possessive, and adverbs, the novelist uses them as detachments of light cavalry which are deployed to hang on the rear of a flying army so as to increase the rout and the carnage. It is his reserve corps, intended at critical moments to make the massacre of the language more complete." Here is irony for you. Chaudes-Aigues may be sure of one thing, and that is that one page of Balzac, even though incorrect, has more force in it than a whole volume of his articles. Our language has been in a transitional state since the beginning of the century, brought about by our literary struggles, and it is a singular thing to try to judge Balzac's style by the rules of La Harpe. Chaudes-Aigues simply denies the modern evolution in the matter of style, this great enrichment of the language, this flood of new ideas, this color, and, I will say, this perfume introduced into the sentence. No doubt there will be necessary some tribunal to regulate all this later. But, to sneer and become indignant over the movement is not to understand it ; it is only a proof of cerebral infirmity.

Let us take up the question of morality. Here Chaudes-Aigues becomes superb. It seems to me as if I heard our critics and biographers of to-day thundering against naturalism. It is abundantly amusing. I am embarrassed with the wealth of quotation. "One of M. de Balzac's pretensions toward which we should be pitiless," he says, "and that which the general title of his works emphatically reveals, is to understand to the bottom the morals of his age and to paint them

with a vigorous truth.   What are the morals which
M. de Balzac paints?   Ignoble and disgusting morals,
with avarice and lust as their only motives.   If we are
to believe the pretended philosophical historian, money
and vice are the ordinary and only objects for which
men of to-day strive; unnatural desires, depraved tastes,
infamous inclinations animate the France of the nineteenth century exclusively, this daughter of Jean
Jacques and Napoleon!   Not an honorable sentiment,
not an honest idea, no matter in what direction you
turn your eyes.   France—for it is the portrait of France
which the author puts before us—is peopled with black-
guards covered with gold lace, bandits more or less dis-
guised by a mask, women who have reached the last
limits of corruption, or are in the course of being
corrupted.   A new Sodom whose iniquities call the fire
from heaven.   That is to say, dungeons, brothels,
the galleys would be asylums of virtue, of probity and
innocence compared to the civilized cities of M. de
Balzac."   Everything is put just as you see it, Sodom,
Jean Jacques, and Napoleon.   And all this is said about
our works to-day, and they throw Balzac at our heads,
saying that Balzac at least allotted a certain space to
virtue, that a high morality is always to be found in his
works!   The truth is that the Chaudes-Aigueses of to-
morrow will throw us at the heads of the twentieth
century novelists, accusing them in their turn of a
shameless immorality.

But wait, this is not the end.   Here is the finest of
all; you could almost imagine that you heard critics
speaking with whom you are well acquainted; you
could imagine you were reading an article published
yesterday on some of the novels whose titles you know:

"Oh, yes ! without doubt there are in the society of the present infamies and disgraces, fortunes whose sources are unspeakable, usurped positions, occupations exercised in a base manner, dishonorable industries, selfishness pushed even to cowardice and to villainy, unmentionable baseness. But to say that there is only this is an unpardonable lie ! To please one's self by putting into a book subjects of this nature, to enlarge upon them, to idealize and caress them, to make them a lasting spectacle for the crowd, to try to make them objects of admiration and enthusiasm, this is the wrong of it all. Happily there are to-day more than ever, in the hearts of a certain class of young men of whom M. de Balzac does not even suspect the existence, disinterested and noble instincts, generous passions, sincere and ardent convictions, which will not follow nor uncover bad examples any more than pernicious lessons. Under this manure which M. de Balzac stirs up with too amorous hands is a virginal and fertile soil, developing in silence at this very moment precious germs. . . But to whom are we speaking? and could the author of ' La Fille aux Yeux d'Or ' be expected to understand us? All that we have to say of M. de Balzac is that he has in no sense unraveled the philosophical spirit of his age nor of its serious literature. . . Placed during his lifetime even between Mlle. Scudéry, whose sickly fecundity he has, and the Marquis de Sade, whose work he continues with rare success in another order of ideas, he will be able to see shortly from his own windows the corpse of his reputation dragged to the gibbet."

Now this is complete. Here is the Marquis de Sade. I have been waiting for him. He ought to be at the

feast. You cannot imagine what use criticism makes
of the Marquis de Sade. He is the finishing touch
of Chaudes-Aigues' past, present, and future. A novelist cannot risk exposing a human sore without their
bespattering him with this absurd comparison, which
proves one thing—the complete ignorance of those who
employ it. But let me amuse myself with the extraordinary clairvoyance of the prophet Chaudes-Aigues.
Where are the youth who were to drag Balzac to the
gibbet? To-day the sons and grandsons of Balzac triumph. This novelist of genius, who had in no sense
grasped serious literature, nor the philosophical spirit
of the age, has left behind him the scientific formula of
our actual literature. If thy equals at the present hour,
O Chaudes-Aigues, prophesy with the same certainty,
those whom they condemn to the sewer may well
rejoice, for there surely awaits them a high and noble
glory.

Let us finish. But I must again make a long quotation. Chaudes-Aigues, in a last paragraph of two pages,
thinks to finish Balzac with a stunning blow. He
blames him for introducing so often his own personality; he speaks of his pride; he calls him squarely a
fool. Read and meditate on these pages:

"We would willingly have witnessed, from the position of impassive and indifferent spectators, the decline
of M. de Balzac, a false meteor about to plunge back
silently into the pool of forbidding octavos whence
he came, if M. de Balzac, in proportion as he declines,
did not do his best to tire the public's patience
by promenading his own personality. M. de Balzac,
as a result of discovering his resemblance, if not his
superiority, to all the great men of ancient and modern

times, has finally reached such a height in his own
estimation that it would show incredible modesty if
he should proclaim himself, as they assure us he will, as a
candidate for the Academy. To consent to thus share
the empire of letters with thirty-nine rivals, to be willing to swap a throne for an armchair — that would
be indeed an abdication. . . The members of the
Institute will not give place, we trust, to a buffoon of
whom the public is tired. . . When M. de Balzac
proclaims himself, by aid of advertisements, an incomparable author, the finest of modern novelists, the
foremost composer of masterpieces, in the lump, or
one by one, it is an absurdity that recalls Lafontaine's frog, but which the booksellers are at perfect
liberty, on the whole, to give to an author so as
to get their money. When M. de Balzac sets himself
up as a writer beside whom Richardson, Walter Scott,
and others are small potatoes, this also, up to a certain
point, can be tolerated as a delicious subject for a
joke. But when M. de Balzac, not content with having
put his name before the public by means of preface
and paying advertisement, seizes upon all occasions to
lavish flattery upon himself, and trumps up such occasions at pleasure—when, under a pretext to-day of
clearing up a question of literary rights, to-morrow of
making known the wrong done to the French book-
seller by the Belgian pirated books, the next day of
refuting an opinion passed upon him in a critical article, another day of proposing the modification of the
civil or penal code—when, in short, M. de Balzac, inces-
santly preoccupied with his own individual importance,
gives expression to this double rôle of Maréchal of
France and emperor, which he plays alternately—

this is a thing which can be tolerated no longer, this is a thing which is no longer laughable, for this is pride pushed to the border of idiocy. To oppose the smallness of the merit to the extravagance of the ambition was, in such a case, a duty which philosophic criticism could not dispense with."

My ears ring. Is it Balzac of whom they speak, or is it another? Did this article appear thirty years ago, or only this morning? Was it by Chaudes-Aigues, or was it by ——? Put a name here. Poor, great Balzac, fallen under the ferule of a dunce because he worked too hard, because his personality overflowed inevitably, because his days were rounded out with the faith of great workers. Ah, what a vengeance is his to-day! But he has suffered, and he is no longer here.

You will say to me: "Enough of this; you are right; this Chaudes-Aigues is an idiot. What made you think of such a strange idea as digging up this mass of folly? It is not funny; it is tiresome; it is beyond all reason. At the present day everybody is agreed that Balzac is the great novelist of the century. It is unnecessary to try to prove it, to display the foolish things which long forgotten critics said on their own account. Give us a respite from your Chaudes-Aigues."

And I shall reply: "Granted that Chaudes-Aigues is an idiot; that the quotations which I have borrowed from him have become silly and tiresome. But it is worth while to point out that Chaudes-Aigues was, in his time, a distinguished critic, listened to and read by a public whose intelligence he spoiled, and who thought as he. His essay is written correctly, except for certain mistakes and much nonsense. He surely thought he was doing a work of justice and morality. But it has proved that thirty years were sufficient to change him into a buffoon whom you cannot read without amusement. Well, how many Chaudes-Aigueses do you think we could number in our own times? and think with what bursts of laughter our grandsons will read the articles of these gentlemen. This makes me happy, that is all."

JULES JANIN AND BALZAC.

L ATELY I amused myself with giving some extracts from a most incredible essay which the now forgotten critic Chaudes-Aigues had formerly written against our great Balzac. To-day I shall take the further pleasure of reproducing certain passages from an article published by Jules Janin upon the author of "La Comédie Humaine" in the *Revue de Paris* in the number for July, 1839.

Chaudes-Aigues was almost an unknown, a man without much authority as a critic, and whose imbecility was of no great consequence. But Jules Janin—*diable!* this is getting serious. Remember that Jules Janin was solemnly crowned the prince of critics, that for forty years the world bent beneath his rod, that nothing has equaled his celebrity, unless it be the oblivion into which he has fallen at once and forever. A prolific novelist, a dramatic critic of acknowledged ability, he seemed big enough to understand Balzac. Well, you shall hear.

It must be said that Balzac had just handled the press roughly in his novel of "Illusions Perdues." Janin thought he ought to take up the gloves for journalism. In those days one was astonished to find that a novelist who had been slaughtered by the newspapers, and dragged in the mud every morning, had the audacity to be dissatisfied and to accuse his defamers of unfairness and ignorance. Balzac did not mince matters;

in the *Revue*, which belonged to him, he squarely
declared that the newspapers assumed an "ignoble"
attitude toward him. Moreover, he never pardoned
them. These are things which we have far too much
forgotten nowadays, when we try to crush the living
under the remembrance of the distinguished dead. Let
us add that Janin, in making himself the defender of
the press, was meanly the executor of the bitterness of
La Revue de Paris, which had just lost its famous suit
against Balzac.

But let us come to the quotations. I give them in
the order in which they present themselves.

In the first place, Janin jokes very pleasantly. He
was forced to read the "Illusions Perdues," and this was
a frightful punishment for him. For one moment he
thought to escape the drudgery, and he cried out:
"Immediately I very happily returned to those old
books which have at once a middle, a beginning, and
an end,—noble masterpieces, the contemplation of which
makes you so much better. On the contrary, all these
modern tortures, written at haphazard, without any plan,
any end, as if one were drawing on paper the most fantastic castles in Spain, make you so impatient that you
can hardly contain yourself." This is his declaration
of faith. "Without any plan, any end" is very good.
This recalls Sainte-Beuve, who preferred "Le Voyage
autour de ma Chambre" to "La Chartreuse de Parme."

Again: "David Séchard considered himself very lucky
to replace his father at any price, so as to be able to
make his friend Lucien foreman of a printing office, at a
salary of fifty francs per month. I forgot to tell you that
Mme. Chardon, the mother, earned thirty sous a day
caring for the sick; her daughter, twenty sous a day

working for a washerwoman.　This sound of money and
this horrible odor of copper coin will often come up in
my story; but whose fault is it but M. de Balzac's, who
makes the destiny of his heroes, indeed of nearly all
his heroes, depend upon a piece of fifty centimes?"
And farther on: "Of the 2000 francs which he had
brought to Paris, there remained to him not more than
360 francs.　He took lodgings in the Rue de Cluny,
near La Sorbonne; he paid 40 sous for a ċab; there
remained to him then but 358 francs.　In order to read
M. de Balzac's novels with benefit you must at least
know a little arithmetic and a little algebra; if not,
they lose a great deal of their charm; also please don't
forget that these minute details are exact, and that I
am incapable of inventing them."

I believe that, by George!　He is intelligent—this
good Janin.　The prince of critics did not understand
that Balzac's great originality consisted in giving money
its terrible modern rôle in literature.

But the most amusing reproach which Janin makes
against him is that he repeats, that he has but one
theme.　This is too droll when you recall the fact that
the aforesaid Janin made over for forty years the same
article in the front page of the *Débats*.　Forty years
of the same empty prattle, forty years of useless and
flowery criticism.　Is it not abominable to come and
accuse the author of "La Comédie Humaine" of uni-
formity, he who has created a whole world?

At last he risks it, he throws himself thoroughly into
the reading of the "Illusions Perdues"; and just see
in what gallant terms: "Again, once more, it must be
done; let us shut our eyes, hold our breath, incase our
legs in the impenetrable boots of men in sewers, and

walk at our ease in this mud, since this pleases you."
I could imagine I was listening to a critic of to-day
speaking of the filth of naturalism.

In his course Janin encounters the name of Walter
Scott, and, once he is started off, he talks about him
for two pages in his fluid style, which runs like tepid
water. Balzac, who felt for Walter Scott an admiration
which it is difficult to understand to-day, having had
the misfortune to say that all the heroines of the Eng-
lish novelist resembled each other, the critic cried out
with indignation: "What blasphemy! And how can
anyone fail to recognize the value of these masterpieces, which all Europe knows by heart? But it is
precisely because he has put woman in the background
in his stories, because he has surrounded his heroines
with the sweetest virtues, because their feelings are
restrained, because their love is pure, because they
always remain quiet and reserved, as honest girls
should, who are to become the worthy mothers of
families—this is why Walter Scott's novels have been
accepted so extensively." Here is profound criticism.
Decidedly the prince of critics had not a brain large
enough to understand Balzac.

He understood him so little that he compared him to
and gave the preference to Paul de Kock. Besides, this
was one of the pleasantries of the time which enraged
Balzac. Janin perfidiously railed at him : " Thus, by
different roads, one by gross gayety and an exaggerated roughness, the other by a most refined feeling and
a politeness that was a little more than exquisite, M.
de Kock and M. de Balzac have reached exactly the
same popularity, the same favor, and the same number
of readers; but to know which one carries the day

over the other, ask that question of the great capitals of Europe. London will choose Paul de Kock; St. Petersburg, the most skillful counterfeit of Paris, will shout for M. de Balzac; Paris is for both of them; Paris is for all those who amuse her; she will never have too many amusers." To-day Paris, Europe, and the world know but Balzac, as Paul de Kock and Jules Janin himself are dead.

Further on this prince of critics is not willing to give the kingly crown to Balzac among novelists. He reveals his temperament in this. I quote the whole page; it is worth the trouble: " I will reply to you that M. de Balzac is not the king of modern novelists; the king of modern novelists is a woman—one of those grand minds full of disquietude which seek their true course—and who, even when she writes her most beautiful novels, produces on me the effect of Apollo guarding the flocks of Admetus. Coming next, sometimes alongside of, and sometimes behind M. de Balzac, sometimes in front of him, are several novelists who, like him, look with great contempt upon society as it is revealed by its behavior —writers of great audacity, of a marvelous fecundity. What work of M. de Balzac's has been more filled with movements and incidents of great diversity than 'Les Memoires du Diable'? What story of M. de Balzac's is superior to 'La Femme de Quarante Ans' by M. de Bernard? When has M. de Balzac developed irony to a finer degree than Eugène Sue? Has he ever written anything which, in the freshness of its descriptions, in the whispering and springlike grace of landscape, can be preferred to the charming fancies of M. Alphonse Karr? Let us not forget, in a higher class, M. Alfred de Vigny's novel, and 'Notre Dame de Paris,' and

"Volupté," which is a book standing alone, without counting all the beautiful little stories which I forget, all filled with ecstasy, imagination, and love. . ." All this has become very droll in these days. This prince of critics lacked any genuine flavor.

Would you like to hear Balzac treated as a tainted naturalist of to-day? "Because the thing exists, does that mean that the novel and the comedy, with hook in hand, are free to occupy themselves with this pandemonium seething under this pile of filth? No, no; there are some things which ought not to be seen, and which are hardly permissible to the philosopher, barely allowable to the moralist, and scarcely permitted to the Christian. A writer is not a ragpicker; a book cannot be filled up like a basket." There is a phrase which has the air of having been written this morning. Oh! these gentlemen do not put themselves to any expense in the matter of imagination. The same phrases have been used for half a century. They have not overthrown Balzac; but never mind, they are still considered good enough to try to crush out the newcomers with.

Upon the whole, as I have said, Jules Janin feigned to believe that Balzac attacked all the leading spirits of journalism, all the well-known names: Chateaubriand, Royer-Collard, Guizot, Armand Carrel, Villemain, Lamenais. The truth was that Balzac spoke of the shameful way of cooking up articles which he had witnessed, the side scenes of the press, of all the abuses to which the rapid success of newspapers had given birth. In this connection let us admire the following passage: "When, merely since 1789, all the principles upon which modern society rests are founded, defended, and saved by the newspaper, it is sad to see your noble and beloved profession attacked, even as regards its shadows, even in its most futile and unperceived accessories. Attacked, and by whom, I pray you? By a book without style, without merit, and without talent." Good Heavens! is it of "Les Illusions Perdues" that this prince of critics speaks? But you do not know your own domain even, you old meddler! After such a judgment they should have seated you on your crown as on a bottomless chair.

Wait a minute; it is not finished. There is a stronger phrase yet. Here it is: "Happily this book belongs to the great number of novels which we do not regret not having read, which appear to-day to disappear to-morrow into the depths of a great oblivion. Never, in fact, at any epoch during the exercise of his talent has the thought of M. de Balzac been more scattered nor his invention more sluggish, his style more incorrect. . ." This is enough; let us stop here, for we have reached the height of the ridiculous.

Well! prince, I think it is you who disappeared the next day into the depths of a great oblivion. Nobody reads your books, and your forty years of criticism have not even left a trace in our literary history. As to Balzac, he is standing on his feet, he grows each day greater. He belongs to the mass of refreshing, healthy reading of the past which does us good. One breathes again in exhibiting the imbecility of criticism, even when it is crowned. Consider further that to-day they have not found one whom they judge worthy to be seated on the throne. If a man makes such a mess as this when one is a prince, what do you think of the judgments pronounced by the great troop of ordinary critics?

A ROMAN PRIZE IN LITERATURE.

A VERY strange scheme has just been projected, that of founding in literature a Roman prize. Fortunately this project seems to have no chance of being realized, and it would be useless to discuss it if it were not a symptom of the ugly disease which we suffer from in France of being protected and encouraged by the state.

Truly we are never free from our life as young folks at college. The arts and letters continue to be for us a series of compositions like Latin themes and Greek translations, and it is necessary that some master should distribute the places, should be always on hand to paste on the backs of the scholars the numbers in their order. If at the end of the year the distribution of prizes, with their laurel crowns, made out of painted paper, should fall short, there would be a general consternation.

Urchins of eight years of age carry a tin cross on their chest. Later their names are inscribed on the honor lists. They are overwhelmed with good marks. Later still, on their entry into life, they go from one examination to another, and diplomas fall upon them as thick as autumn leaves. But this is not all. Medals, titles, and crosses made of all kinds of metals continue to rain upon them. They are ticketed, given certificates, recommended. They bear on every part of their body the signature of the administration, declaring in due form that they have genius. You become a package duly

registered for glory.   What childishness, and how much
more healthy it is to be alone and free, with your breast
bare to the clear bright sunshine!

Now there are some writers who were not protected
enough.   They had no examinations, except that the
Academy permitted itself to distribute to some ladies
and quiet men some insignificant prizes.   They did not
feel the guardianship of the state, as did painters and
sculptors, for example, who depended upon the administration absolutely.   From that springs up an enormous
jealousy.   We long for chains also.   Our liberty hampers us ; we do not know how to write *chefs-d'œuvre,*
and we hold out our hands to be manacled.   The artists
are too greedy, and keep all the fetters for themselves.
We will begin with polemics, we will hold conferences
if necessary, but we shall exact nothing less than our
corner of the dungeon.

Just think of it !   The painters and sculptors have a
school in which professors teach them the latest method.
They pass their youth in the midst of examinations.
Then a jury admits them, or does not admit them, to
the public.   Each year they compose, and the first ones
have medals given them.   When the medals are
exhausted there are exceptional compensations.   This
is at least an enviable career.   The successful students
taste all manner of pleasures.   Talk to me of this way
of understanding the life of an artist, and then understand how colorless a writer's life seems beside it.   The
poor man has not one medal to cheer him up.   His
house is left desolate.

At this moment they do not ask for medals; they
would be satisfied if the state would only found in literature a Roman prize.   This prize would consist, the

same as the Roman prize in painting, of a certain income, which would be paid for four years to the winner. Naturally it would be awarded as the result of an examination, and the winner would be required to furnish each year a work of some kind, to prove that he is not eating the administration's bread in idleness. This is the project in general. It remains to fix upon the style of the composition. Shall it be a novel, an historical study, or a poem? They have spoken, I think, of a comedy or a drama in verse. This would restrain the Roman literary prize in a very singular manner, for it would thus become a Roman dramatic prize. I suspect the inventors of this project have some youthful tragedies in their drawers. But truly I think they have not yet seen the comical side of the invention.

When the Prize of Rome was created, the idea especially was to furnish young artists with the opportunity of making a stay in the city, which was then looked upon as the tabernacle of art. The journey cost a great deal; on the other side, they wished to assure to the winner a home, relations, artistic supervision. Finally, the school had a flag and intended raising soldiers to defend it. All these reasons explain its foundation.

But in letters, who could make verses for such a prize? It could never enter the thoughts of anyone to send the literary prize winners to any city whatever; they should remain in Paris, in this Paris which attracts all minds. I could thoroughly understand the large cities of the provinces founding a Prize of Paris. On the other side, writers have no heavy expenses. With a quire of paper, three cents' worth of ink, and one

penny's worth of pens you can write a *chef-d'œuvre.*
Finally there is no longer a state literature whose flag
anyone wishes to defend. The two cases are thus completely different, and I cannot understand what connection anybody can see between them.

The only reason which has been given is that this
Roman prize in literature will relieve great despair and
discouragements. And they mention Hégésippe Moreau, and all the poets in story who have died in the
hospital from poverty and suppressed genius. Now
the idea of this undertaking ought to be clearly set
forth. If it is a question of giving an income to a poor
young writer, it would be necessary to make such a
rule that only poor young writers could compete. The
mayor and the commissary of the ward might deliver
a certificate of indigence, which must be handed in to
the secretary with the other papers. In truth, the successful candidates, even if they should only have an
income of twelve hundred francs or a small family
allowance, would commit a very villainous action if
they came and, by reason of equal merit, disputed the
prize with a man who was dying of hunger. The
poverty of the candidate would have more weight
with the mass of the jury than his absolute merit.

If you set aside this sentimental reason, no other serious argument can be quoted in favor of this foundation. But this is not all, because, even if there were for
the Roman prize in literature the same arguments which
had decided the Roman prize in painting, it would be
wise, before going into a second venture, to ask if the
first had produced good results.

To-day the rôle which our Roman school has played
in the art of the century can be clearly exhibited. This

rôle has been absolutely nil. Certainly a great artist who went to Rome would return, no doubt, with his genius ; only Rome is so little necessary to our painters that the greatest among them, Eugène Delacroix, Courbet, Théodore Rousseau, Millet, Corot, and our whole great school of landscape painters have never been there. From this nursery, which should be so fertile in masters, hardly anything has come out but mediocrities. The great movement of art in the nineteenth century has developed outside of and apart from the administrative hothouse.

This is so true, the Roman school is to-day so useless and unstrung, that the students live in complete anarchy as regards doctrines. Every year, at the exhibition of its studies, you can ascertain the confusion of the different individualities. The Roman school has no longer even its æsthetic stubbornness. You might as well send the prize-winners to Pontoise ; they would be nearer modern life. Otherwise their stay in Italy is a very pleasant thing. It weakens their judgment a little, but with a more or less commonplace painter that does not make very much difference. As to the danger of genius going astray there, it would always withstand any such tendency. My opinion is, then, that our Roman school is neither dangerous nor useful.

Thus, as the experiment has been made, what would be the use of recommencing it in literature ? It is well known that arts and letters gain nothing by being patronized and coddled. It only serves to keep mediocrities alive. A writer of slender ability is always troublesome by himself ; if he were licensed, he would become dangerous. We are already too much overrun by the makers of phrases for us to open a school of rhetoric. The day on which we found the Roman prize in literature I know very well what will come to pass; it will not go to the poor ones, it will not go to original talent: it will go to those middling and flexible minds who know how to pluck all the flowers along the roadside. What is the use of encouraging these gentlemen, who already have too much courage?

I have a theory which may be a little barbarous on these matters: it is that strength is everything in the battle of letters. Misfortune to the feeble! Those who fall are wrong to fall, and so much the worse for them if they are crushed. They only need the power to stand upright on their feet. Each time that a *débutant* is stranded, that a conqueror of the day before is vanquished, I conclude that he bore within him the germs of his defeat. The victory goes to those who hold the reins firmly, and that is just. Talent should be strong; if it is not strong it is not talent; and it is essential that this truth should be made manifest for talent's own sake. When it is a question of art things must be said out squarely, so that art may discover in man the passage to failure or to success.

I find, for example, that they exaggerate the cases of Hégésippe Moreau, Chatterton, and others in an unwarranted manner. Hégésippe Moreau was a second-rate poet. His great cleverness was in dying as he did. If he had lived no one, perhaps, would have known his name. You can pity the poor devils whom literary ambition kills in the garrets; but it is silly to regret their talent. It is a crime to support the pride of men of no ability. The writer who is big with a world always brings forth that world.

I spoke in the commencement of this contemptible

necessity of protection which we have in France. One
hand rests on titled ladies, the other on the constituted
bodies; you mount thus, little by little, the ladder of
a pretty success; you start with diplomas and college
prizes, and you end with crosses and titles. To climb
this ladder you must have a supple backbone and know
how to please everybody; a bow to the right, a bow to
the left, a tirade on morality every now and then, and,
above all, a selection of phrases which can displease no
one.

Ah, but contempt is far preferable! To despise all
these conveniences, to feel none of these wants springing from our vanity, this is, perhaps, the supreme force
in our trade of writer. You stand alone; you rise, but
by your own talent. A book is good, and you write it
because you wish to write it. No consideration will
determine the change of a phrase. Why should there
be a change when you have given up all compensations?
The greatest pleasure is to will and to create. Your
spirit goes on before you and sees the completion of
your desire, and this is the only route which leads to
masterpieces.

THE CONTEMPT IN WHICH LITERATURE IS HELD.*

WHEN I was struggling, and getting my articles accepted after a great deal of trouble, I can remember the emotion which the appearance of a new journal caused me. There was one door more which might open; literature was perhaps at last going to show a little streak of hospitality. It may be for this reason, but I still have the refreshing sense of pleasure when I see Paris speckled with placards. It may mean bread for some beginners.

This year the appearance of new journals coincided with the end of summer. No more sitting of the Chamber, hardly any politics, and not an incident of any note far or near. As the number of newspapers was

---

* This chapter and the following one have a history. They were the decisive cause of my breaking with *Le Voltaire*, the editor of which, without giving me any warning, took it into his head to enter a protest against me, declaring that I was wanting in respect for our political men and affecting to believe that I defended obscenity. This was done so as to bring about my resignation abruptly and before everybody. A proceeding so foreign to letters—did it come from a man who served as an instrument, with more or less consciousness, to the literary vermin whose political appetites I denounced? Or did this man act from his own whim merely for the sake of a bold stroke so foreign to our world, and from not having really understood what I wrote in his newspaper? Everything is possible. Here are my articles; you can judge them for yourself. It is a fine rôle to play, that of falling for literature. I have only one wish, and that is that this extraordinary editor should live through me, and I bequeath his name to future generations. He is called M. Jules Lafitte.

growing just at the moment when politics were dull, they had, doubtless, decided to give some space to litera- ture, for you cannot disguise the fact that literature has become simply a thing to fill up with. Between two sittings of parliament they insert an article on biog- raphy in justification. As to any variety, any literary studies of any great length, they remain for months in the pigeonholes. The newspapers which have the rep- utation of being the most hospitable to letters, the *Débats* and the *Temps*, for example, have allowed them- selves to be eaten up, like the rest, by politics. There are but five or six obstinate personalities in the press to-day who persist in talking literature and nothing but literature, in the midst of the abominable uproar which the different parties let loose around them. Later, I think, they will get the benefit of this laudable obsti- nacy. Just now I do not know whether their articles are even read. They are granted a great favor in being permitted to occupy three hundred lines of the news- paper every week which could be employed to so much better advantage in discussing the revision or the *scrutin de liste.*

Thus, in the slackness of politics, and as the news- papers had become more numerous, I dreamt that they would turn as a last resource to literature. Not at all. Politics, which rushed like a torrent, simply takes the form of a stagnant sea; it sleeps and rots on the spot, that's all. If twenty new papers were created politics would be only the freer to stretch and overrun everything, and the journals would empty themselves of all but advertisements that it might thin itself out so that it could fill them from top to bottom with its slow and muddy stream. It alone is sufficient. Politics is the fatal disease of our age of troubles and transition.

I was talking one day with the editor of a new journal. He spoke bitterly of his circulation, which, he said, was far from being satisfactory to him, and asked me if I did not know some young writers of talent. I named over several, but he shrugged his shoulders, murmuring:

"Oh, a *littérateur* . . . I wanted a young man who had great talent and who occupied himself exclusively with politics."

"Ah, indeed!" I ended by saying to him impatiently; "do you think that a young man who has talent enough to be a writer will ever consent to smear himself with mud in the 'dirty kitchen' of your politics?"

It was brutal, but it was, and is still, the exact expression of my thoughts. I admit frankly that the ambitious spirits who carve out for themselves a high position in politics are oftentimes powerful and original natures. But observe that they make their triumphs especially in action, and that you find often at the bottom but a poor writer. Great poets and prose writers have always made a beggarly appearance in government service. If we put to one side the extraordinary political successes, if we keep to the crowd of journalists and agitators, to the troop of those elected by universal suffrage, from the simple municipal councilors to the deputies, we shall always find among these hirelings of the state the name of a writer or an artist who has failed in his vocation. This fact is constantly observed; politics is recruited to-day from the ragged edges of literature.

How sure I am of this and how many stories I could

relate to prove it. This man started out with a volume
of verse, samples of which can still be found on the stalls
of second-hand booksellers; that one sent his MSS. to
editors' offices and theater managers for ten years;
another has been an obscure journalist since his early
youth without obtaining an audience, and, exhausted
by his exertions, has never got any farther than beer
saloon celebrity; still another eaten up by ambition,
has tried everything from history to criticism, from
poetry to novels, but was obliged to renounce his dreams
one by one, until at last he found in politics a mother
compassionate toward all mediocrities. And I do not
speak of those writers who were full of intellect one
day, who on the next awoke so knocked up that they
have never been able to find their lost talent again.
All the same, these are excellent recruits for politics,
whose right hand is stretched out to the helpless and
her left hand to the sick.

This is the hospital, the menagerie, and so much the
worse for them if they are angry at me for calling it
thus, for I really know of no word strong enough to use
in my indignation. Yes, I grow indignant at such a display of wretched and foolish ambitions. Bring me a
scrofulous man, an idiot, a brain misshapen, and you will
find at least in such a man the making of a politician.
I know among them men that I would not have for servants. You need neither mind nor force nor originality, only a "pull," and a certain nonentity cast of
character. When you have failed in everything and
everywhere, when you have been an unsuccessful lawyer,
an unsuccessful journalist, an unsuccessful man from
head to feet, politics will take you in hand and make
you a minister as good as another, reigning, from the

position of a more or less modest and amiable upstart, over the French intelligence. These are the facts.

Mon Dieu! the facts are still acceptable, for there are strange things happening daily around us. The observer becomes accustomed to it, and contents himself with smiling. But it makes me sick when these men pretend to despise us and patronize us. We are only writers, we hardly count; they limit our share in the sunshine, they place us at the foot of the table. Ah! when the situations are finally determined, gentlemen, we intend to pass in first, to have the whole table and all the sunshine. Understand that one page written by a great writer is more important for humanity than a whole year of the agitation of your ant-hill. You make history, it is true, but we make it with you and beyond you; for it is through us that it remains. Your life is commonly passed in the infinite littleness of a personal ambition, without the nation, as a whole, being able to derive anything useful and practical from it, while our works, by the mere fact of their existence, aid in the civilization of the world. And besides, see how quickly you die. Look into a history of the last years of the Restoration, for example, and ask yourself where so many political battles and so much eloquence have disappeared to; a single thing survives to-day, after fifty years — the great literary evolution of the epoch, that romanticism whose leaders have remained illustrious, while the statesmen have already faded from memory. Listen to us, you men of little stature, who are making such a noise: it is we who shall live and who shall give immortality.

It is necessary that this should be clearly stated; literature is on top with science; then comes politics, very low down in the scale of human productions. In a day of anger, exasperated by the ridiculous ambitions and odious hubbub which surrounded me, I wrote that my generation would end by regretting the great silence of the Empire. The words exceeded my thought; I am willing to confess it to-day. But in truth did I not have extenuating circumstances? The condition of tumult, of shock, of frightful and senseless preoccupation in which politics has made us live for ten years—is it not an intolerable condition, in which the mind ends by becoming suffocated? Reread our history. At each convulsion, during the Ligne, during the Fronde, during the French Revolution, literature was struck dead, and it can come to life again only a long time afterward and after a period of more or less bewilderment and imbecility. Doubtless social evolutions have their necessity and their logic. We must submit to them. Only it is a veritable' disaster when they are prolonged. To-day the republic is founded; it is trying to attain the solidity of a true state by assuring to the nation the free use of its intelligence. Its duration, its glory, depend on this. The politicians will kill it by their extravagance, while it will live by its artists and its writers.

I speak less for my own generation than for the generation which is to follow us. We others, we have made our mark after a fashion, amid the most vexatious circumstances. But how I pity the beginners of to-day. Is it not frightful, this multiplication of newspapers, of which I have spoken, and this indifference, this contempt of literature? Not a paper which gives one corner to a serious literary question.

They are all grinding the most discordant airs on the political hand organ. And the airs are badly composed; they are tiresome and they nearly kill the public; for the public, it would seem, hardly listens. I should be delighted to see them perish through that very thing in which they sin so deeply, to see them die of a political indigestion brought about by a final desertion on the part of several hundred readers, of whom they dispute the possession with the greediness of shop-keepers, dreaming of a night at the Elysée. You are not ignorant of the fact that there is a President of the Republic underneath every newspaper editor. After Napoleon's defeat all the ambitious ones wanted to be lieutenants. To-day, after Messrs. Thiers, Grévy, and Gambetta, cracks begin to appear, and there is not an unsuccessful man of letters or arts who does not dream of being the chief magistrate by means of the bar or the press.

A momentary folly, but for all that very tumultuous and trying. All this will pass away and we shall remain. It is this thought that gives us a little pride. Pride, whatever may be said of it, is healthful in these flat, shrunken times in which we live. When the editors of newspapers demand young men of talent, and when they shrug their shoulders if you mention a writer, a pure man of letters to them, it is right, it is sound if the literary men rise and say: "We beg your pardon; it is you who are nothing, and we who are everything."

OBSCENE LITERATURE.

WE have just been witnessing a very singular occurrence. Paris has just been seized with a fit of virtue. I speak of a fit in its acute sense: one of these nice crises which spread out to full view all the ignorance and foolishness of a public. When the disease shows itself, the most intelligent are attacked; they do not all die, but they all yield to the contagion. It is a sort of fashion for about a fortnight. This time the press has made the startling discovery of what it calls in its indignation obscene literature.

The story is so droll that I feel obliged to relate it in all its details. A newspaper had been started, *Le Gil Blas*, which at first sold very badly. Once in a while I questioned, through curiosity, the editors of rival sheets as to the chances of the newcomer's success, and these editors, shrugging their shoulders contemptuously, declared that they feared nothing, for the paper would never sell. Then all at once I saw the editors' noses lengthening: *Gil Blas* was selling; it had adopted a specialty of light stories which gave it a certain public. I mean, if you like, the public at large —men and, above all, women who did not dislike questionable stories. From this in a few weeks arose this great storm of virtuous indignation on the part of the press.

I do not wish to defend *Gil Blas*, but it seems to me it is a case which can be very easily analyzed. Certainly it was not founded with the avowed intention of corrupting the nation. It simply felt its way with the public; new newspapers all know this period of hesitation. Success does not come ; everything is tried until something is found which the public bites at. Well, *Le Gil Blas,* having ventured among other things a few coarse articles, realized that the public bit at the bait. From that time it did not sulk at its success—it gave to its readers the stew that was to their taste.

Ignoble speculation, school of perverted tastes, cry out its indignant colleagues. *Mon Dieu !* I would like to see the paper that would refuse its subscribers what they clamored for. In these times of groveling at the feet of the public, is not the press a great toady to the tastes of its readers? In politics, in literature, in art, where is the paper which plants itself squarely in the center of the road and resists the great current of nonsense and human obscenity ? Since all the follies, since all the appetites have their mediums of expression, why should not doubtful stories have theirs? Among its colleagues who are shocked are many who have worked in other ways for the demoralization of the public. To flatter an imbecile aristocracy, to flatter the robbers of the stock market, to flatter the ambition of the *bourgeoisie* or the drunkenness of the people—this is more disastrous than flattering everybody's coarse tastes.

I have subscribed to *Le Gil Blas* to find out what there was to it. I have read in it some charming articles : for example, sketches by M. Théodore de Barville, full of a poetic charm ; little novelettes, fine and spirited in their style, by M. Armand Silvestre ; highly colored studies by M. Richepin. Here are three poets whose company was highly honorable. It is true that the rest of this issue was of a lower literary order. There were, besides, some stories in it which were positively gross. Not that I blame this source of inspiration, for I should have to condemn on such a ground Rabelais, Lafontaine, and others still whom I esteem; but in truth these stories were too badly written. This is my whole quarrel. You are highly blamable when you write badly. That is the only crime which I can admit in literature. I do not see where they can put morality, if they pretend to put it elsewhere. A well-made phrase is a good action.

I was then in the middle of my study of this question, charmed when I read an article by a true writer, and absolutely disgusted when I came across the obscenity of a casual journalist bungling his work. In my opinion the unworthy begins where talent ends. Only one thing disgusts me—stupidity. But my age had still another surprise in store for me. I suddenly learned that *Le Gil Blas* is my work, the child of my womb. It is not Voltaire's fault, it is Zola's. In any case, *Gil Blas* would be a very unnatural child, because he eats his father every time he mentions him. I have not yet found a line about myself, that is, I will not say kind, but that is even polite. Three men, at least, could be counted who publicly profess to detest me. Admit, then, that this child would make my old age wretched if I had the least certainty of being its father.

But no; I examine myself. I question my heart, and no answering throb confirms any such claim. Ashamed of my sterility I must surrender the child to Boccaccio and to Brantôme. I do not feel myself at all gay or sprightly; I am incapable of pleasing the ladies; I am a grumpy tragedian, a man dressed in black, whom gallantry does not tempt; and they must understand the laws of heredity very badly to try to seat on the knees of a hypochondriac like myself this gayly be-ribboned baby who is already playing pranks with his nurse. Are you not astonished at the extraordinary judgments of the present criticism? I speak of the current criticism which fills up the newspapers. It does not put a single writer in his proper place; it does not study; it does not classify; it starts from a word, from a ready-made idea, without taking into consideration the real temperament, the true work of a writer. *Gil Blas*, the child of "L'Assommoir" and of "Nana"! But, great God! it is Jeremiah giving birth to Piron. I say this *sotto voce* for fear they will accuse me of including myself among the prophets.

What pretty articles my friends send me. I have about a dozen under my eyes. In them I am accused of corrupting the age. One especially is incredible; it is said there in plain words that I invented obscene literature. Alas, no, monsieur! I have invented nothing, and I have been bitterly reproached on this very account. It will be necessary, however, for you to settle things with your colleagues. If I copy all the world, if I am only a falling off from my elders, my influence would hardly be either so terrible or so decisive. Why do you not also say that I invented vice? That would put me at one bound as a third in the company of Adam and Eve in the Garden of Paradise. It would be ridiculous for a lad who prides himself upon having finished his lessons to cross out with one stroke of the pen so many strong and charming works, written in all the languages of the world, and to pretend to begin

with "L'Assommoir" and "Nana" what you so innocently call obscene literature.

And remark that these accusations are not made
without a great display of the finest sentiments in the
world. They speak especially in the name of justice;
they protest against the proceedings through love of
equality. A piece of nice hypocrisy which does not take
even with fools. Since they prosecute the newspaper,
why not prosecute the book? Since one novelist has
been brought into court, why has not such another?
Unquestionably that would be the only logical way.
But it is very weak, this logic of repression. Ah, monsieur! since you are in favor of entire liberty, rejoice,
then, on the day that justice has a caprice in the way of
liberalism; there is, at least, some gain. What would
you say of a man whose wife beat him and who wanted
to be beaten every evening for the sake of being
logical? When one of us has brought about a triumph
for liberty of thought by escaping from the judges,
whom you declare incompetent, should we not all
rejoice? I do not speak of those men whom the quick
success of a colleague irritates.

In short, a whole group of writers are accused of
speculating in obscenity. They hoot at them, they
gather up handfuls of mud from the gutters to throw it
in their faces; and not content with soiling them, they
try to attack their talent, swearing that their books are
the easiest things in the world to write, that all you need
to do is to pile up horrors. Well, then, try this; it will
be very droll!

It is certain that there are speculators everywhere.
In *Gil Blas* you find speculators in obscenity. They
are journalists with no talent whatsoever, who concoct

a coarse story, just as they would get up a paper upon the reward of virtue, with tears at the end of each phrase. The coarse stories are accepted; they continue to make them. To-morrow they will go so far as to defend the Jesuits. All journalism, all the utensils of our reporters, I repeat, this is what it has come to, with more or less exactness. In the novel it is the same thing. Speculators make money with their neighbor's success, seeing only its tumult and acquiring only its crudities, and making it revolting through their lack of talent. This has always been and always will be.

But if we should also speak of speculators in virtue, do you think the subject would be less vast or the traffic less to be condemned? How many novelists and dramatic authors I know who boldly work virtue just as they might a granite quarry. I do not pry into their private life; I simply say that these jolly fellows have a fine time with their morality, from which they only mean to make an income. With virtue, in the first place, there is no necessity for any great talent; you tap your chest before great ladies, swearing never to say or write anything which would make them blush, and that is sufficient. Then you are decorated, you are certain of the Academy, you give yourself airs as a pure and patriotic man. And have we not heard enough bad patriotic dramas, and do they not force enough silly novels upon us whose fine sentiments burn to the last pages, like Bengal lights? Is all this convincing? I suppose not; it would be too simple. Pure trickery— shrewd men, born in the school of hypocrisy, and who have perceived that there are still more solid profits for working in virtue than in vice.

Now between those who make it a specialty not to make the ladies blush and those who make their living by causing them to blush, there are true artists, writers bred to the occupation, who do not ask for one second whether the ladies will blush or not. They have a love for language and a passion for truth. When they work it is for a human end, superior to the fashions and disputes of these dabblers. They do not write for a certain class; their ambition is to write for the ages. The proprieties, the sentiments produced by education, the welfare of young girls and wavering women, police regulations, and the morality patented by amiable natures, disappear, and do not count. They go straight for the truth, for the masterpiece, in spite of everything, over everything, without worrying about the scandal caused by their audacities. The fools who accuse them of cunning calculation fail to understand that their only object is genius and glory. And when they have built their monument the gaping crowd accepts them in all their superb nudity, understanding them at last.

I do not urge morality on anyone; but I wish a great deal of talent to my adversaries, which would certainly be more agreeable for us. If they had talents that would calm them down, and they would ask less of virtue. In any case, they may be sure that the year 1880 is not more vicious than any other; that the really obscene literature does not spread itself any more than in the eighteenth century, for example, and that years may roll by before *Le Gil Blas* advances perceptibly the rottenness of our society. All this skirmish is a bit of ridiculous prudishness, which makes me anxious about the fate of our famous French spirit. Is it, then, seriously ill? Are we to see Rivarol turn into Grandison? It is Protestantism which is overrunning us. They put iron bars on their closets; they create concealed refuges for monstrous passions, while our fathers innocently exhibited theirs in broad daylight.

THE INFLUENCE OF THE REPUB-
LIC IN LITERATURE.

THE INFLUENCE OF THE REPUB-
LIC IN LITERATURE.

I.

I HAVE no attachment to the political world, and I
expect neither place nor pension nor recompense
of any kind from the government. This is not pride;
it is, at the outset of this study, a necessary statement.
I am alone and free; I have worked, I work still; my
bread comes from that.

On the other side, I must establish a second point.
I am a republican of former days—I mean to say that
I defended republican ideas in my books and in the
newspapers while the second empire was still in existence. I could have had my share of the spoils, had I
had the least political ambition.

My position is thus clearly defined. I am a republican who does not live by the republic. The idea has
occurred to me that the situation is an excellent one in
which to say out aloud what I think. I know why many
hesitate to speak. One is expecting a cross; another is
anxious about the place which he occupies in the administration; a third hopes for advancement; a fourth
expects to become Attorney-general, then deputy, then
minister, then—who knows?—President of the Republic. The necessity of daily bread, the longing for honors
are terrible ties, which bind down the most simple lib-

erties. As soon as you have a desire or an ambition you belong to the first comer. If you judge certain political characters too frankly you close all doors in your face ; if you dare to tell the truth on such a question you turn your back on some powerful party. But be ambitious for nothing, have need of no one to enable you to live, and all at once the shackles fall and you walk freely, as you please, to the right or to the left, with the calm joy of your regained individuality. Ah, this is true happiness : to live in your own corner, on the fruits of your little field, where you labor ; not to depend upon your neighbor; and to speak out aloud in the open air without being afraid that the wind will carry away and sow your words.

In political parties there is what is called discipline. This is a powerful force, but an ugly thing, for all that. In letters, happily, discipline cannot exist, especially in our time of individual production. If it is essential for a politician to group around him a majority upon whom he depends for support and without whom he would not exist, the writer, on the other hand, lives for himself outside of the public. His books may not sell, but they exist, and they will one day have the success which is due them. This is why the writer, whose conditions of living are not subjected to discipline, is particularly well placed to judge the politician. He stands superior to what actually exists; he does not speak under the pressure of certain facts, nor to bring about certain results ; he is free, in a word, to stand alone with his own thought, because he does not form part of a group, and can say everything without upsetting his life or risking his fortune.

I would never have ventured into this mess we call

politics, had I not wanted to study what is in my opinion a very grave question. This question is to find out whether the republic and literature will live happily or unhappily together. I mean our contemporary literature, this large evolution, naturalistic or positivist, as you will, which was started with Balzac. For a long time I have hesitated, because the ground seemed burning. Then for eight years the tumult has been so deafening, the complications which presented themselves so rapid, that it was difficult for a studious man to risk a serious inquiry, and, above all, to conclude wisely. But to-day, though the noise continues, the period of incubation has ceased, the republic exists in fact. It is in working order, and you can judge it by its acts. The hour has come, then, to place the republic and literature face to face; to see what the latter ought to expect from the former; to examine whether we analyzers, anatomists, collectors of human data, savants who admit only the authority of facts; whether we are to find in the republicans of the present time friends or enemies. The solution of this question is one of extreme gravity. It seems to me that the existence of the republic itself depends upon it. The republic will live or the republic will not live according as it shall accept or reject our method. The republic will be naturalistic or it will not be.

I am going then to study the political situation in its connection with literature. This will of necessity lead me more than I could wish to judge the men who govern us. But, I repeat, my intention is not to pronounce on the destinies of France or to add my opinion to the confusion of other opinions. I start from this point, that the republic exists, and I simply wish, as a writer, to examine how the republic behaves with regard to writers.

I must first study the way in which the republic was founded in France. Nothing could be more characteristic. Without entering into the history, so complicated and troubled, of the last eight years, we can easily run over the principal outlines. First, there is the crumbling of the empire brought about by the rottenness and imbecile arrangement of the framework which held up the government. Picture to yourself purple and gold decorations held up by frail, badly planted, worm-eaten pillars which one shock would reduce to powder; the war of 1870 was this shock, and consequently the empire was crushed to the earth at the height of its pomp. After our disasters came Bordeaux and the attempt of the loyalists. I was there. I saw the arrival of that majority who shrugged their shoulders when the republic was mentioned. They seemed strong, all-powerful; they thought it was but necessary to have a vote cast in order to re-establish the monarchy. They also accepted M. Thiers' presidency without any uneasiness, certain of remaining masters of France. However, on the next day the classification of the parties was made. If the republicans were in the minority the monarchists were divided among themselves. When the details of the votes came in there were legitimists, Orleanists, imperialists, and neither one of these parties remained in the majority while it stood by itself. From this arose a radical weakness which could settle nothing. Later came the long intrigues and parliamentary struggles at Versailles. M. Thiers had said with his business tact that France would finally belong to the wisest. At bottom he already foresaw the final triumph of the republic; he realized that the three pretenders would destroy one another. The drama of the Commune, and the violent repression which had followed it, served to consolidate the republican government instead of overwhelming it. A much graver danger menaced it, however: there was a question of reconciliation between the two representatives of the House of France; the fusion of the legitimists and the Orleanists was on the point of being brought about. Finally comes the crisis of the 24th of May, the overthrow of M. Thiers, the triumph of the monarchists. For one instant the republic seemed lost. Henry V. was about to re-enter Paris; the state carriages were already ordered. Then at the moment of voting there was a supreme split on the part of the royalists on the question of the white flag. The republic carried the day on the vote.

Certainly this was not yet a decisive vote. But you could easily see that the monarchy was condemned, for each day it went a little further in accomplishing its own destruction. Then, under the presidency of Maréchal MacMahon, was seen this singular spectacle of a monarchial majority, whose members devoured each other, and which worked in spite of itself toward the foundation of a republic. Its violent attacks, its stupid plots, its most clever and strongest plans, all tended to make more solid the government which it wished to destroy. The explanation of this phenomenon is very simple. A great republican sentiment had declared itself throughout the country, logically, because the republican party alone seemed reasonable and possible. While the royalist majority in its weakness was exciting a useless agitation to re-establish the monarchy, it rendered itself more and more unpopular, and the entire country rose and chased it from parliament. Hence the continuous work of elections replacing every monarchist by a republican; then the legislative elections of the 14th of October, and the senatorial elections of the 5th of January, which, after the desperate adventure of the 16th of May, finally made the republic a regular government, working like all established governments. It must be said that the Left of the assembly had retained and put into practice M. Thiers' words: "France will belong to the wisest." Without doubt a minority of the extreme Left pushed toward extreme measures; but M. Gambetta, who was the undisputed chief of the party, had put forth the word " opportunism" to characterize how greatly the situation demanded patience, cleverness, and wisdom. If M. Grévy is to-day President, if the republicans are to-day masters in both Chambers, it is because the republicans allowed the new evolution to work its way with the nation without trying to hasten the *dénouement*.

These are the facts briefly stated. There is no necessity for me to enter into details; I simply wish to reach the conclusion that the republic, in order to exist, had to be the logical result of certain facts, and not the arbitrary formula of a political school. In the eyes of many republicans the republic exists by divine right; one government only is legitimate, the government of all; there is but one sovereign possible—the people. This is my opinion also. But here we are in pure abstractions. A mathematician can alone reason thus, because numbers have no will. Think of attempting to apply this theoretical formula of a republic to a people—everything is at once put out of order. This is because you then introduce a new element, that terrible human element which is not obedient like numbers, and which is full of somersaults and whims. You cannot make of a people an equation. Look at France in '89. Behind her were centuries of monarchy; customs, usages, a way of thinking, a manner of living which constituted what we call French society. The race, the surroundings, the institutions work toward the slow formation of a people, give it its genius, stamp it with an impress which remains its own. Ah, well! it was no use to wish to violently transform France in '89; she became once more a monarchy, after one of the most terrible shocks which had ever overturned a state. Without doubt the old world was not able to resurrect itself. A new century opened out; the gains of freedom were considerable. But the empire was about to bend all heads, and the revenge of the Restoration was bound to follow. It was simply that the human element, petrified for so long a time by centuries of monarchial government, could not adapt itself to the republican change, notwithstanding the violence of the revolutionary pressure. The fanatics, the sectarians, all those carried away by the exaltation of a faith and in a hurry to enjoy the ideal state of which they dreamed, knew well what they were doing when they clamored for one hundred thousand heads, and when they wished to establish a reign of terror. They felt the necessity of brutally subduing the human element; of crushing in man what the past had deposited there; of purging man, by bleeding him, of everything which race surroundings and institutions had put in his blood. Vain hope, nevertheless. There is no example of a nation thus transformed in an instant. Blood flowed from our scaffolds, and out of the red puddles Napoleon is seen to rise, who came, in his hour, to arrest the revolutionary movement and perform his work. Two other revolutions were produced, still without being able to found the republic; one ended in the monarchy of July, the other in the second empire. For all this there is only one explanation, and that would be easy to establish by history; thé social and historical facts did not tend toward the republic; the human element in France did not as yet adapt itself to republican rule. And look at the actual facts; that which terror was not able to effect, the slow evolution of minds is in the way of realizing to-day. Suppose that the frightful shock given by the Revolution to the old French society was necessary in order to plow up the field in which the new society was to grow, yet what long cultivation was needed to ripen this society. All our history for the last eighty years is here included. We see the discredit of dynasties increase at each attempt at restoration; there is the elder branch which breaks, there is the younger branch which can bear no flowers, there is the empire which is overthrown by a second invasion. During this time the people made a study of liberty; a slow and steady growth pushes the country toward the republican rule; and, as always happens when a historical force sets the nation in motion, the smallest incidents, even those which seem as though they were going to arrest the onward march of the nation, soon precipitate it forward with a much greater impetuosity. In a word, when the facts demanded the republic, the republic was founded.

There is what I wished to clearly establish at the

commencement of this essay. In all political problems there were two elements: the formula and the man. In my opinion, the republican formula is the only scientific one, that in which all nations must of necessity end. If men were mere abstractions, soldiers of lead, or quills, which one could arrange to his liking, nothing would be easier than to transform in an instant a monarchy into a republic. But as soon as men come into play they upset the formula; they complicate the question terribly by the chaos of ideas, of wills, of ambitions, and of follies which they bring with them. From this politics is born; the least evolution demands sometimes hundreds of years for its accomplishment in the midst of incessant struggles. Happily changes go on, some gain is accomplished, the formula is realized according to certain laws. Nothing would be more interesting than to study this play of the human material adapting itself to a new political and social formula by taking up the history of French society toward the middle of the last century. There would be in that a very great labor. I have contented myself with pointing out rapidly how, since the Revolution, we have been carried toward a republic, and how in these last years a republic has been founded by force of facts in the midst of obstacles which seemed at every hour about to barricade the route. Now it remains for me to study the different groups in the republican party. Then, knowing the make-up of our actual republic, I can study what connection it has with contemporary literature.

Of course I should soon lose myself if I tried to classify all the shades of the republican party. I must confine myself to three or four characteristic types. Naturally I choose the influential groups. Besides, I am not writing a polemic—I am but a savant and an observer. You will, therefore, not find here the name of a man nor the title of a newspaper.

In the first place, there is the formal republican. This individual belongs to a chapel of some kind. Often he is Protestant with Puritanic leanings. He aims at the Academy, prides himself on his beautiful language and happy equilibrium. He is the liberal, with the balance of a clever man, who has sworn never to swerve to the right nor to the left. When he has made up his mind he is generally hard-headed and narrow-minded; he is then a formalist, a *bourgeois* who fears the people and who despairs of a monarchy of its making. But when he has not made up his mind, he shows a singularly supple intelligence. His gravity, his big words, his correct attitude, his phraseology of the serious and bashful man hide the most amiable of skepticisms. In fact, he has but his ambition. He has said to himself, as a practical man, that the surest means of governing is to frighten no one and to tire everybody. He has also created journals in which the gray in literature and politics flourish—sheets of thick paper which never sacrifice anything to wit, which cram their readers with very indigestible articles. All this is sufficient in order to have weight. It is only a question of putting a white cravat on with common clothes. A whole public has been formed around this majestic emptiness, this liberalism living on academic formulas. The exact word is never used there. It is a *bourgeois* salon, with its prejudices, its stiff attitudes, its vague religiousness, its importance, and its *ennui.* Its object is the solemn cultivation of the middle classes. From this point start its dogmas, its

reassuring cut and dried opinions, its continual alle-
viations, its declarations as experts. I propose to
give these formal republicans the name of Protestant
Jesuits. They have dreamed of power from the first
day, and their long campaign has been but a slow march
toward coveted situations. They are men of expedi-
ency. Be certain they will accept nothing from the
republic but etiquette. All scientific formula is repugnant to them.

I will now pass to the romantic republican. This
one, though less dangerous, is much droller. He
unhappily holds a big place in the tumult of the day.
This entry of romanticism into politics is a whole history in itself. I have already recounted it elsewhere.
It so happened that certain dramatists in 1830, finding
their receipts in the theater growing less and less, conceived the idea of throwing themselves into journalism,
with their rubbish and their plumes. This happened
toward the end of the empire, at the moment that the
public was devouring the newspapers of the opposition. At this time of passionate attacks against the
government romanticism made great headway in the
press. The tirades at which they had commenced to
smile on the boards seemed quite new printed at the
head of a newspaper. It was *Hernani* who demanded
liberty, proudly lifting his brick-colored mantle with
the end of his sword ; it was *D'Artagnan*, it was *Buridan*,
wearing their broad-brimmed felts with long, sweeping
plumes, who hailed the people "sovereign" and styled
them lords. No carnival has ever been more quickly
successful. The people unquestionably did not recognize their favorite heroes of "La Tour de Nesle" and
"Les Trois Mousquetaires"; they were tired of

applauding them at the Ambigu and the Porte Saint
Martin; but all their old-time tenderness awakened
again; they were touched to the heart, and cried out
willingly, " Bravo, Melingue!" From that time romanticism had full sway in the market, and a very formidable sway it was. The receipts were such that the romantic republicans, satisfied with this fortune which had
come to them so late, were content to coin money with
their plumed phrases without caring to become deputies
and ambassadors like so many others. The process
offered great simplicity; it was merely a question of
transporting into the discussion of public affairs the
"tra-la-la" of great, empty phrases, the juggling of
antitheses, the disheveled airs of the imagination let
loose through all manner of fantasies. In a word, it
was necessary to be poetical at any odds; to mingle
" Triboulet " with " Ruy Blas "; to take a ride on Pega-
sus above the astonished lands. You comprehend what
politics has become, this science of facts and men,
in passing through the romantic formula. At once
all serious basis of observation has disappeared, rhetoric has replaced analysis, words have devoured ideas.
The romanticists have set out at a galloping pace after
humanitarian dreams, the universal fraternity of nations,
the approaching end of conflicts and wars, equality
and liberty shining upon the world like suns. On
the other side, as they coined money by the people,
they knelt in adoration before them, and there was no
blarney with which they did not delude them; the
people have become an emperor, a Pope, a god
inclosed in a triple tabernacle, and whom it was necessary to adore on one's knees under pain of the greatest
punishments. The workmen would certainly have

shown little gratitude had they refused to pay two cents for all this adulation. But what sorry masquerading, what shameless money-making. The romantic republicans ridiculed good sense, modern science, exact analysis, the experimental method, those powerful tools which are at this moment reforging society. They were like tight-rope dancers, covered with spangles and tinsel, executing marvelous bounds into the ideal for the greater amusement of the crowd.

Alongside of the romantic republicans there are the fanatical republicans, those who have put on Robespierre's frock coat or worn Marat's boots. These are shut up in an historical figure and cannot emerge from it—strange brains who wish to cut out the future by the past, without understanding that each evolution comes at its time, and that history never repeats itself. Further than this, I say again, it would be a difficult task clearly to classify the republicans, the groups are so numerous, from the impatient ones of the extreme Left, to those satisfied with "opportunism." There are among them some able men; men of the past, and men of the future a whole crowd. I shall content myself with having touched upon the formal republicans, the romantic republicans, and the fanatical republicans. These are the most powerful groups, who in every case have the most widely circulated newspapers, and, consequently, have the most influence. My opinion, in all simplicity, is that they would ruin the republic to-morrow if they were masters. The formal republicans would bring us back to a constitutional monarchy, while we should have a dictator inside of six months with the romantic republicans and with the fanatical republicans. This follows mathematically. Whoever does not walk with truth loses his way and goes of necessity toward error.

There exists, then, in my. eyes, but one republican who is the real worker at the present hour, and that is the scientific or naturalistic republican. If I had not promised to mention no names I could make my meaning clearer by quoting examples. The naturalistic republican, who is represented by some very powerful individualities, bases himself, above all, upon analysis and experiment. He does the same work in politics that our savants have done in chemistry and medicine, and that our writers are in the way of accomplishing in the novel, in criticism, and in history. This is a return to man and to nature : to nature considered in its action, to man considered in his needs and his instincts. The naturalistic republican takes into consideration the surroundings and the circumstances. He does not work on a nation as in clay, because he knows that a nation has its own life and a reason for existing, the mechanism of which should be studied before trying to manipulate it. Social formulas, like mathematical ones, possess a certain rigidity, so that a nation cannot be bent from one day to the next; and political science, such as it exists to-day, consists simply of the attempt to lead a country by the shortest and most practical paths to the form of government toward which it is moved by its natural impulse, aided by the force of the conditions. The naturalistic republican has not the stiff hypocrisies of the formal republican : he does not use one class for the benefit of another, but says what he ought to say, at the risk of scandalizing the *bourgeoisie*. The naturalistic republican understands nothing of the romantic republican's gibberish, whose false rhetoric and ideal of gilded pasteboard make him shrug his shoulders. For him all these comedians are charlatans, whether they wear a white cravat, or whether they are decked out in the leather jerkin of the Middle Ages.

Even admitting that there are some sincere men amid the formal and romantic republicans, these are exhausting their strength in trying to construct a monument in the air, which has no foundations; they are exciting themselves about delusions, they are applying false formulas to men who do not exist, to pure abstractions conceived about an ideal; thus it is not astonishing that their work crumbles, and that after each of their attempts the country has need of a dictator or a king to sweep the soil clear of the rubbish which they have heaped upon it. On the contrary, the naturalistic republican does not build until he has studied and sounded the ground; he knows that each stone hé places will be solid, because it fits on all sides, and because it is placed just where the nature of the ground and the construction of the building demand that it should be. He is a man of facts, and he will make a republic, not a Protestant temple, not a Gothic church, not a prison opening upon a place of execution, but a large and beautiful mansion, where all classes may be accommodated, full of air and sunlight, and so appropriate to the tastes and wants of its inhabitants that they will remain there forever.

This is but an essay indicating the broad outlines. But it is evident that the history of this century in general, and the events of the last eight years in particular, lead us logically to this scientific solution. The naturalistic movement cannot put in motion all human intelligence without communicating itself to political science. It has made over history, criticism, the novel, and the theater ; it ought to take a decisive start in politics, which is but made of history and living criticism. Politics, purged of the doctrines of empirical thinkers and the idealism of the poets, based on analysis and experiment, employing its method as a tool, taking for goal the normal development of a nation studied in its surroundings and its being, can alone found in France a lasting republic. This ought to be boldly said : there are no principles, there are but laws. There simply exist organized beings living on the earth in certain conditions. The republic will never come to be in a country until it becomes the condition even of the existence of that country. Apart from this fact, all attempts are but temporary and artificial arrangements, which will fall through and cause catastrophes.

II.

LET us consider now the attitude in which the different groups of the republican party stand toward contemporary literature.

For many years a great many foreigners have been coming to see me, Russians and Italians especially. I like to listen to them, because they present me with such original judgments upon us, and which nearly always strike me forcibly. They always express the greatest surprise at learning that the republican party shows itself so hostile to the new developments in literature, attacking writers who have freed themselves from tradition and who advance forward, and angrily discussing works conceived in an analytical and experimental spirit. The naturalistic novelists, more than any others, are maltreated with a veritable fury by the most influential newspapers of the party. And the foreigners do not understand it. Why is it? Why this strange contradiction, of new political men so set against the new writers? Why desire liberty in matters of government and deny to writers the privilege of enlarging their horizon? I have tried several times to explain to my visitors so singular an anomaly. But they only half understood me, so that to them the situation remained strange. To-day I wish to get at the real heart of the business.

In the first place, there are many characteristic precedents. During the first Revolution, from 1789 to the empire, the literature of the period remained classic; not one effort was made to break the old mold; on the contrary, there was a more and more insipid dilution of the old formula of the seventeenth century. Is it not curious? Here are men who abolish the king, suppress God, and who make a clean sweep with the whole ancient society, and yet who retain the literature of a past which they wish to efface from history; they do not seem to suspect for one moment that a literature is the immediate expression of a society.

It was much later that the reaction of the Revolution made itself felt in letters. After the empire and during the Restoration the romantic insurrection burst forth like a literary 1793. And what see you then? You see the republicans, or rather the liberals—those who claimed the conquests of the Revolution, those who fought the battles of 1830 in the name of menaced liberty—you see them defend classical literature and attack the triumphant romanticism, Victor Hugo's dramas and novels, furiously. It is sufficient to read an old file of *Le National* to be convinced on this subject. Such are the facts. In France, every time that politicians have desired the emancipation of the nation, they have commenced by defying the writers and by dreaming of shutting them up in some old formula as in a prison. They break a government, but they intend to regulate written thought. Their audacity stopped at the more or less violent transformation of power; they did not admit that you could transform letters. They precipitate the political evolution, and they strangely wish to deny the literary evolution. However, I repeat, the two hold together, one cannot be affected without the other, hand in hand they accomplish the same good. What is there, then, at the bottom of this attitude of the republican party?

Remark, however, that the law appears constant. In 1830 the liberals refused romanticism; to-day the republicans refuse naturalism. You could almost think there was a fixed element in this bad feeling, in this face to face defiance of these new literary formulas. Evidently this fixed element exists, and I shall try shortly to determine it. But I think the accidental causes, the causes of the moment, are more numerous and powerful. I will leave the past and I will only study the present hour, examining in what manner the different republican groups, of which I have already spoken, behave toward naturalism.

First let us speak of the formal republicans. These, as I have already said, remained classicists. One of them, a man of weight, a journalist whose solemn carriage has brought him to the senate, wrote, a short time ago, that Balzac and Stendhal were equivocal writers, unworthy of appearing in an honest man's library. Another, an old professor, who has been made a high dignitary, formerly distributed criticisms and blows from the ruler in a review with the pallid rage of an impotent schoolmaster. I could quote twenty such examples. They are a group of puritanical Jesuits, buttoned up in their cassocks, afraid of words, trembling before actual life, wishing to reduce the vast movement of modern inquiry to the narrow p..th of moral and patriotic readings. I know that practical Catholics do not like us, for we carry the hatchet into their beliefs; I know that the old world revolts against the cruelty of our analysis, which reduces it to dust; but these men who assert they accept the spirit of the age, these men whose speeches claim liberty of thought, why are they against us when we work more actively than they do for the society of to-morrow? There is a great deal of hypocrisy in their case. Our work is done too much in the daylight; we tell too many truths; we trouble them by our frankness. They have been in the opposition and seen humanity in all its ugliness; but if they get into power humanity becomes beautiful. This is enough; they govern; it is necessary to throw a veil over human nature. The truth is, an abyss separates them from us. As men of equilibrium or men of doctrine, prejudiced *bourgeois* or clowns playing the comedy of virtue, skillful men, who wish to increase the circulation by publishing sheets for the family, a mixture of academic minds and pedagogic brains, they all detest by instinct or from interest the attractive freedom of letters, the living style and highly colored images, the audacities of analysis, the powerful assertion of the personality of the writer. As a great stylist of our days often repeats, they have *la haine de la littérature;* hatred which causes them to prance before a poet's phrase as a horse balks before an object which he is afraid of.

With the romantic republicans the misunderstanding became simply a quarrel of school against school. Naturally the romanticists, who have thrown themselves into the republic to protect their receipts, show themselves very uneasy at the movement which operates with the public in favor of the naturalistic writers. This growing love for reality, this curiosity which attaches itself to all the work of contemporary analysis, makes them think, and with reason, that the crowd is turning from them and their works. What will become of them

if the cuirasses and the plumes are no longer the fashion;
if their tirades no longer suffice; if their readers demand
clear and scientific ideas, real characters under the dra-
peries of style? Not only their novels and their dramas
are attacked, but they even begin to smile at their politics; they are on the point of no longer taking them
seriously. Then, menaced in their pride and in their
purse, they become angry, they affect to be full of disdain and disgust for the new writers. Instead of admitting that the romantic evolution had been but the period
of the first impulse of the great naturalistic movement,
they denied this; they wished to stop French letters
with the productions of 1830. The necessity of shutting themselves up in an epoch, of embodying a literature in a formula, or in one single man, of pretending
that now the future was fixed is very characteristic;
and you can hardly quote a more striking example of
this contradiction on the part of men who admit all
the progress in politics, and who absolutely refuse to
letters the right to march onward or be renovated. But
there is still another and graver matter in the hostile
attitude of the romantic republicans against the naturalistic writers. They try to belittle them by throwing
mud in their faces, styling them disgusting and
obscene novelists. Understand by this that these
writers studied man unclothed, dissected and analyzed
him entirely, working as savants in this contemporary
inquiry. In the main, under the gross words by which
their defamers tried to soil them, they are simply workers in the truth, while the romanticists are workmen in
the ideal. There is in all this only a difference of method
and literary philosophy, but it is all-important. The
romanticists believe it is right to embellish and arrange

human data for the pleasure and the profit of the nation; we are convinced, we others, that it is better to give human data such as they are, so that one can seize the nation by its vitals, and thus to leave behind us works which will remain eternal. Evidently any understanding is impossible; these must kill those. I am very tranquil as to the issue of the quarrel. I only make the remark that it will be us, the savants, who will establish the republic on logical foundations, while the romanticists will have compromised it by dragging it into I cannot tell what humanitarian carnival.

Finally, the fanatical republicans, and I designate under this heading those burning and narrow brains who look upon the republic as a state by divine right which one is bound to impose upon men—these fanatics treat letters in general with a certain amount of contempt. They are not far from being for them a useless luxury. They refuse them an important rôle in social mechanism, and when they do accept them they try to make them bow to a common rule and to assign to them definite limits by law. Proudhon, one of the most powerful brains of our epoch, could not withstand wishing to treat art as a part of political economy. He dreamed of casting down high personalities; he longed for a people of draughtsmen, well disposed and learned, in order to hold with credit the place occupied by that rebel of genius who was named Delacroix. You can easily understand that these republicans, so contemptuous toward letters, showed themselves but little disposed to welcome new literary formulas. At bottom they had, in fact, a historical ideal for the republic, the black broth of Sparta, the patriotic stiffness of Brutus, the deadly spite of Marat; and this republic, which they wished for, black and somber, leveled and authoritative, this republic of purely classical imagination, impossible as an actual condition in our modern times, would fit in very badly with a literature of analysis and observation, needing an absolute liberty in which to develop itself. These men we still wound, because we are not in the nightmare they keep up even when awake; because we refuse to tell ourselves off, to take our place in the ranks, to obey the words of command, to consider man a stick whom you can plant where you please, and who ought to grow wherever he is placed. They are in favor of a ready-made formula; we are for a continuous inquiry and for due respect for human data.

I have said that outside of the accidental causes there are general causes that explain the visible hostility of the republican party to the new literary formula. These causes are working under all governments. As soon as the republicans came into power they did not escape that common law which brings it about that all men, when masters, begin to tremble before written thought. When one is in the opposition one cries out enthusiastically for the liberty of the press, and death to all censorship; but if, the next day, a revolution seats our man in a minister's armchair, he commences by doubling the number of censors and by wishing to regulate matters, even up to divers facts in the newspapers. Certainly I well know there is no ephemeral minister who does not burn with the zeal of bringing back in his own time the age of Louis XIV. But this is merely an air of music which he plays at the *fête* of his accession to power; arts and letters in reality count for nothing; politics possesses him entirely. Then, if he does worry himself over the desire to make his administration speak, if he really concerns himself about writers and artists, it is a great calamity; he meddles with questions which he knows nothing of; he astonishes his deputies by extraordinary actions; he distributes rewards and prizes to such mediocrities that even the crowd finally shrugs its shoulders. This is where every man ends who comes into power, however good his intentions at the start; he fatally encourages the men of · no ability, while he leaves the strong on one side when he does not persecute them. There may be a state reason in all this. Governments are suspicious of literature, because it is a force which always escapes them. A great artist, a great genius hampers them, frightens them from the moment that they feel that he stands outside their discipline armed with a powerful tool. If they accept a novel, a picture, a drama as an honest recreation, they tremble when this ceases to be pleasure permitted in the family, when the novelist, the painter, the dramatist brings forth an original work, expresses a truth which stirs up people. Always this "hatred for literature." You must not stand alone and be strong; you must not write in a living style which has a sound, a color, and a perfume; you must not, above all else, bring about a new evolution; if you do you disquiet the government and you make the ministers in their cabinets indignant. Kingdoms, empires, republics, all governments, even those who pride themselves upon protecting letters, have repulsed original writers and innovators. I speak more especially of modern times, in which written thought has become a redoubtable weapon.

Such is the situation, and I will make a *résumé* of it. The naturalistic writers have the republic against them.

because the republic is to-day an actual government, and because from the moment that it became so it has been attacked by that particular disease which I have called "hatred for literature." Further opposing them are the formal republicans, the romantic republicans, and the fanatical republicans—in a word, the most powerful groups of the party whom they hamper in their hypocrisy, their interests, or their beliefs. Is it necessary for me to say more? Will strangers, ignorant of the under side of the cards and not being able to see aught but the exterior lines, will they still be astonished at finding that the republican party "cut up" so furiously the young writers who have grown up with it and who are doing a work similar to its own? I could have stated the facts more precisely, but it is sufficient to have pointed out the general reasons. We really only have the naturalistic republicans with us. Those who desire the republic only through science, through the experimental method, know well that we are walking with them. These are the superior men of the age; naturally they are not numerous, but they command or they will command later; and if they have to employ inferior soldiers from that want of men which is common in all parties, they at least regret the foolish acts committed; they hope to make more truth and more force enter into the government each day.

I will quote here a very typical example, which will show the strange intelligence of certain republicans. The most awful reproach which they address to naturalistic literature is that of being a literature of facts, consequently a Bonapartist literature. This is a little vague. I will try to explain it. For the republicans in question the empire based itself on facts, while the republic bases itself on a principle; thus a literature which admits only facts, which represses the absolute, is a Bonapartist literature. Must we laugh? Or must we get angry? On reflecting upon this I find the matter a very grave one, for beneath this astonishing accusation there is a question of the existence even of the republic.

There exist a great many republicans who declare positively that the republic is absolute. The fanatical republicans make this assertion with the force of an axiom. The romantic republicans push right up to the ideal, waving their plumes, and make the republic an apotheosis of paradise, God the Father bonneted with a Phrygian helmet, radiating in a sun. In my opinion nothing is more childish or more dangerous. I am willing that there should be principles, as there is a police force to tranquilize honest people. However, the absolute is simply a philosophical amusement, upon which you can reason between the fruit and the cheese. As to taking it for a basis for human affairs, that is to try to build upon nothingness, that is to raise a building which will certainly crumble at the least breath. As I have explained, you enter into the relative as soon as man appears with his multitude of wants. From that moment facts alone govern. It is imbecile to think that the empire is crushed when you style it a government based upon accomplished facts. Does there exist a government outside of facts? Is not the republic of to-day a government based upon accomplished facts? Is it not precisely facts which founded it in a positive manner?

Let us take the second empire. We can speak the truth out aloud to-day. The second empire was because the republic had wearied France. It held its own course without regard to facts; it did not bother itself to respond to a want; it lost itself in empty declarations, in fatiguing quarrels in the cloudiest and least practical theories. Recall that period of the republic of ''48. All its attempts failed, because not one was planted on solid ground; it was devoured by humanitarianism, by a purely speculative socialism, by a romantic rhetoric and the religiousness of theistic poets. It never had a clear idea of the France which it wished to govern. It pretended to experiment upon her as upon a dead body. Indeed, the words were superb : liberty, equality, fraternity, virtue, honor, patriotism, But these were but words, and acts were needed for a successful administration. Imagine men, the best intentioned in the world, very worthy, very good, who fall upon a country of which they are totally ignorant, and of which they wish to remain ignorant, and who have conceived the strange notion of applying to it a form of government which is purely theoretical. It will happen of necessity that this country, rudely disarranged in its daily life, will end by rejecting the experiment. The dictatorship is an end. This was what happened on the 2d of December. France accepted a master, tired of being turned round and round for three years without being able to find a comfortable position.

Study the eighteen years of the second empire, and the all-powerfulness of facts is here again perceptible. Greeted as an experiment, as a relief, it killed itself, it ripened the republican idea, and when it fell it was through facts that the republic was definitely founded. I repeat these things because you cannot dwell upon them too often. If to-day the republic is in existence it is not by means of the absolute, it is not by principles, it is only because the facts willed it, made it the only government possible in France, finding in it the immediate and exact satisfaction of the needs of the country. Without doubt right exists, but right is only a superior fact, which is, if you so wish it, the final fact, toward which all nations tend across all the intermediary facts. Admit that we have attained the social truth, the republic; this republic is no less based on facts than were all the other governments which have led us to it. It is absurd to try to dig up the soil in order to plant in it vague poetical ideals or the absolute philosophy of the sectarians.

You can see what weight the accusations of these republicans carry who reproach us with holding simply to the facts. Yes, facts alone hold for us any scientific certainty. We believe only in facts, because it is solely upon facts that all modern science has grown. The human document is our solid basis. We leave to dreamers the ideal, or the absolute, as they prefer to call it, having the conviction that it is precisely this absolute which during all these centuries has stopped and led astray men in their search after truth. We expose facts, we do not judge them, for judging is not our work, as we are observers and analyzers. We have exposed the facts of the empire, constituting ourselves the historians of this historical period, as we shall expose the fact of the republic when it shall enter into our history, and when it shall bring to pass new manners. To style naturalism Bonapartist literature is one of those splendidly foolish notions which gain a lodging place in the small brains of the wordy gentlemen of the ideal. I affirm, on the contrary, that naturalism is a republican literature, if you look upon the republic as the true form of human government *par excellence*, based on universal inquiry, determined by the majority of facts, responding, in a word, to the observed and analyzed needs of a nation. All the positivist science of our century is contained therein.

At the bottom of these literary quarrels there is always a philosophical question. Such question may remain vague ; we do not touch upon it ; the writers we have been discussing cannot often tell what their beliefs are ; but the antagonism between the schools proceeds no less from the first ideas which they form of the truth. Thus romanticism is always deistical. Victor Hugo, in whom it is incarnated, was brought up a Catholic, from which religion he never really disengaged himself. Catholicism in him became pantheism, a cloudy and poetical deism. God always appears at the end of his verses, and he not only appears in the light of an article of faith, he appears, moreover, as a literary neces   Let us turn to naturalism now, and you will soon find yourself on actual ground. This is the literature of an age of science, which grows but by facts. The ideal is, if not suppressed, at least set to one side. The naturalistic writer believes that there is no necessity to pronounce on the question of a God. He is a creative force, and that is all. Without entering into a discussion as to the subject of this force, without wishing still further to specify it, he takes nature from the beginning and analyzes it. His work is the same as that of our chemists and our physicists. He but gathers together and classifies the data, without ever referring them to a common standard, without drawing conclusions about the ideal. If you wish to call it so, it is an inquiry about the ideal, about God himself, a research into what is—instead of being, as in the classical and romantic school, a dissertation about a dogma, a rhetorical amplification about superhuman axioms.

Let the classicists and the romanticists and the deists drag us through the mud with the fanaticism of religious passions—I understand it perfectly; it is because we deny their God, we empty their heaven in not taking account of their ideal, in not referring everything to this absolute. Only what has always surprised me is that the atheists of the republican party attack us with such violence. How is that? Here are men who cast aside the dogmas, who deny God, and yet absolutely cry out for an ideal in literature. They need a trumpery heaven, with celestial paintings and superhuman abstractions. In social science they declare that we no longer have need of religions; they go so far as to say that religions lead to an abyss; but as soon as there is a question of letters, then they become angry if one does not profess the religion of beauty. But, in truth, one religion goes not without the other. Pretended beauty, absolute perfection, traced according to certain lines, is but the material expression of a divinity dreamed of and adored by men. If you refuse this divinity, if you have the desire to bring the philosophic problem down to the study of the world of nature and of man, you must accept our naturalistic literature, which is precisely the literary weapon of the new scientific solution demanded by the century. Whoever is with science should be with us.

III.

I NOW reach the practical part. I have only raised these great questions incidentally in order clearly to exhibit the actual literary evolution. In fact, the real point of all this is the question of the attitude of the republic in regard to literature.

One of the last Ministers of Public Instruction, a very clever man, seemed to be animated by the most active and fearless intentions when he entered into. power. He had, moreover, an extraordinary zeal in questioning all those who came to him, saying: " I beg of you to tell me what I ought to do; point out to me, enlighten me as to what artists and writers expect of the government." ⸱ This bespoke a very great wish to know our real needs and to satisfy them. One day I was present as the minister uttered these words before a number of my colleagues. He went from one to the other; he wanted to have the opinion of each one. The first asked for the cross for men of talent whose personality until then had frightened those in power; the second wanted a fund in order to create a vast encyclopedia, summing up history and science; the third spoke of sending a mission to certain convents in Lower Russia, where he suspected that literary treasures were hidden. Certainly all this was excellent, but I must admit that this did not satisfy me; therefore when the minister questioned me in my turn I simply replied: " Make us free, and you will be a great minister."

Liberty—this is all a government can give us. I do not deny that the rôle which an intelligent minister is called upon to fulfill is a hard one. He has under him schools, he conducts examinations, distributes orders and medals, and grants pensions. According to the kind of man in power the mediocrities profit by all this, more or less, but they are the ones, in spite of everything, who get the largest share. But what true benefit do art and literature derive from this intervention, this protection by the government? These are but the details of the administrative cookery, which have no influence either on the development of minds or on the birth of great talents. A pension is given to someone who is poor; he who is agreeable is decorated. Letters thrive neither better nor worse. Again, some painters or composers are fed. But all this decides in no one way the coming of a master who shall transform painting and music at the given hour. Master minds grow alone in the soil of the nation without any aid from the government, and it often happens that the government rejects them, so that they are thrown upon the strength of their own genius. Therefore ministers cannot really have any direct influence. Putting things at their best, if they were strong enough to disentangle themselves from all questions of routine and from all politics, if they could sweep the mediocres out of their pathway, and distribute their medals and orders, their pensions, their crosses, to really original talent, they would still be but an enlightened Mæcenas, a friend to letters, who gave to writers as much encouragement as possible.

Let them listen to us! We workers who do not need medals, who are not ambitious for crosses, who look to the public for recompense, we ask but one thing of politicians—liberty! They talk of leaving the nation to itself. Well! let them first leave literature to herself; let them loose the bonds with which the old *régimes* have bound her. What shall we say to these republicans who desire entire liberty, and who do not begin by proclaiming the liberty of written thought? They can keep their flowers, their pensions, and their ribbons; we refuse their examinations, we shrug our shoulders before their hothouses, we will not submit to their police, and we forbid their encouraging us. What we want is liberty; we have a right to it; we demand it; it is our due. Politicians keep our liberty from us; let them give it back!

I will quote three facts among many others. Is it not shameful that the press should not be entirely free, that there still exists an examining commission, that theatrical censorship still exists? And here an incredible fact presents itself: this censorship has just been reconstructed, and publicly put under severe police discipline.

I cannot enter into an examination of the actual laws concerning the press. Everyone knows how restricted it is. Our French republic is as hard on the newspapers as the most absolute monarchies. As long as the republicans were not in power they were very loud in their cries for perfect liberty; we shall see if they will remember it. As to this examining commission, it is not only hurtful to liberty, it is foolish. Can you, for example, tell me of a more puerile distinction than that established between the bookstands in a railway station and those in a neighboring street? Everybody walks on the sidewalks, I have the right to spread my works out there ; a special traveling public passes through the station, running generally for its trains, and I cannot sell my books there unless a commission has pronounced them inoffensive. Under the empire this police supervision of books and pamphlets was easily understood, putting obscenity where it was not ; but in a republic such a commission plays an odious and inexplicable rôle. That is a small question, you say ; the question is not a small one for writers, who miss just so much advantage. They hinder us from reaching the public, they cut off from us a certain sale, and all this is a blow to equality and right. Besides, it is sufficient that this examining commission attacks the liberty of thinking and writing in order to show that the republic should suppress it. And the theatrical censorship, will it be eternal ? Governments fall, but the censorship remains. Here the question enlarges itself. I know very well that the censorship poses as a good woman. Successful authors pretend that they always manage in the end to conciliate the censors ; they grant a few cuttings, and afterward revenge themselves by getting off some good joke upon them. A conciliating man once said to me : " Mention the works of talent which the censors have prevented from being played." I replied to him : " I cannot tell you the titles of masterpieces of which the censors have deprived us, for the very good reason that these masterpieces have not been written." The whole matter lies here. If the censor does not play a very active rôle, he does harm as a scarecrow ; he paralyzes the evolution of dramatic art. Every author knows the pieces which may not be written, those which cannot be played, and therefore he does not write them. Thus a fruitful theme, political comedy, is forbidden unless it keeps within the narrow limits of simple banter. This is so much the more grave for the reason that in my opinion all modern comedy is to be found in politics. They reproach our authors with producing nothing new, with repeating the same well-known types, with not knowing how to bring forth modern laughter, and they forbid them to touch upon the political world—this world, noisier and noisier each day, which fills the century. Comedy should live by the everyday life around us. With us, where is the everyday life if it is not in politics? It is only there that our authors will find the characteristics of the epoch, the new forms of appetites, of interests, and the ridiculous things in our French society. In forbidding them this vast field, unknown in the last century, and which goes on enlarging every day, you reduce them to impotence. It is like order-ing a sculptor to carve you a statue, and then refusing him the block of marble he needs.

I repeat, let the politicians give writers entire liberty. They cannot do more, and they can do no less. Any-thing else is a farce and unimportant. But I must first confess one thing: if the republic refuses us these lib-erties we know how to take them. Only I think it would be more logical to see literary liberties founded by the republic. The republic, whose formula is scien-tific, and one which facts impose on us to-day, ought to be able to understand the attitude which it should hold before the actual literature—the attitude of a power which casts forth all state literature, which is in favor of no one school, which simply desires that the free development of his ideas should be assured to each citizen. Let it not make pretense to direct nor encourage nor recompense; let it simply allow the genial and creative forces of the century to do their work. This rôle seems very easy to play. Well, no government up to the present day has had enough intelligence to resign itself to that rôle with a good grace. Will the republic show itself superior? We shall know to-morrow.

In the first place, we must have really strong men in power. I cannot understand a republic governed by inferior men. It seems illogical. In the government of a country by the people, the men who receive from their fellow-citizens the delegation of power ought to be of necessity the most honest and the most intelligent of the nation. Otherwise why should they be chosen? If they are mediocrities, of doubtful honesty, and with no intellect—if, in a word, they amount to nothing—I demand that they give me back the old *régime ;* at least the ministers under the monarchy were men of titles, belonged to an aristocracy of race, existed apart from and above the crowd. The misfortune is that the things of this world do not result in the greatest honor and the greatest profit of humanity. I find here again this terrible human element, which upsets the most beautiful theories based on logic and right. Men still battle for themselves more than for the truth. Thus it is that the chief of a party comes into power with all his followers. He is superior, but the followers are oftenest complaisant nonentities, fools whom you must notice, clowns who have had the strange good fortune of making people look upon them as serious, and who become the most insupportable and dangerous supernumeraries in power. In fact, it often happens that the supernumeraries kill the chief of the

party.   Politics in troublous hours is thus the refuge
for all disappointed ambitions, the ground on which the
useless ones and the impotent gather together to mount
to the topmost rung of success.   This explains the
immense number of candidates.   Nearly all of them
have their pockets filled with the manuscripts of
dramas and novels which have been refused twenty
times over by managers and editors; or again there is
among them an embittered journalist, an unsuccessful
historian, a misunderstood poet.   I mean to say that
they tried their hand at letters, and even when politics
satisfied their ambition, and even when they governed,
they still preserved for letters a tenderness turned into
spite.   They are schoolboys turned into teachers.
Letters remain in their eyes an orgy of youth which
needs watching; they speak of them with dull,
unquenched desires; they are not far from agreeing
with those *bourgeois* who accuse writers of passing their
days on' divans, served by sultanas, in the midst of the
most sensuous debaucheries.   This explains their
wielding of the rod, their discourses on morality, their
work of regulating these letters as they regulate prosti-
tution, with a police force and arrests.   These are the
ones, these terrible mediocre men, these dry fruits
mounted upon the stilts of authority, who make all the
trouble.   They are unhappily the parasites of the
republic.   They are always among the first in revolutionary times to put themselves forward, overrunning
the small and great situations.   But we must hope that
a clearing out will soon take place.   The republic can
only live on the condition that it is the government of
superior intellects, the scientific formula of modern
society applied by logical and free minds.

It remains for me to express a wish which my whole generation will second. They beset us, they crush us with their politics, and decidedly we have had enough of it. I remember that under the empire men melancholily regretted the time of parliamentary battles; the tribune was mute, they said, the press muzzled, and the discussion of public affairs forbidden. Well, to-day they have turned us so completely around that we are beginning to regret the great silence of the empire, when politics were not barking under our windows from morning until night, and we at least had time to think. Indeed, we were patient. During eight years we were resigned. We understood that we could not come out tranquilly from a crisis such as that of 1870; we said to ourselves that a republic was not an easy thing to found in the midst of the anger of all parties, and we must endure the hubbub of the struggle. Only, now that the republic is founded, let us have peace !

Yes, we all of us, men of science, writers, and artists, we hold out our hands toward the politicians, begging of them not to murder our ears any longer. The republicans have conquered, have they not ? They are to-day masters of every situation. Then, for God's sake, let them come to an understanding ; let them dance with the ladies instead of still quarreling. We shall be very thankful to them.

Nobody really thinks of us. No one seems to notice that the present generation, men of thirty and forty years, find themselves strangled between the last convulsions of the empire and the laborious childhood of the republic. Can a writer exist when a politician takes up all the sunshine ? Can one busy himself with

books when the newspapers are overrun with parliamentary debates, with the longest and emptiest discussions? Politics, and always politics, and in such
enormous doses that even the ladies in their salons talk
nothing but politics. Here is where we are : they are
stealing the best part of the century from us, they are
wasting our best years; to-morrow, when they will tell
us, at last, that our hour has come and we can speak,
we shall be very old, and our youths will claim our
places. Thus it is that generations have their life
crushed out by revolutions. Naturally we cannot show
any very great tenderness for politics, in the same way
that the crushed man does not smile at the wheel
which has passed over his body.

Without doubt we must accept historical necessities.
But what puts us out of humor is the superabundant
amount of space which the mediocre men, of whom I
have already spoken, have captured during these last
years. Corneille, Molière, or Balzac never made such
a shameful hubbub in the newspapers as these imbeciles
are making at this moment. Any fool, rising to the
tribune, takes upon himself an importance greater
than that of a writer giving a master work to the public.
I know that the noise does not count for much, that
the fool remains a fool—even when he is known from
one end of France to the other; but how much
time is lost reading these badly written speeches, what
a misapplication of truth and justice, what errors
put into circulation! It is just because of these easy
triumphs in politics that so many of the unemployed
and unsuccessful throw themselves into it to carve
notoriety from it; and it is just on account of the
victories of these insignificant fellows, the swelling out

of certain absurd characters, the parade before an astonished France of these statesmen of a day, that we look contemptuously on politics, we other workers, who believe only in genius and study.

We have had enough noise. Let us rejoice in our republic. Let the workers and ambitious ones, who live upon her, go to America to seek a throne or make a fortune. Let us have music, let us dance, cultivate our flowers, and write beautiful works. It must be admitted that there is among writers and artists a defiance against the republic. Until now they have not felt that they were beloved by the republicans, who have always shown the stiffness of soldiers toward arts and letters. They freely assert that the republic is the worst government for us, with its puritanical airs, its need of teaching and preaching, its thesis of equality and utility. But they should add that we have never really seen the republican government in working order, for up to the present in France it has not possessed the necessary stability.

My conclusion shall be simple. Every definite and durable government has a literature. The republics of 1789 and 1848 did not have any, because they passed over the nation like a hurricane. To-day our republic seems well founded, and from now on she will have her literary expression. This expression, I think, will be strongly naturalistic. I mean by that the analytical and experimental method, modern inquiry based on facts and human data. There must be harmony between the social movement, which is the cause, and the literary expression, which is the effect. If the republic, blinded about itself, not understanding that it exists solely by the force of a scientific formula, turns to persecute this scientific formula as exhibited in letters, that will be a sign that the republic is not ripe for the facts, and that it will disappear once again before a fact—the dictatorship.

THE END.